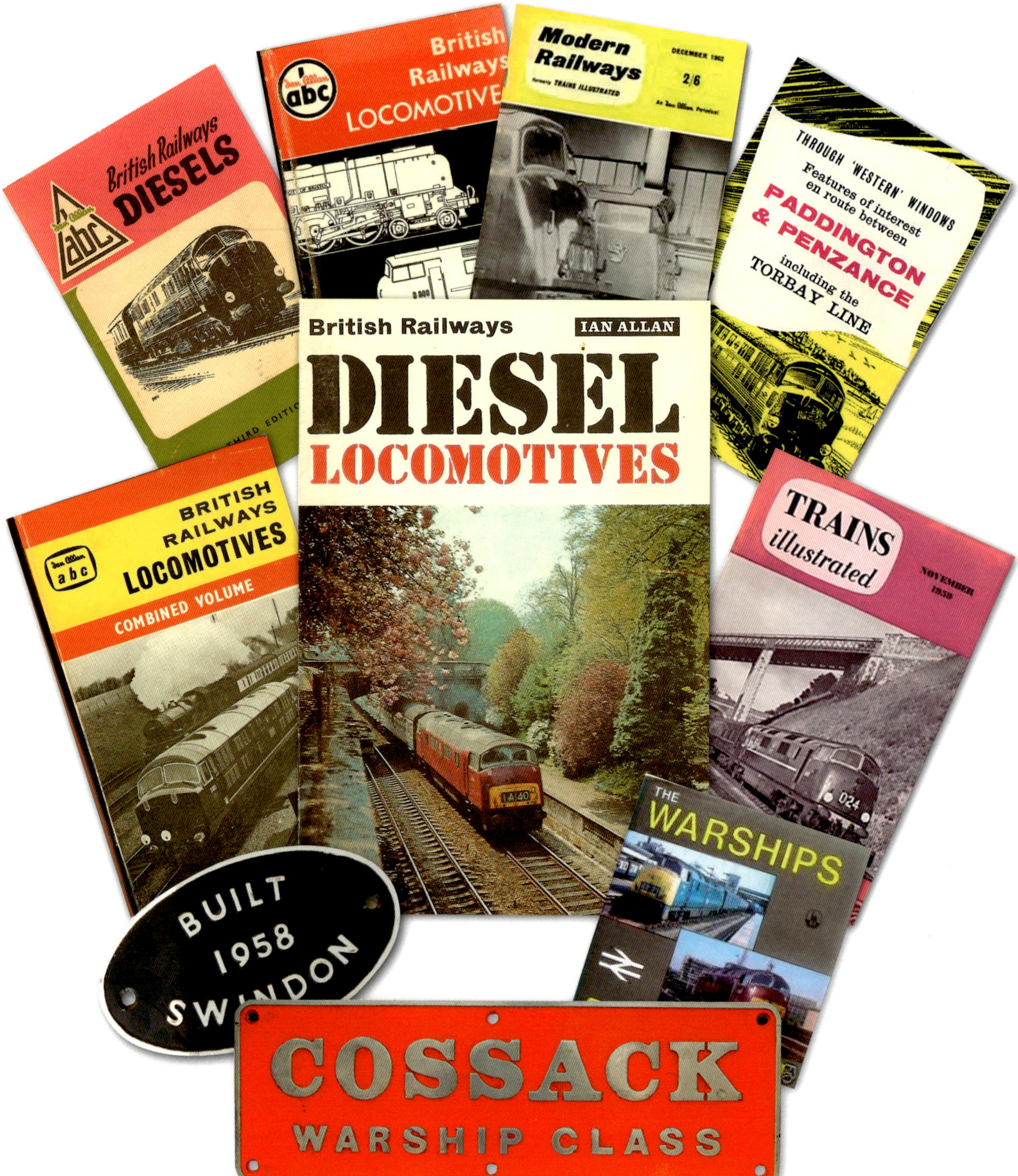
British Railways
DIESELS
Ian Allan
abc
British
Railways
LOCOMOTIVES
Modern
Railways
DECEMBER 1962
2/6
THROUGH 'WESTERN' WINDOWS
Features of interest
en route between
PADDINGTON
& PENZANCE
including the
TORBAY LINE
British Railways
IAN ALLAN
DIESEL
LOCOMOTIVES
BRITISH
RAILWAYS
LOCOMOTIVES
COMBINED VOLUME
TRAINS
illustrated
NOVEMBER
1959
THE
WARSHIPS
BUILT
1958
SWINDON
COSSACK
WARSHIP CLASS

Looking back at WARSHIPS

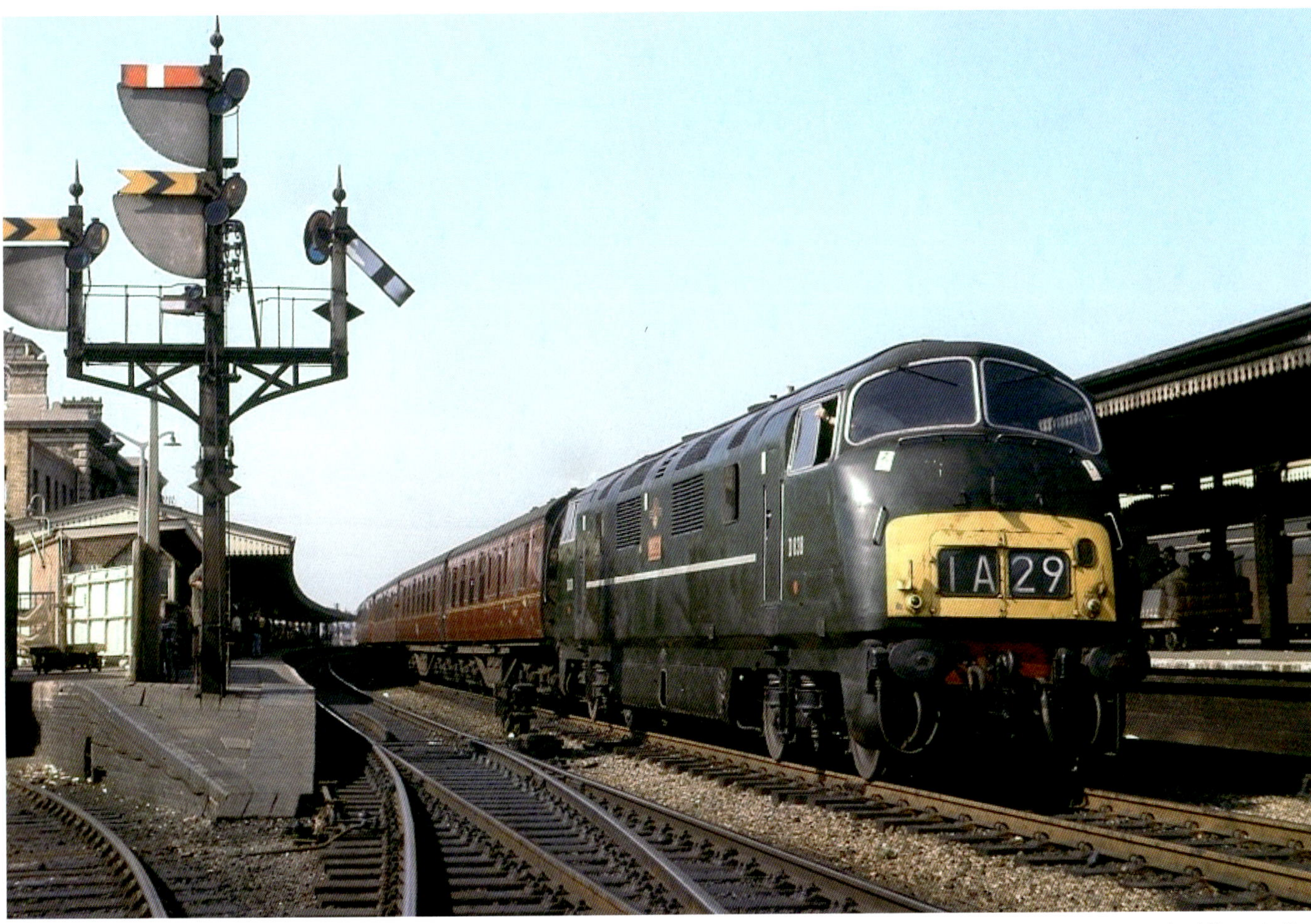

Its a cheery wave from the crew on board D838 Rapid as they pass through Reading on the up fast in June 1962. The signals for the down routes have sighting boards to help pick them out against the background of the station buildings. ***H.J Ashman F.R.P.S/Adrian Vaughan Collection.***

Kevin Derrick

Strathwood

Looking back at WARSHIPS

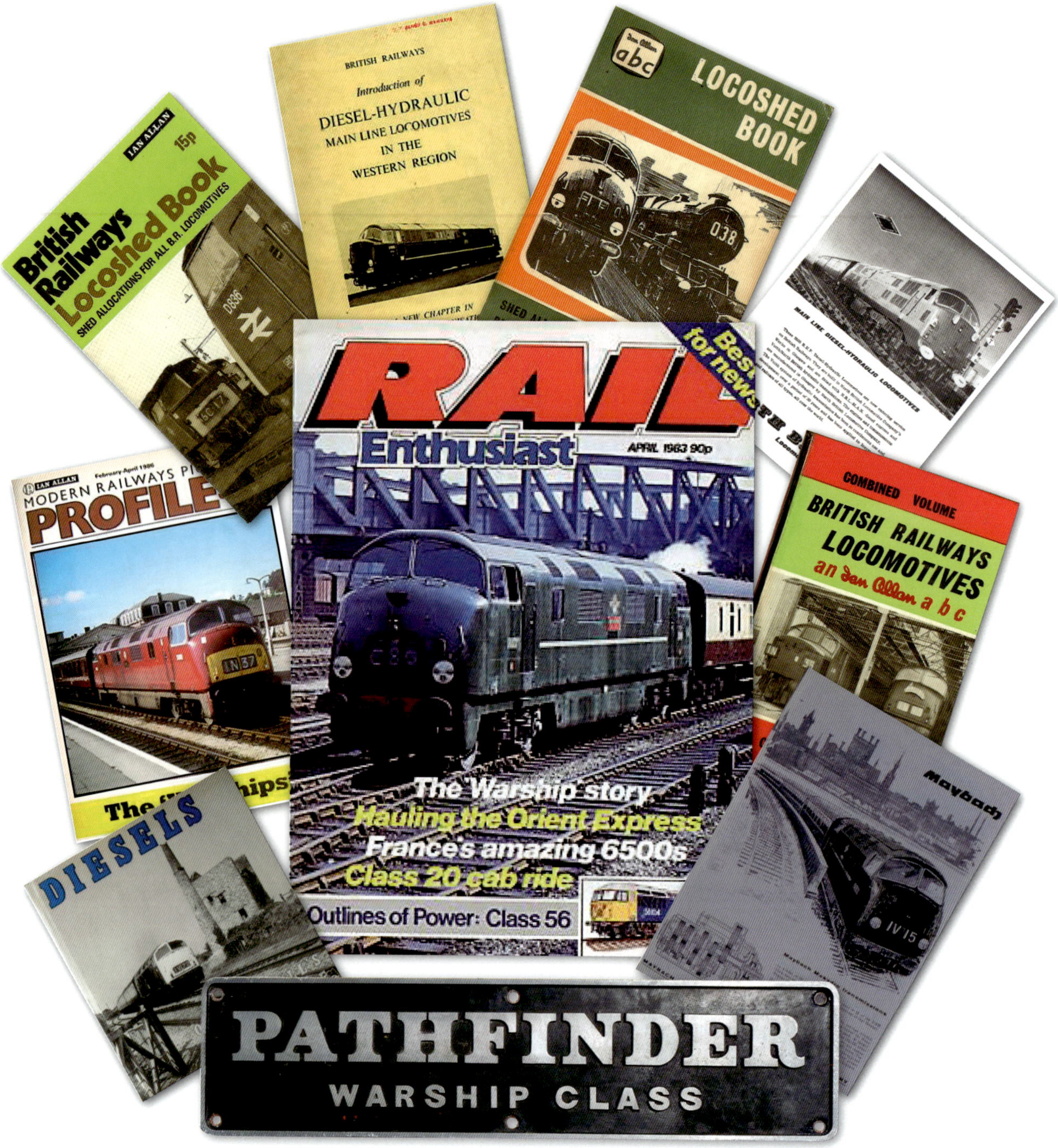

First published 2011

ISBN 1-905276-49-4
ISBN 978-1-905276-49-3

Published by Strathwood Ltd, Glenavon House, Kinchurdy Road, Boat of Garten, Inverness-shire, PH24 3BP. Tel 01479 831139

Proudly printed in the United Kingdom

Contents **Page**

Introduction

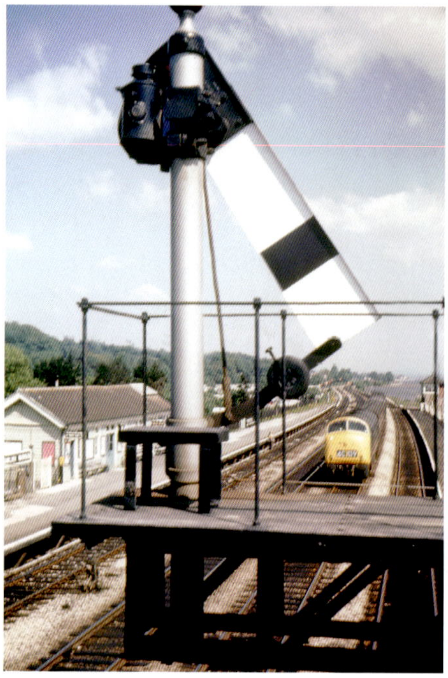

We will all have our favourite classes of locomotives, perhaps influenced by something from our formative years or just because we like the shape, sound or names of the locomotives. Well for myself it was all of those that brought about my enthusiasm for Warships to be my favourites.

Growing up in South West London, I was within easy range by bicycle, bus and train to both the Western Region mainline from Paddington and the South Western mainline from Waterloo. Add to this my school backed onto the Hounslow loop which used to experience a large number of inter-regional freights and diversions often sending Warships to me where ever I went. Whilst Class 33s and 73s were treated with disgust the sound of a Warship always lifted the pulse to one young school boy.

Southall and Old Oak Common were also within easy reach and the late 1960s and the first year or so of the 1970s were a treat for hydraulic enthusiasts, but it was the shape, sound and those evocative names that truly won the Warships over for me.

As they were amassed for scrap at Old Oak Common, Marsh Junction and Swindon Works, visits were arranged as often as funds would allow to visit the corpses of old friends. Although if the truth be told at one time myself and others were often fed up by seeing the likes of Swift, Temeraire and Tenacious it seemed on every visit to Old Oak Common. Whilst the likes of Majestic, Vanguard and Formidable were nowhere to be seen.

Much has already been written on the reasons for and against the hydraulics generally and the Warships too, as to the politics of how thay came about and so forth. The Looking back at series does not pretend to be great techinical tomes of historical significance and importance to be written about by the editors and reviewers of magazines with huge reverence. Instead, it serves one hopes as the author of the series to be an enjoyable photographic record of times gone by and a worthy source of inspiration for modellers.

In compiling this volume within the series I must pay huge thanks firstly to all of the photographic contributors, but especially to Bernard Mills in particular, not only for his generous help in allowing access to his collection of slides, but also to say thank you from all of us who were too young or too poor at the time to record photographically the best of the hydraulic era. Also thanks are sent to one of the country's foremost enthusiasts of all things to do with Warships, namely Martin Street. With their help and the support of others involved within the preservation movement we can enjoy the sights and sounds of Warships still today. To this end Strathwood will be donating a generous proportion from the proceeds from this publication to the Diesel Traction Group to help in their valliant efforts to keep hydrauic power alive for future years.

The Looking back at series has developed into a collectable account using colour photographs of the various designs and specific classes in the era since nationalisation, with the emphasis upon the service years rather than preservation. A further dip into the archives is planned to look at additional types in more detail. If you can help with even a single shot of anything for the future and in particular any futher hydraulic images, please get in touch.

Kevin Derrick
Boat of Garten 2011

This page; Just two of Bernard Mills wonderful photographs of Warships from 1969.

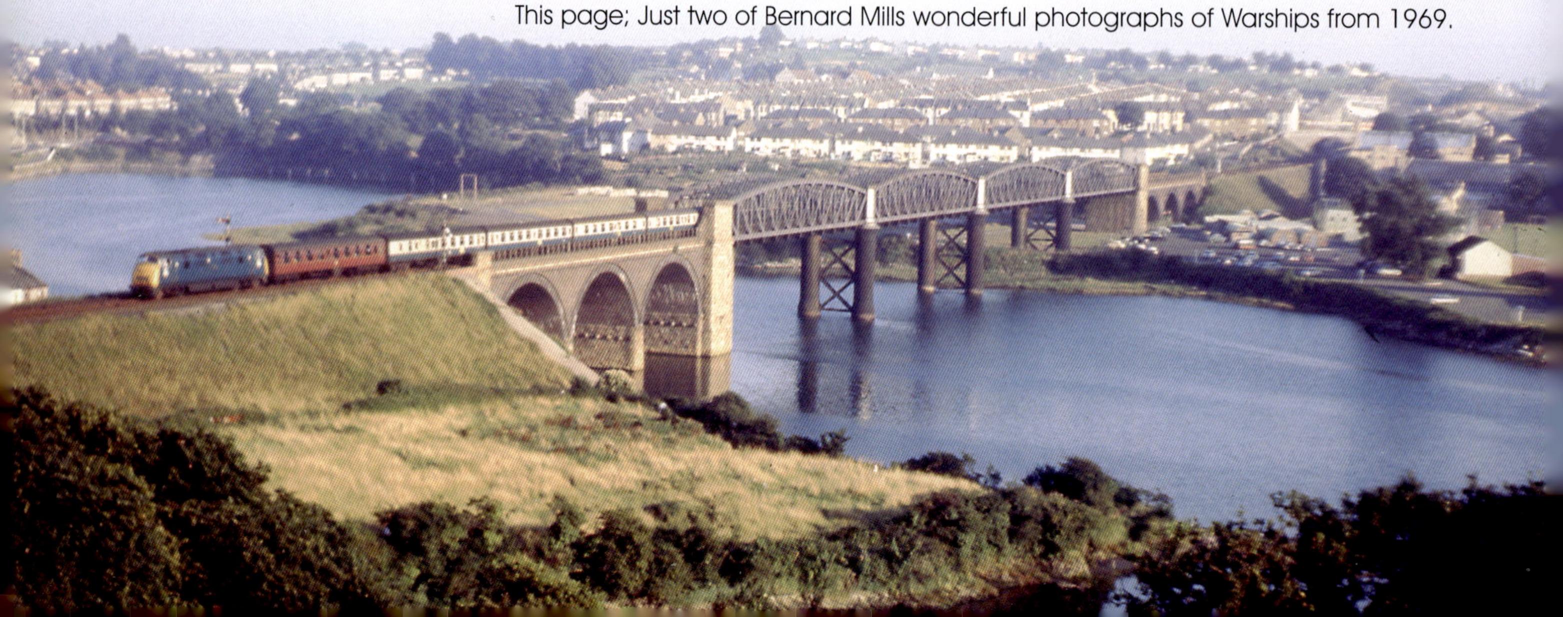

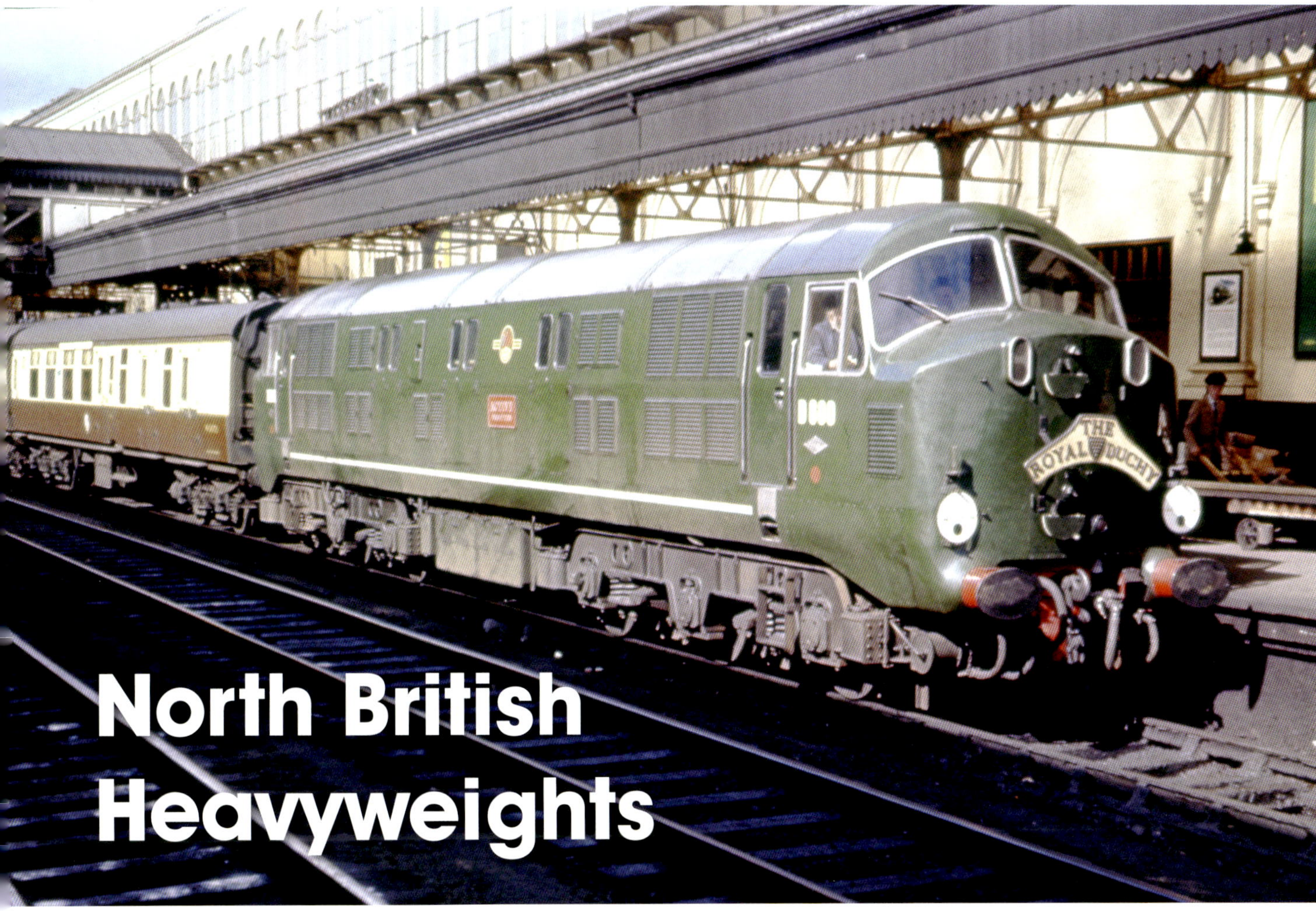

North British Heavyweights

When first into traffic in January 1958 D600 Active found itself put to work on the prestige named trains of the day on the Western Region, such as here at Exeter in 1959 on The Royal Duchy. As built all the locomotives had horizontal louvres on their main side grilles and the first two in service lacked front footsteps below their bufferbeams initially. ***Strathwood Library Collection***

By the summer of 1967 the writing was on the wall for this non standard batch of five locomotives. Even though D600 Active was seen here at Laira after a recent works visit to Swindon, and painting into blue. It had been updated with modified grilles and headcode boxes a few years earlier. ***Strathwood Library Collection***

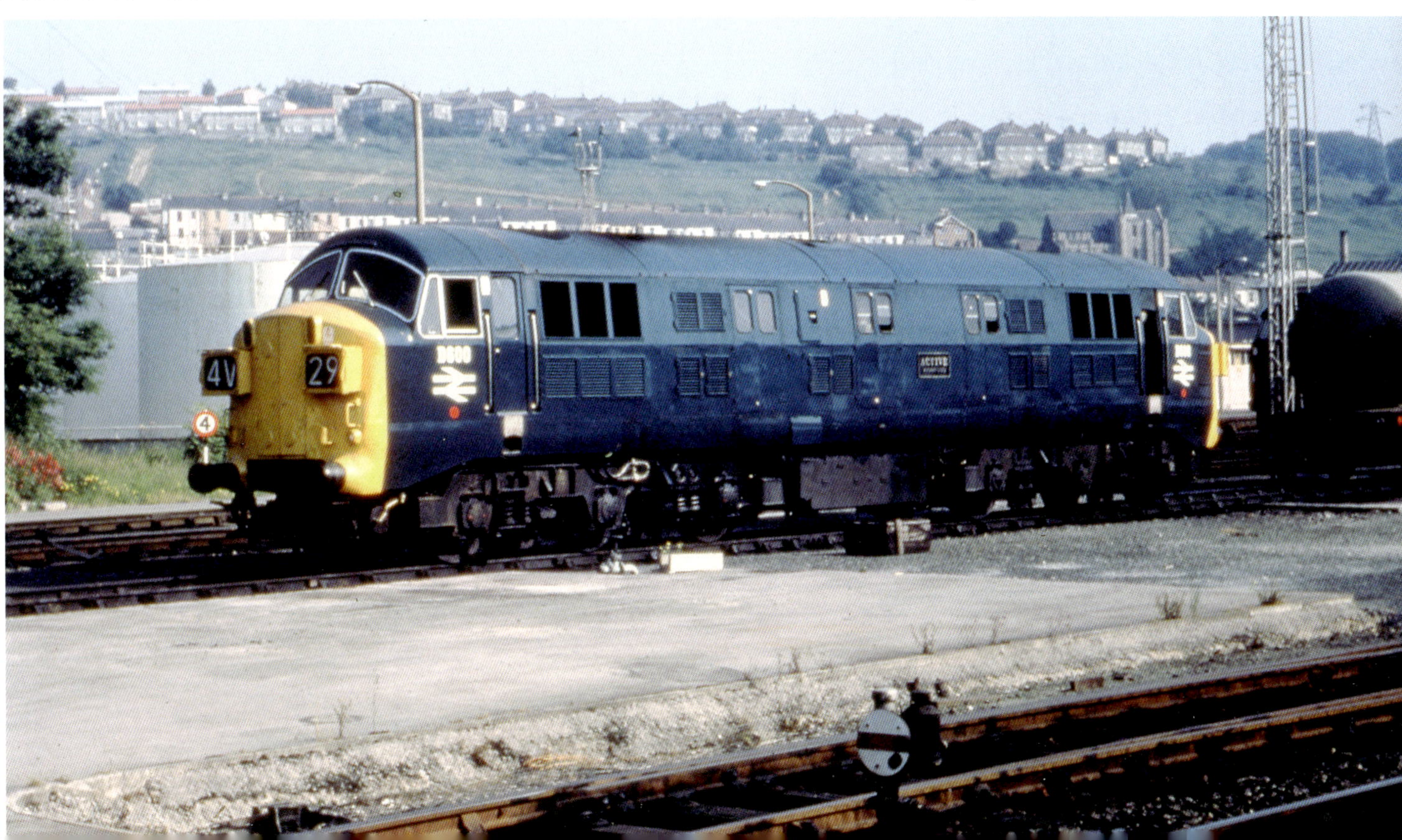

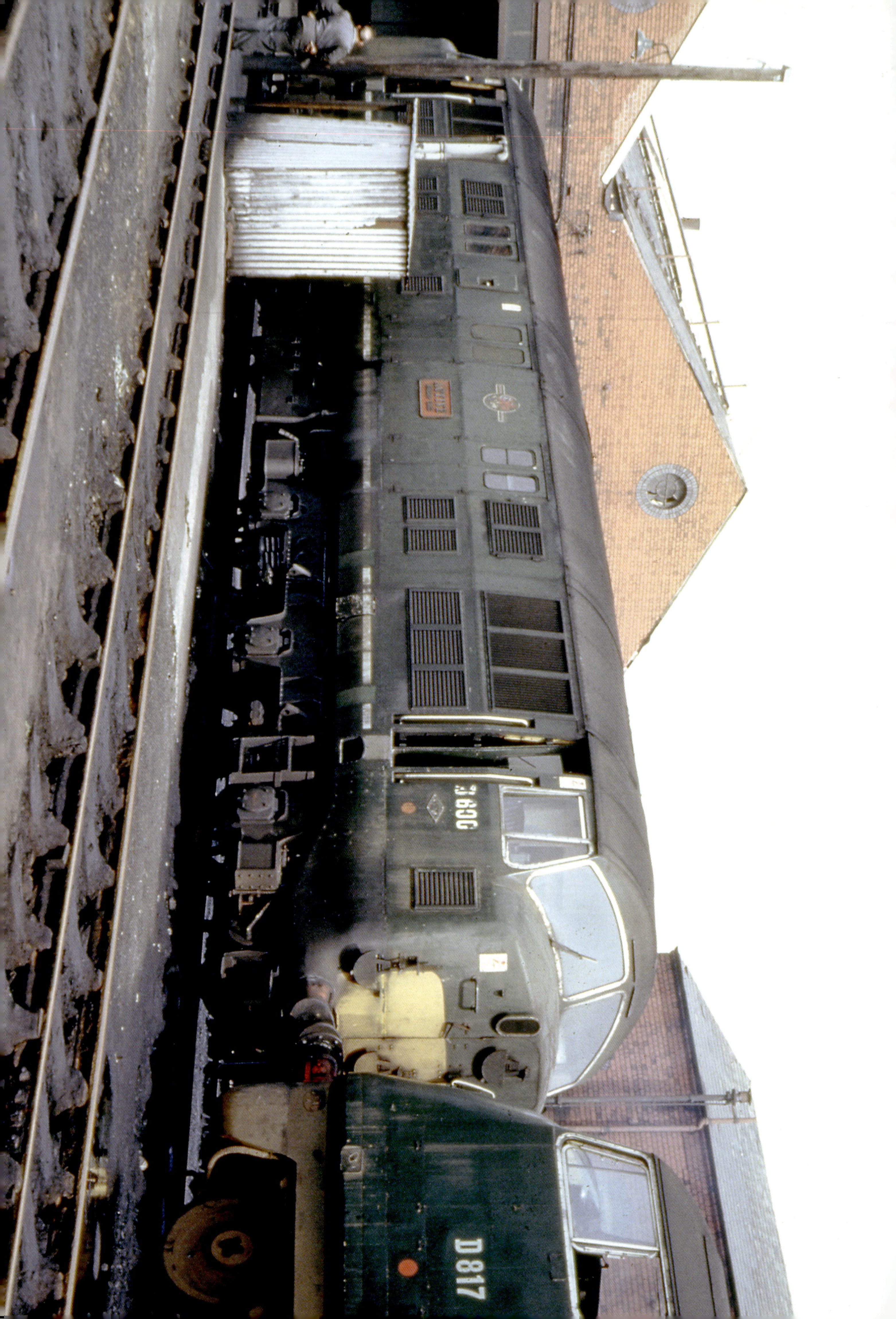
D 817

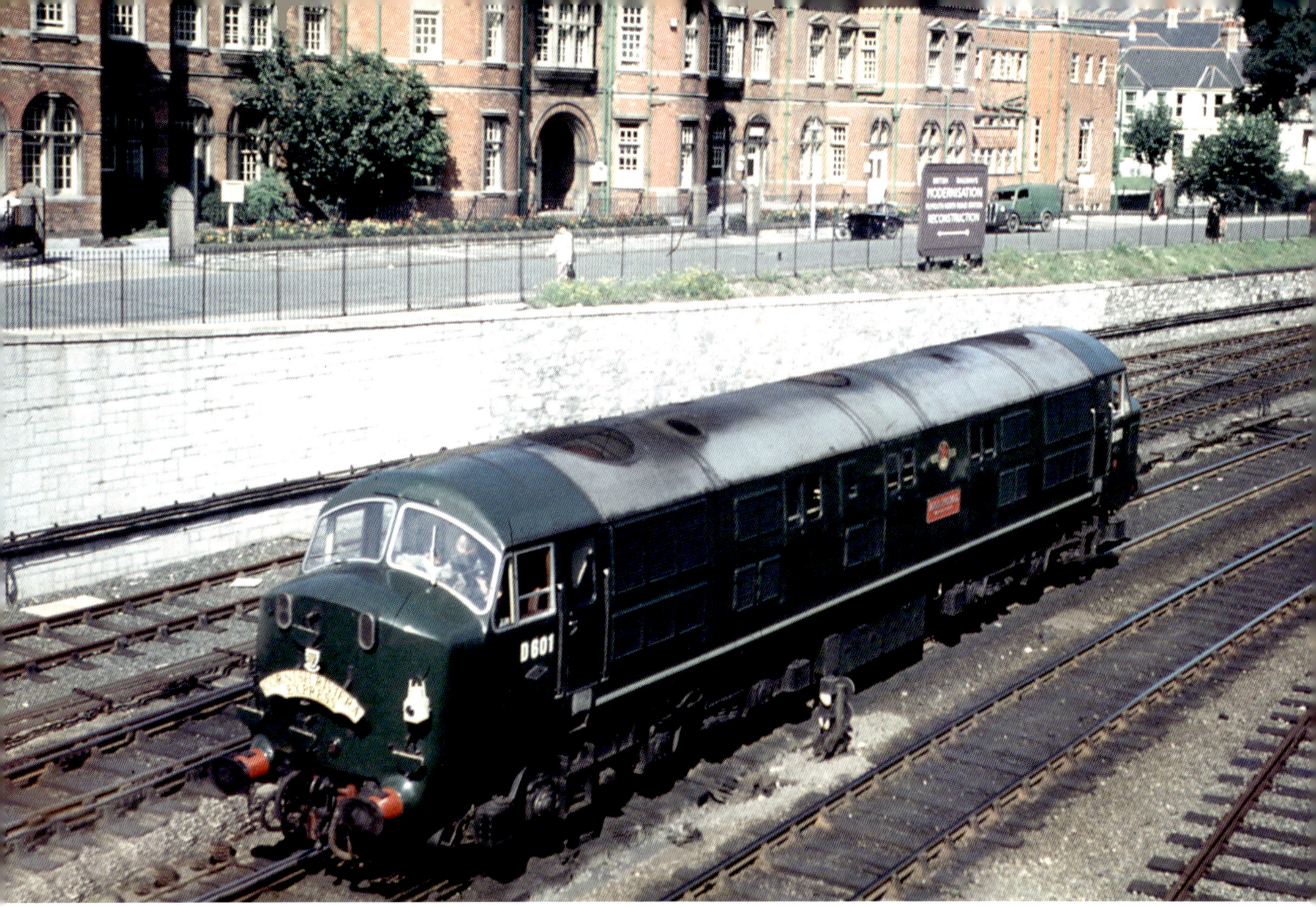

Two shots of D601 Ark Royal both from June 1958 firstly at Plymouth and then at Dawlish Warren. At this point just the first two locomotives were in service and the pair acccrued 150,000 miles per year in their first few years based at Laira. ***Transport Treasury and Strathwood Library Collection***

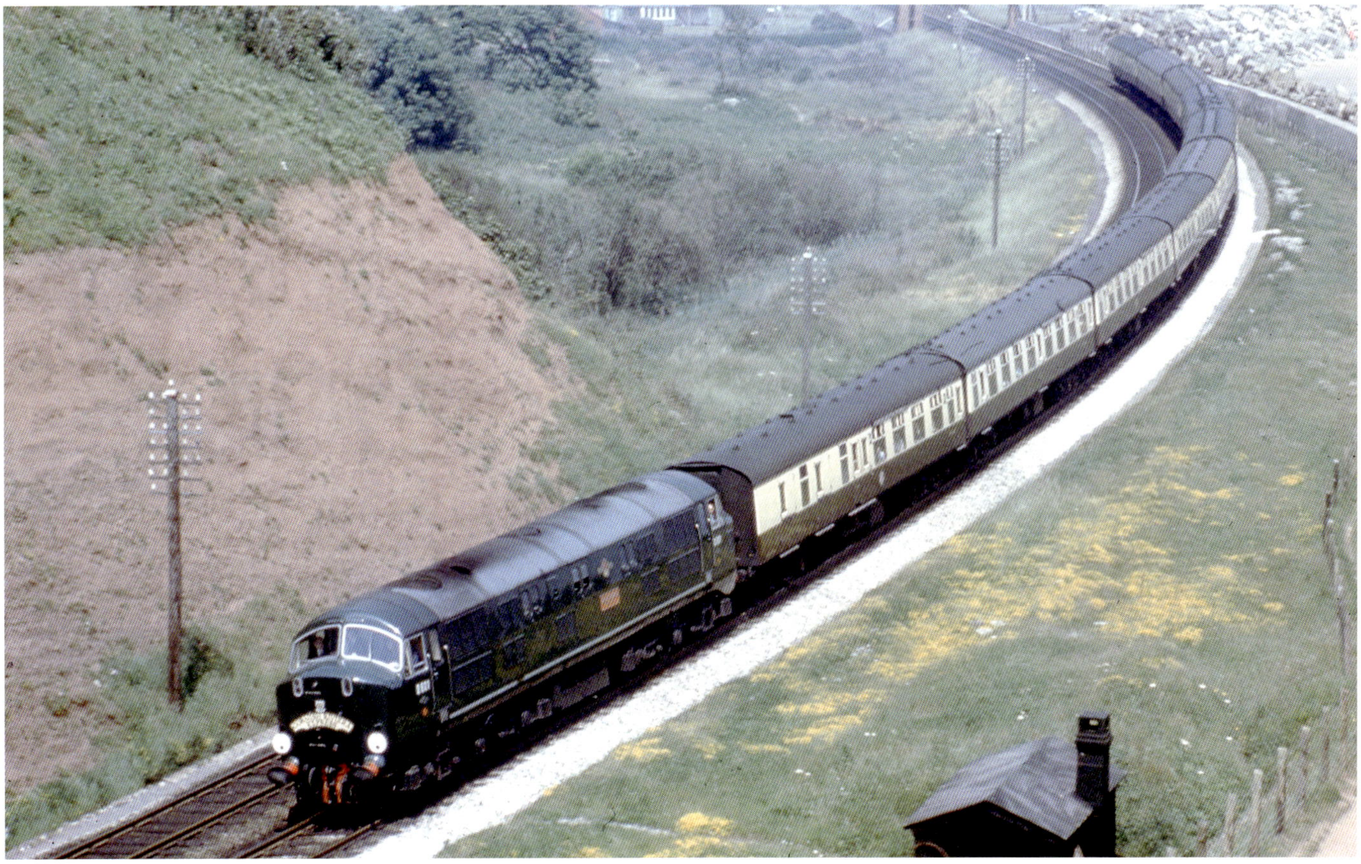

Page left: Interim condition for D600 Active at Penzance on 18 June 1965, still in green before the headcode boxes went on, but the grilles have been changed, and front footsteps added to allow staff to change the head code discs when not in a station platform. ***Frank Hornby***

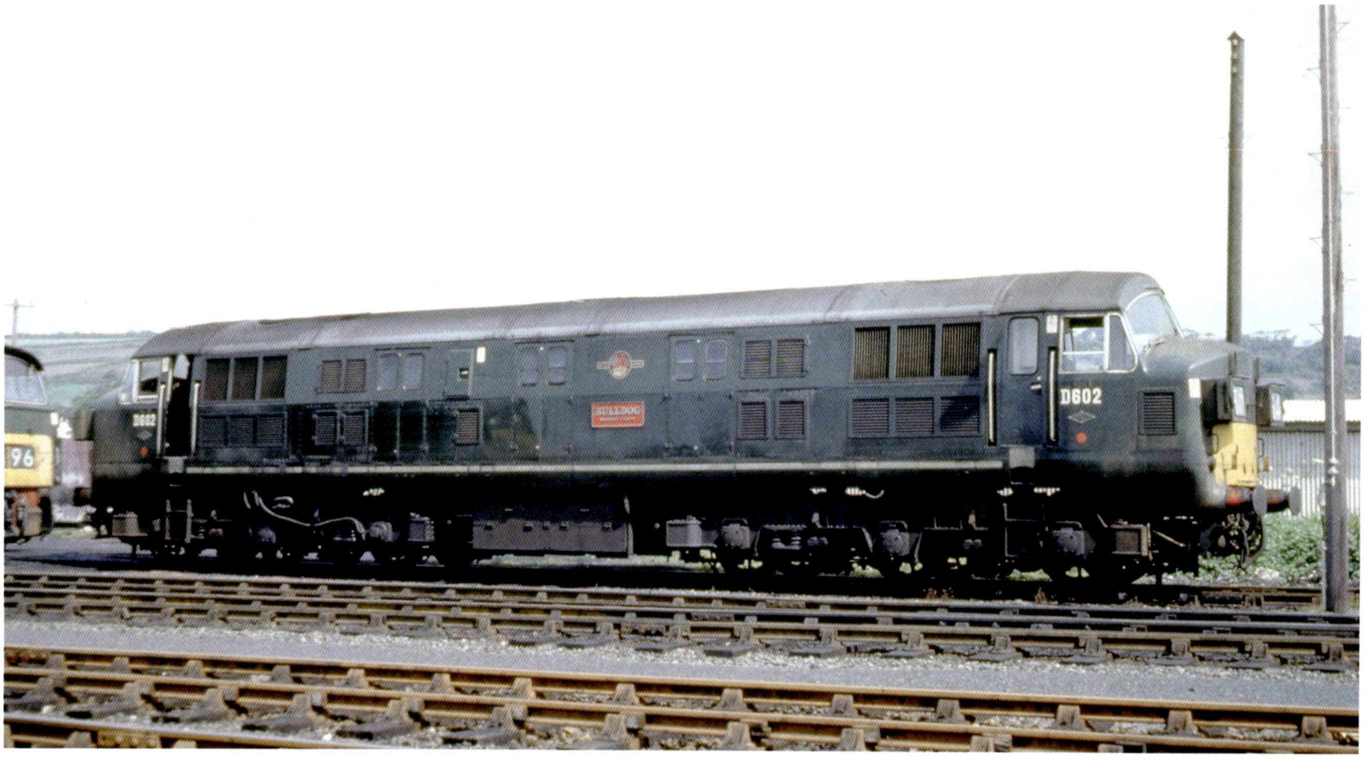

A gap of eight months would ensue in deliveries from North British in Glasgow after the first two, as the engines for the locomotives were now being built within the United Kingdom, rather than Germany. Sadly the standards of these later locomotives was not so good, and a number of engine and transmission faults occured with the need for the componants to be returned to Glasgow for repairs due to contractual agreements. This was the scene at Laira in late 1965 for D602 Bulldog before a visit to Swindon Works in 1966, where it would be overhauled and repainted into blue alongside D600 Active. ***Strathwood Library Collection***

Whilst D600 Active left Swindon in blue with a full yellow front, D602 Bulldog made a return to service with just a half yellow warning panel as seen here light engine at Plymouth's North Road station in the early summer of 1967. ***Grahame Wareham Collection***

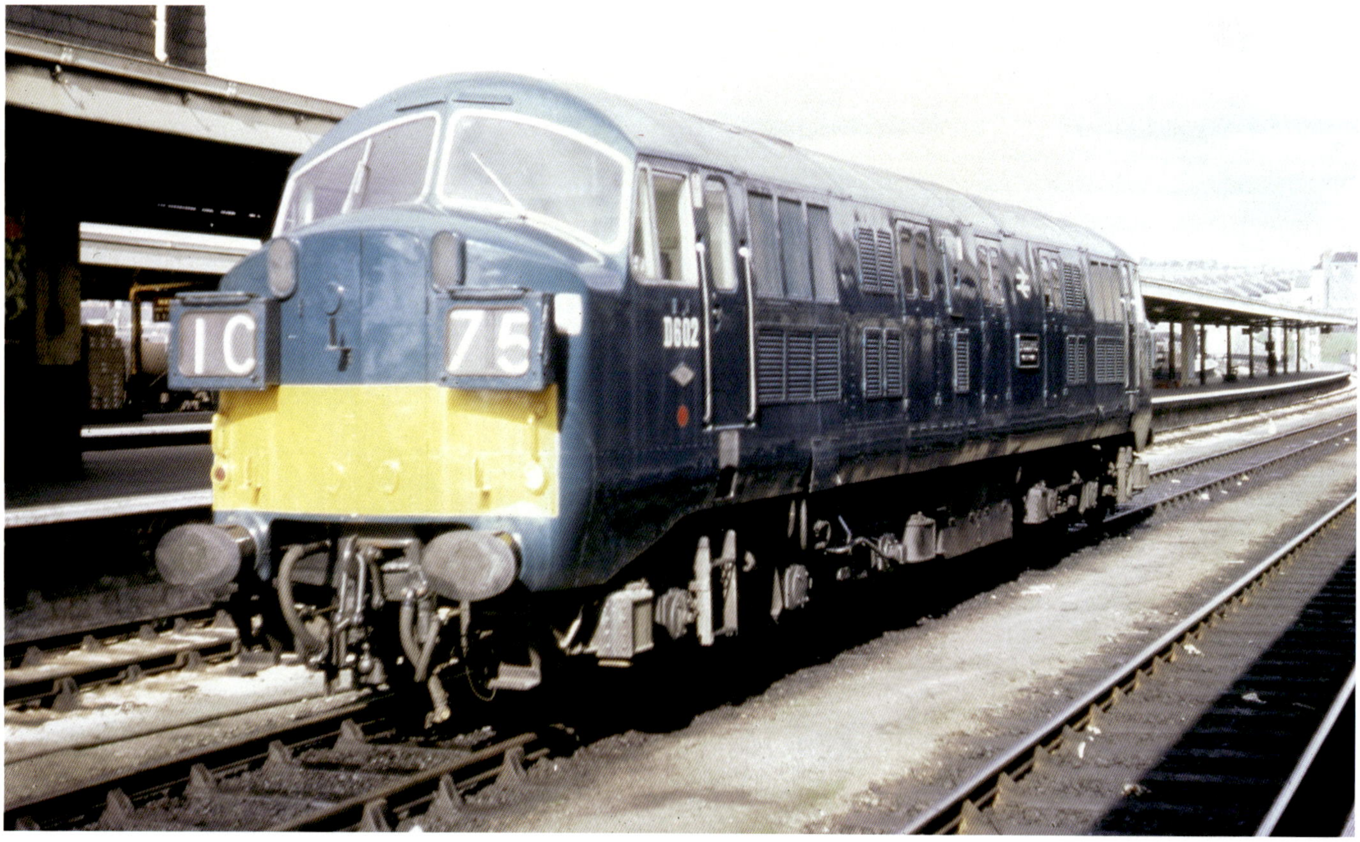

Page opposite: After 1964 the class were rarely seen east of Exeter which kept them close to hand for Laira's experienced fitters should things go wrong, this also kept their mileage down to below 70,000 miles per year which was still more than many Class 40s or Peaks would manage. This is D602 Bulldog drawing into Saltash during 1965. ***Bernard Mills***

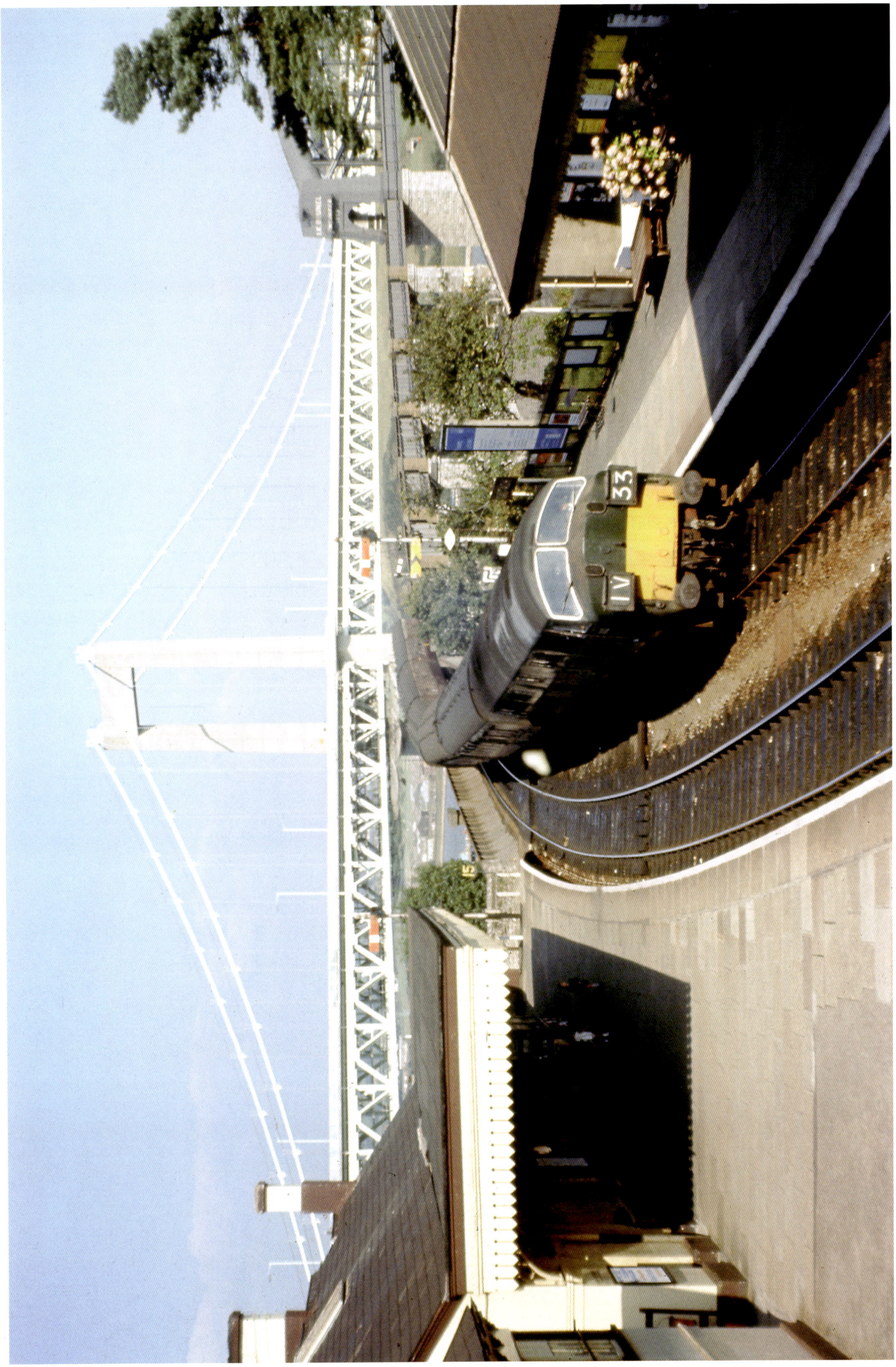
1V
33

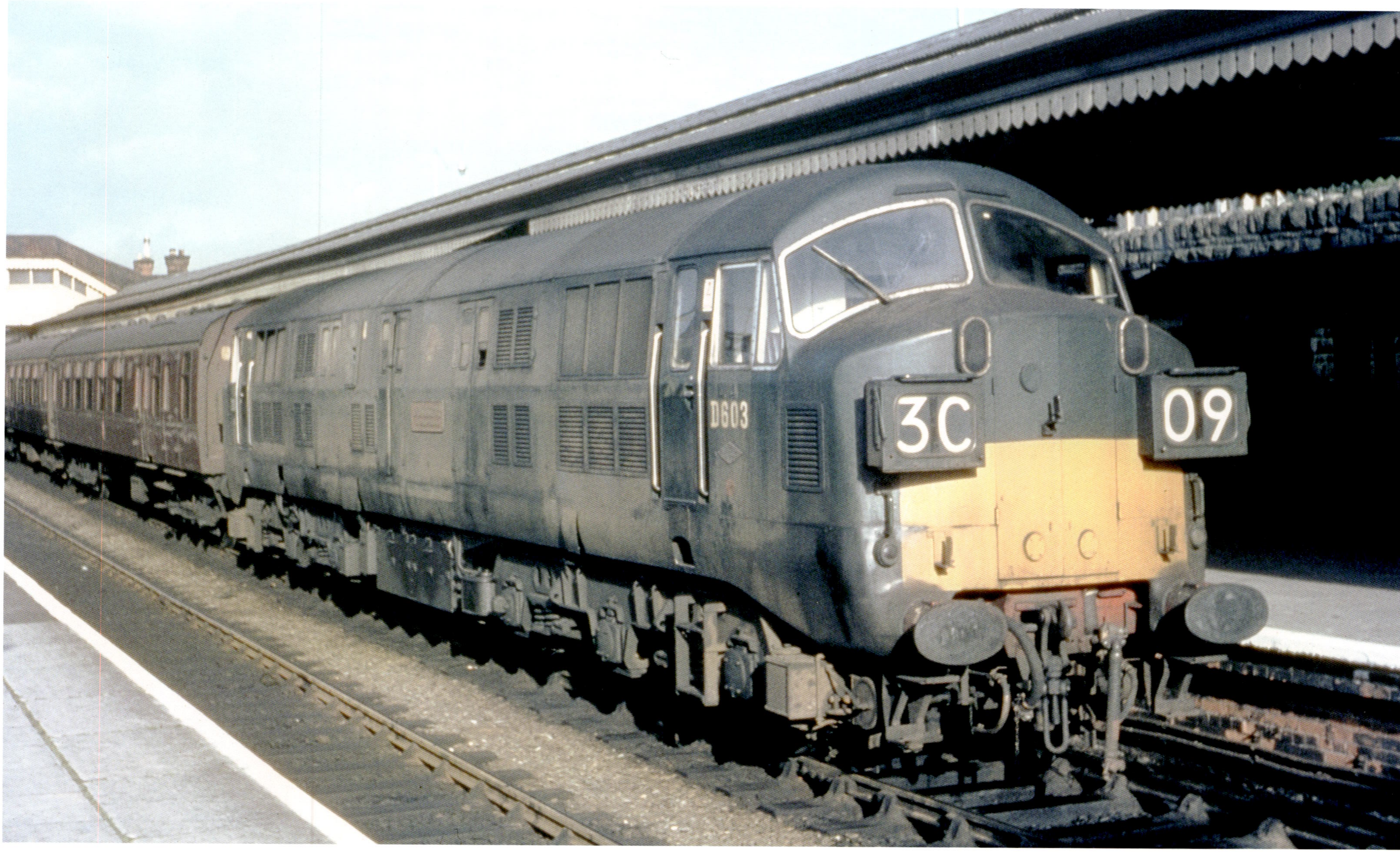

Perhaps the least photographed of the five locomotives was D603 Conquest looking pretty grubby when recorded at Exeter St.Davids in May 1966. If the original plans had gone ahead, and the order for another thirty three of these A1A-A1A Warships D605 to D637 not been cancelled in 1958 with NBL, and instead changed to the lighterweight B-B locomotives numbers D833 to D865, we might have seen D605 named as Eagle. ***Strathwood Library Collection***

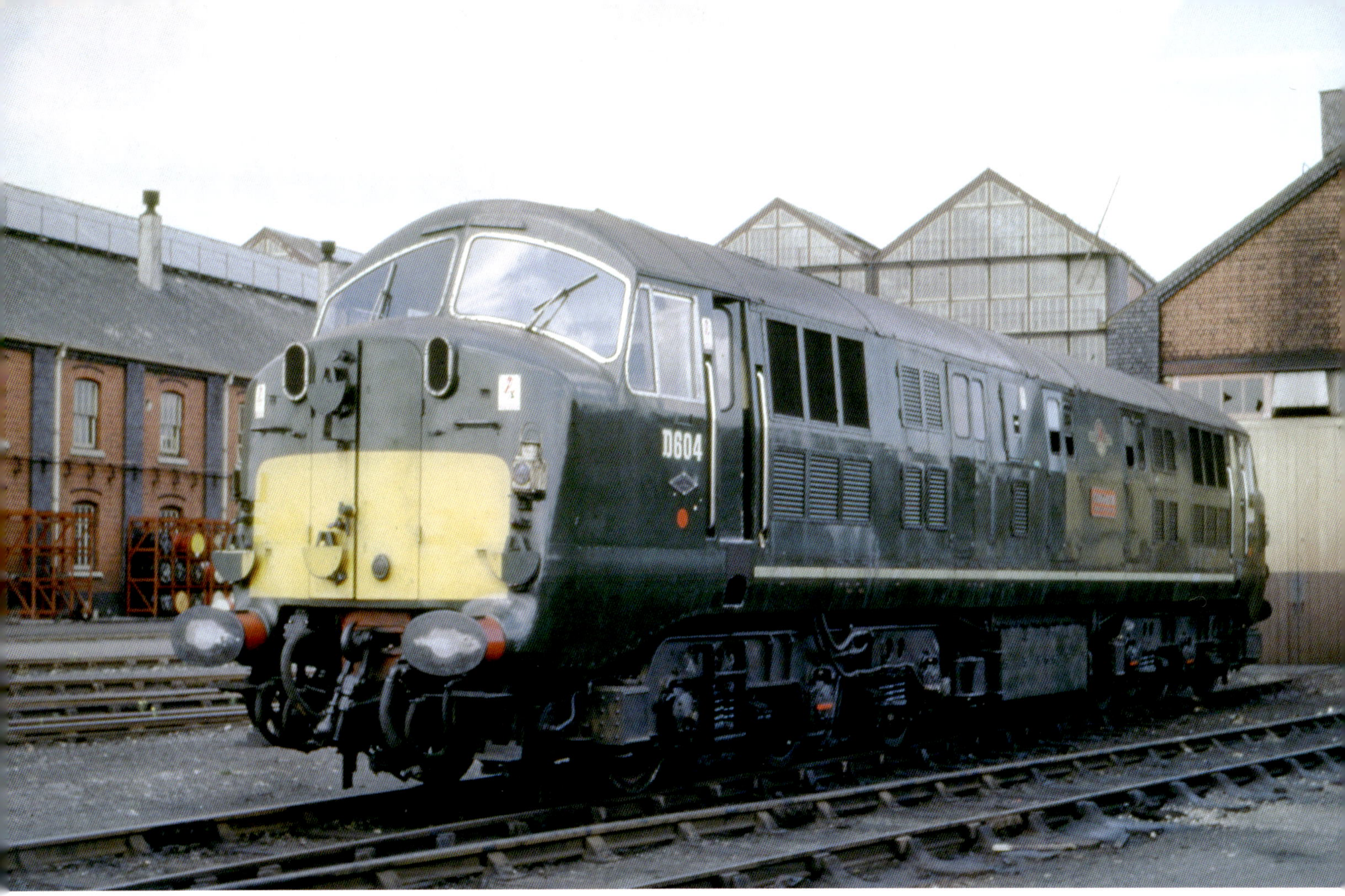

Seen firstly at Swindon Works on 3 June 1962 and then at Laira in August 1965, D604 Cossack shows the extra handrails affixed in 1959 to the fronts of the locomotives, just above where they would all be later fitted with headcode boxes by 1966. ***Strathwood Library Collection***

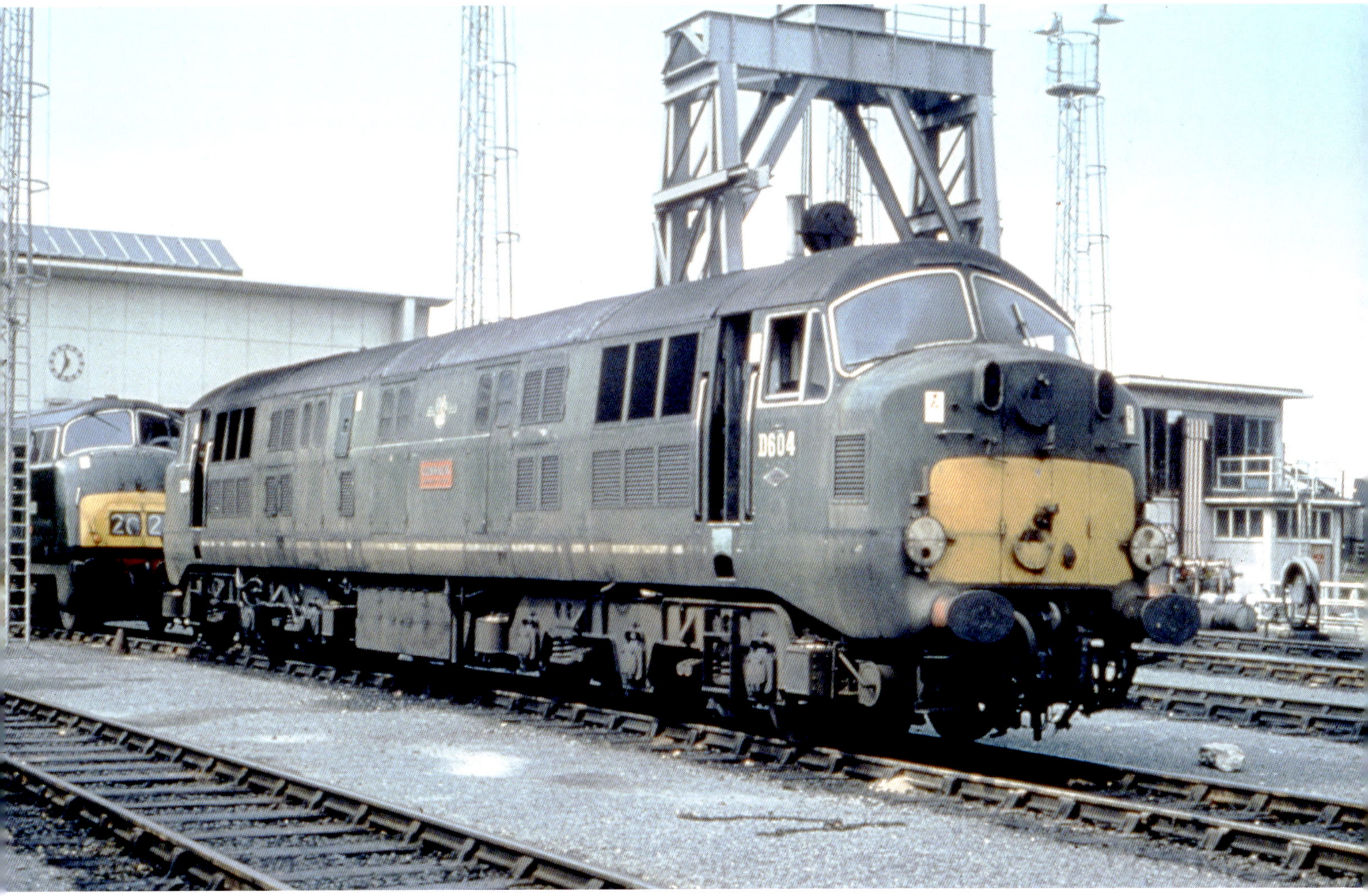

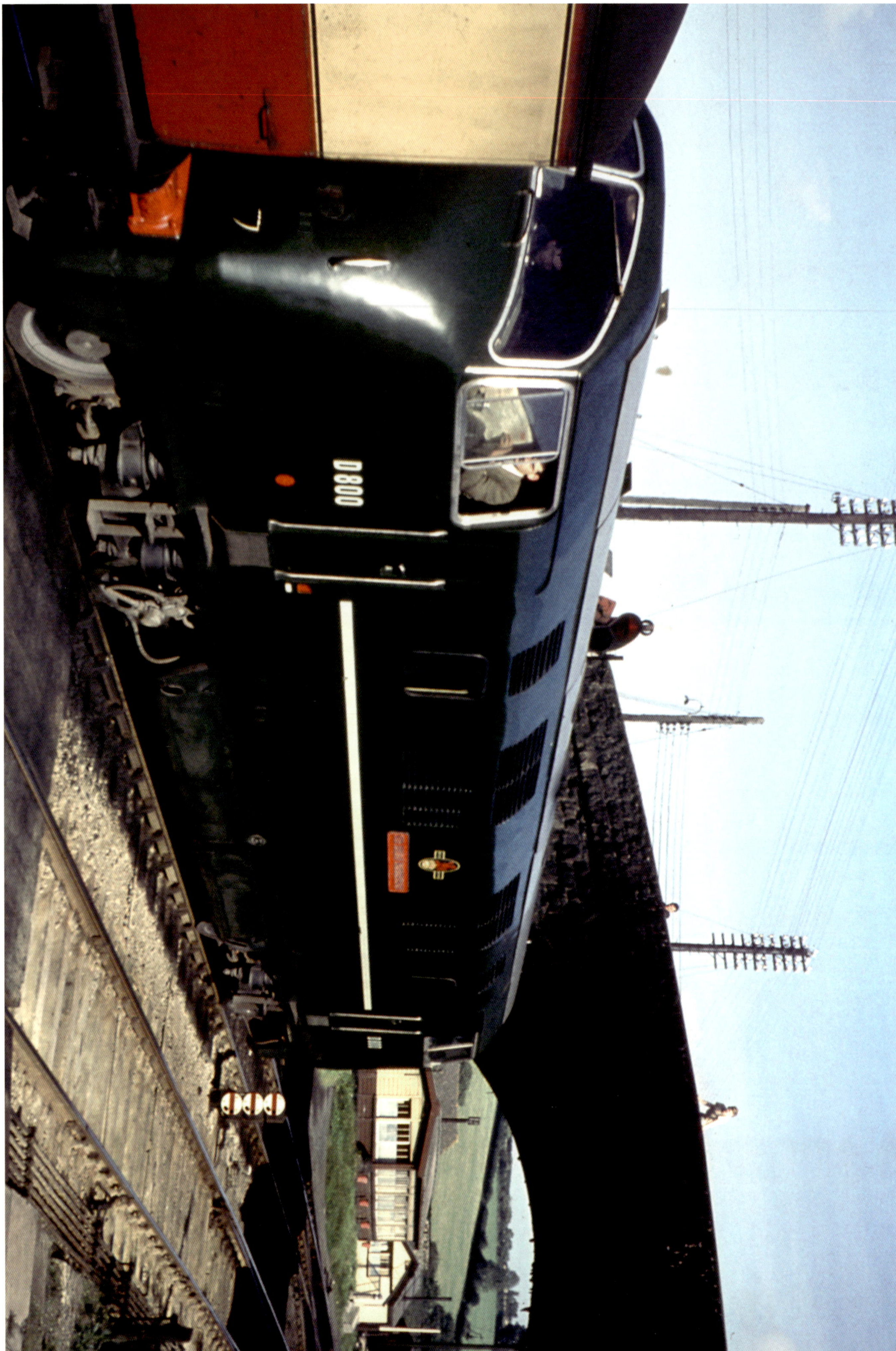
D800

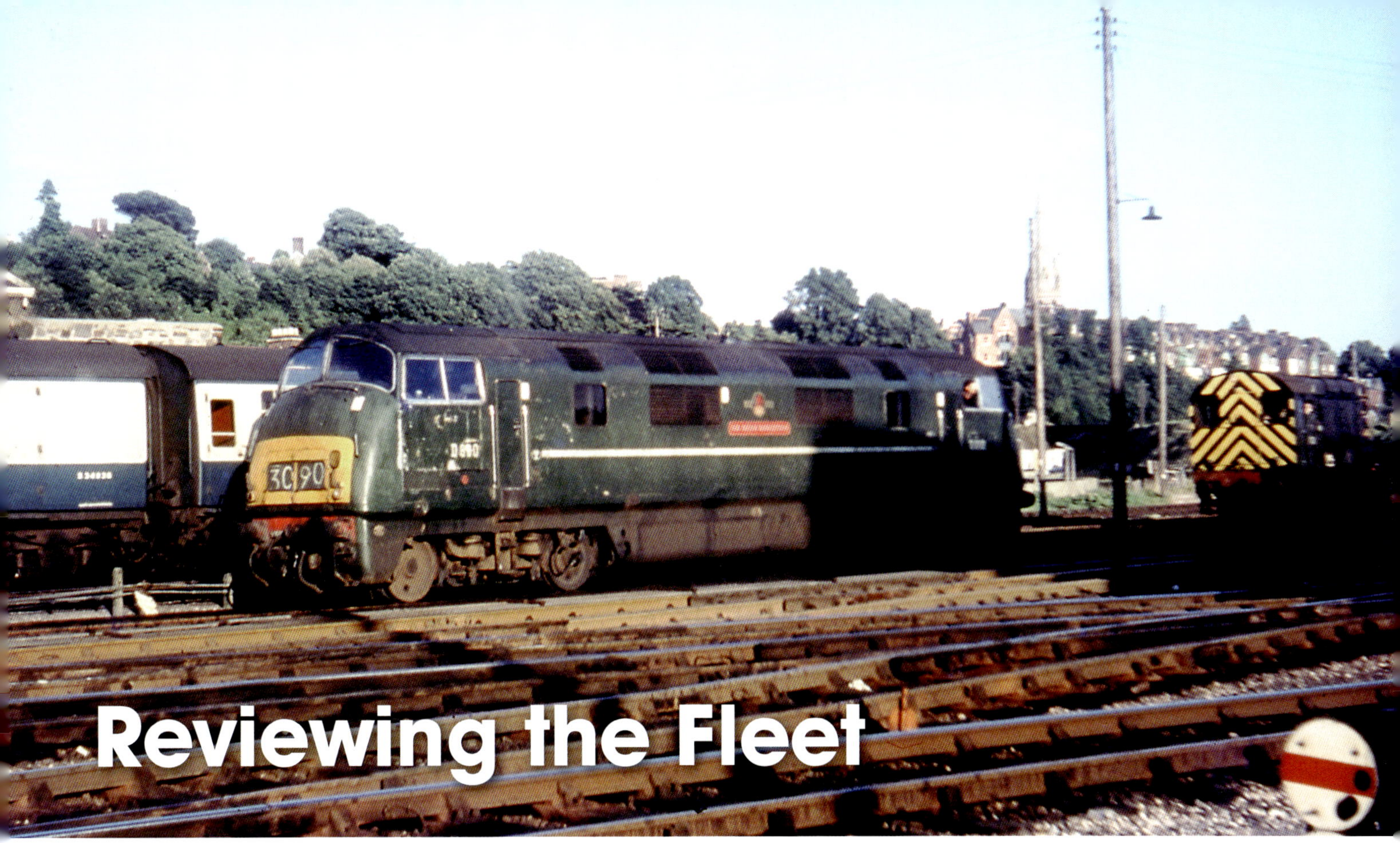

Reviewing the Fleet

The only Warship not to have Warship Class emblazoned on it's nameplates was D800 Sir Brian Robertson seen here at Exeter St. Davids on 20 July 1968. This was the only non-Naval name in the D800-D870 range, honouring the British Transport Commission chairman of the time who lived at Far Oakridge near Stroud in Gloucestershire. This would also be the only lightweight Warship to go for scrap still in green livery. ***Exe Rail***

Smartly turned out at Laira in the May sunshine of 1967 was D801 Vanguard which by June of the following year would be stored here and officially withdrawn on 3 August 1968, along with D800 and D802 following it on 5 October 1968. ***Strathwood Library Collection***

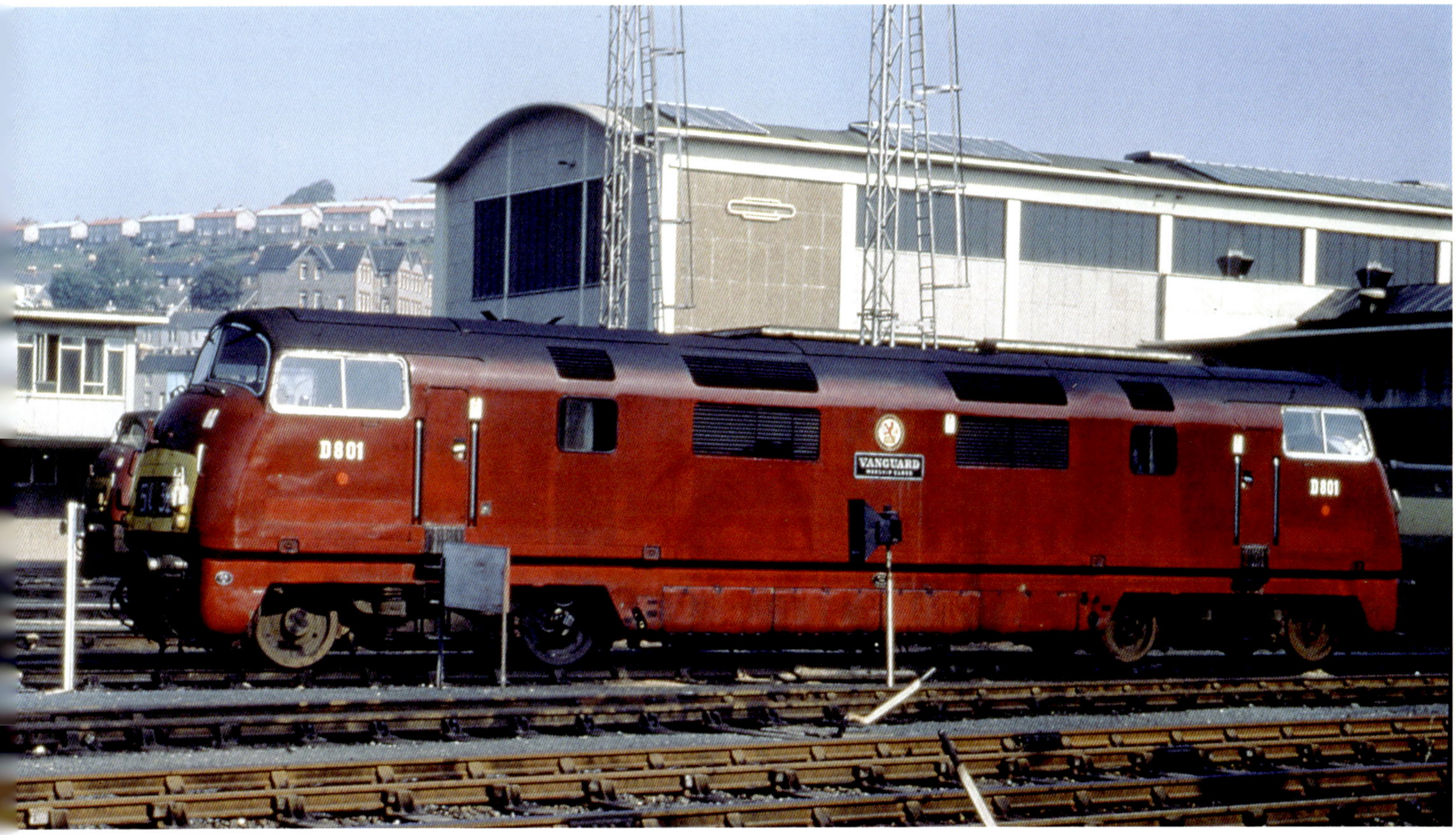

Page left: We believe this shot of D800 Sir Brian Robertson was taken at Par in July 1958 on test with fitters and inspectors on board even if one is reading today's newspaper, so all must be going well. ***Transport Treasury***

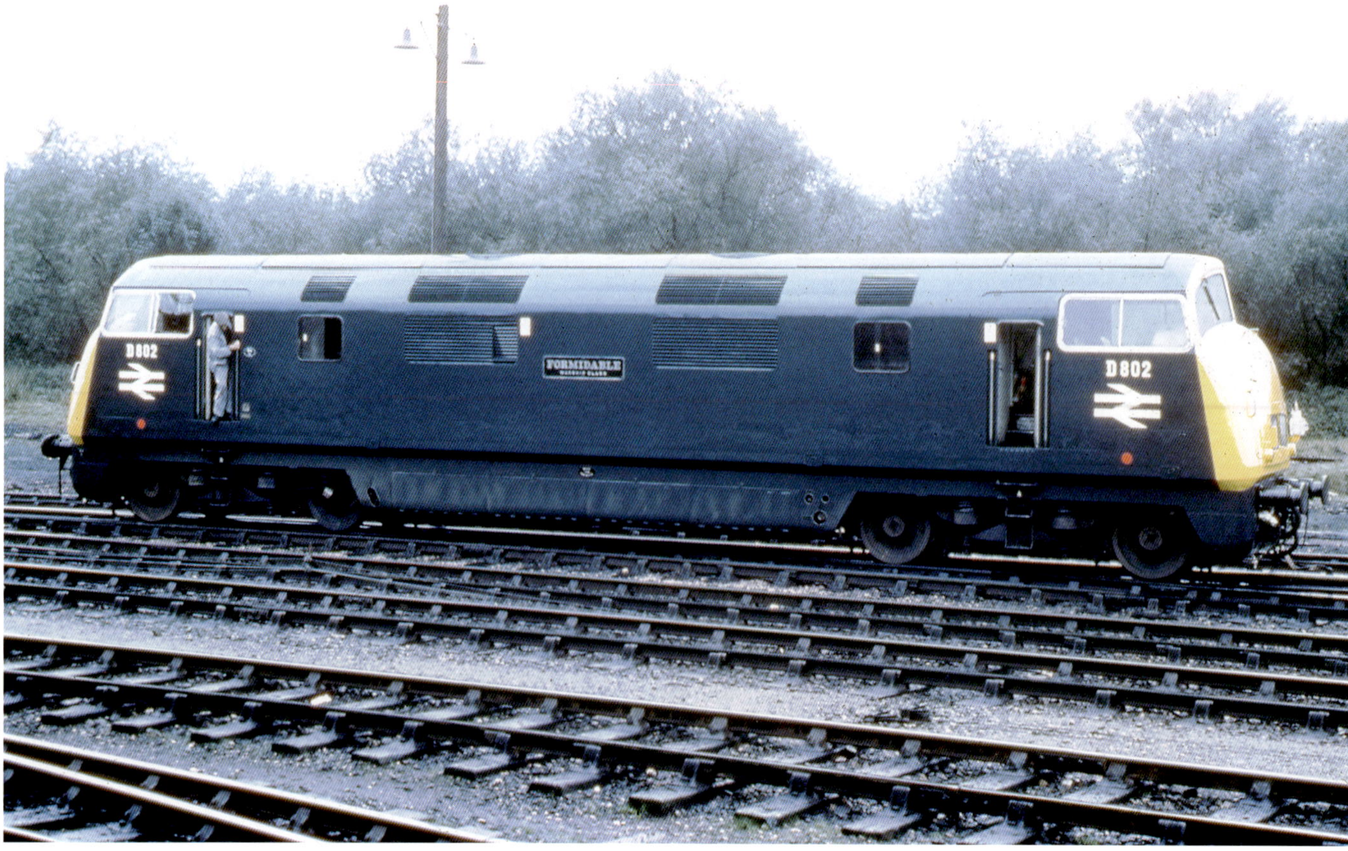

Even though D802 Formidable was among the first casualties for withdrawal it still made it into blue as seen here at Exeter St. Davids shuffling around the stabling point in early 1968. ***Strathwood Library Collection***

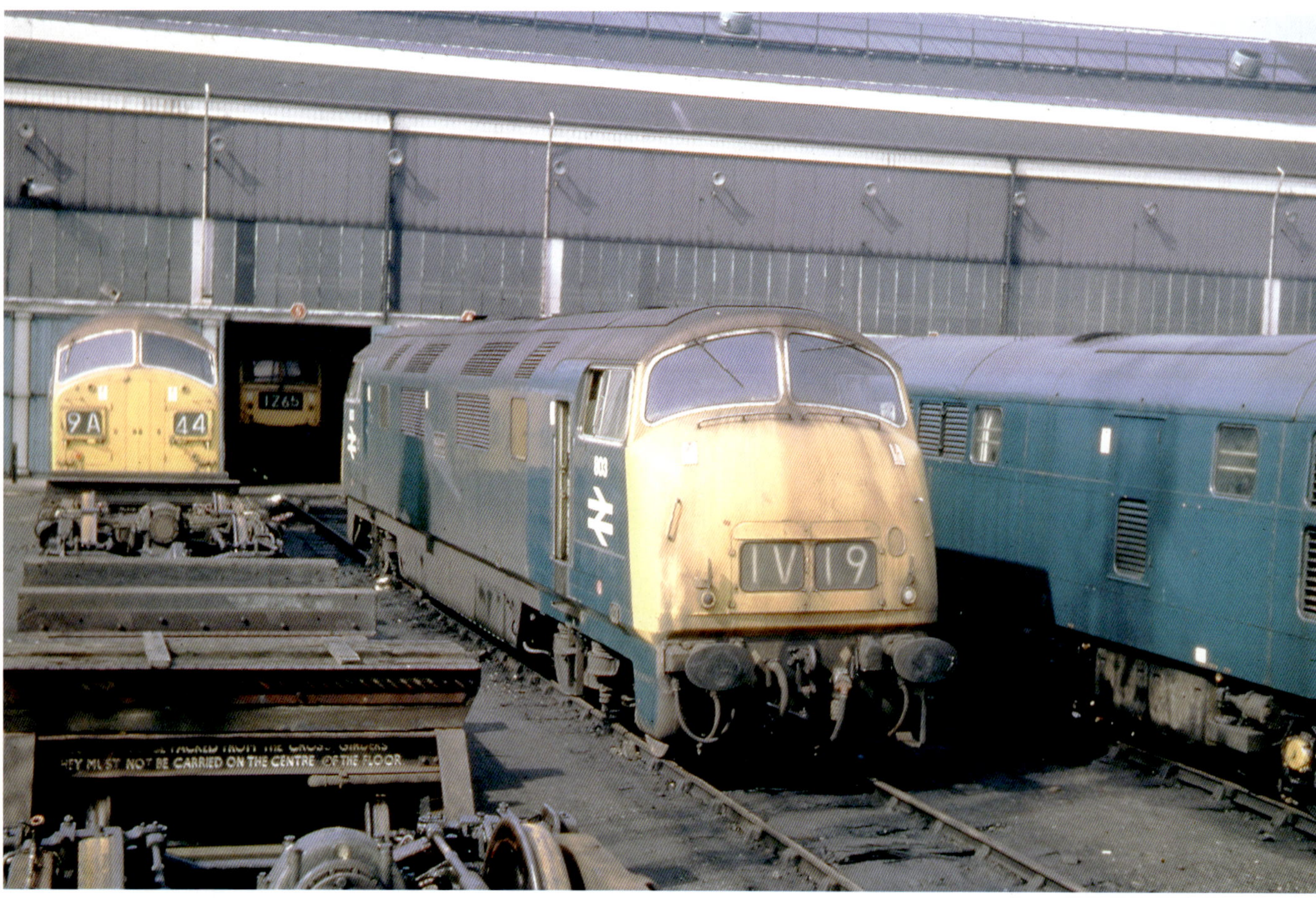

After the first three Warship prototypes an attempt to name the rest of the class in alphabetical order was made, starting with D803 Albion in March 1959. It was a Laira engine when seen at Old Oak Common in April 1970 before a final switch to Newton Abbot which was made in October the following year just before withdrawal. ***Strathwood Library Collection***

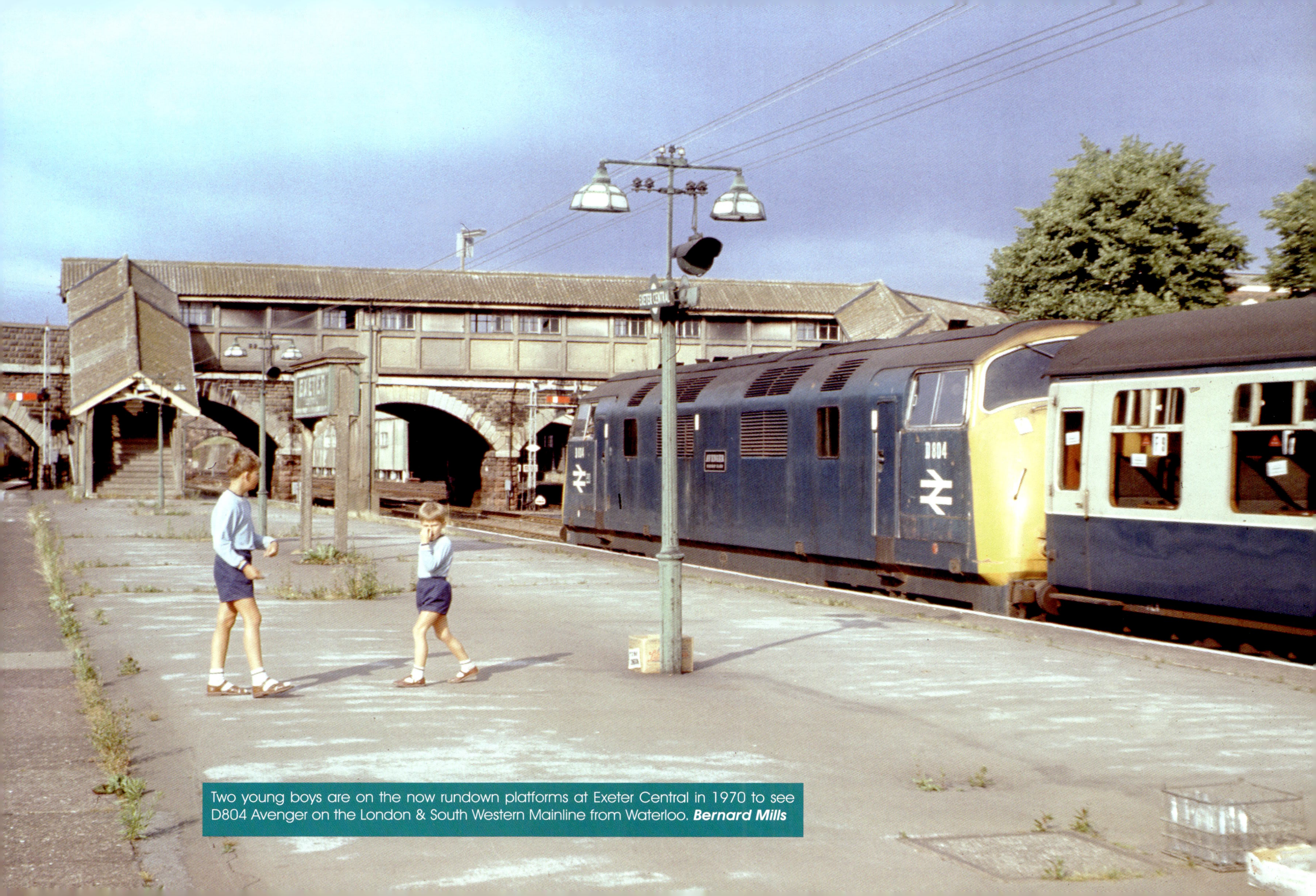

Two young boys are on the now rundown platforms at Exeter Central in 1970 to see D804 Avenger on the London & South Western Mainline from Waterloo. ***Bernard Mills***

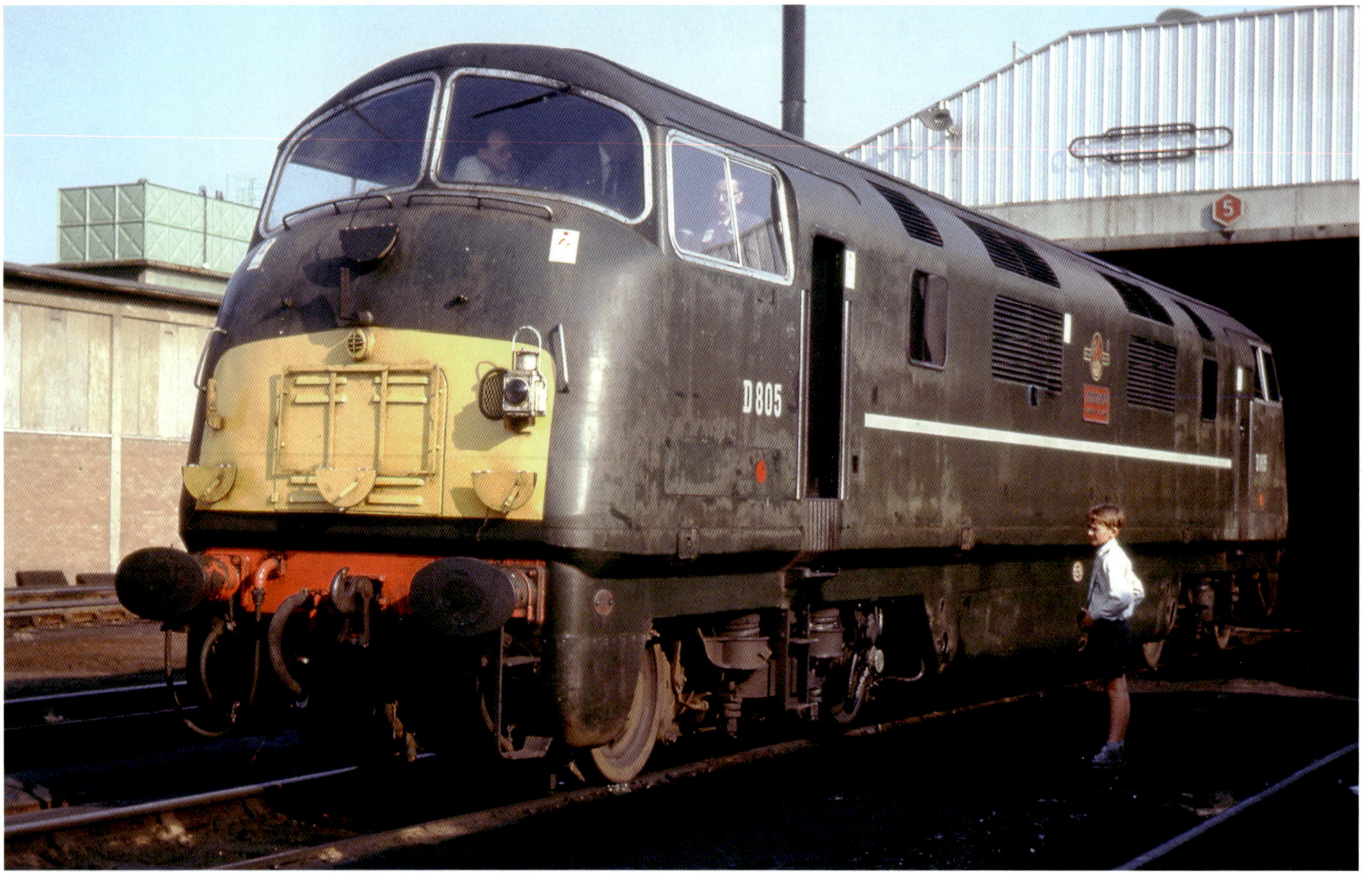

Another young lad admires D805 Benbow still with the headcode discs and the cumbersome route shutters outside Bristol Bath Road in 1965, although a bright yellow warning panel has been added to aid visibility for trackside workers and trespassers alike. This locomotive was the first of the class to be seen with overhead livewire warning flashes fitted in the summer of 1961. ***Strathwood Library Collection***

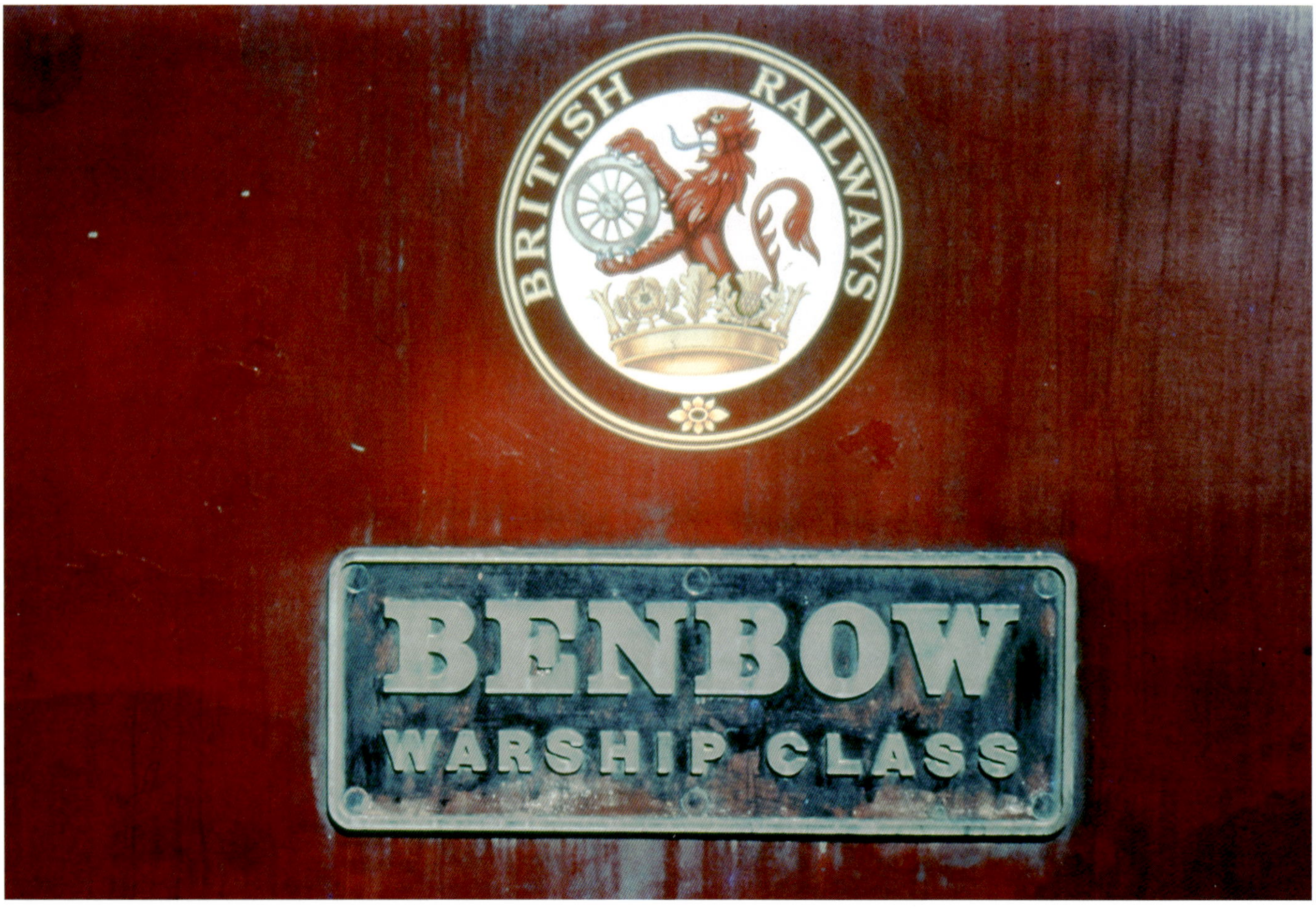

The next repaint would take the locomotive into maroon firstly with a half yellow panel and after early February 1968 a full yellow front was added. Although it is the nameplate that looks like it could do with a touch of paint in this view from 1968. ***Strathwood Library collection***

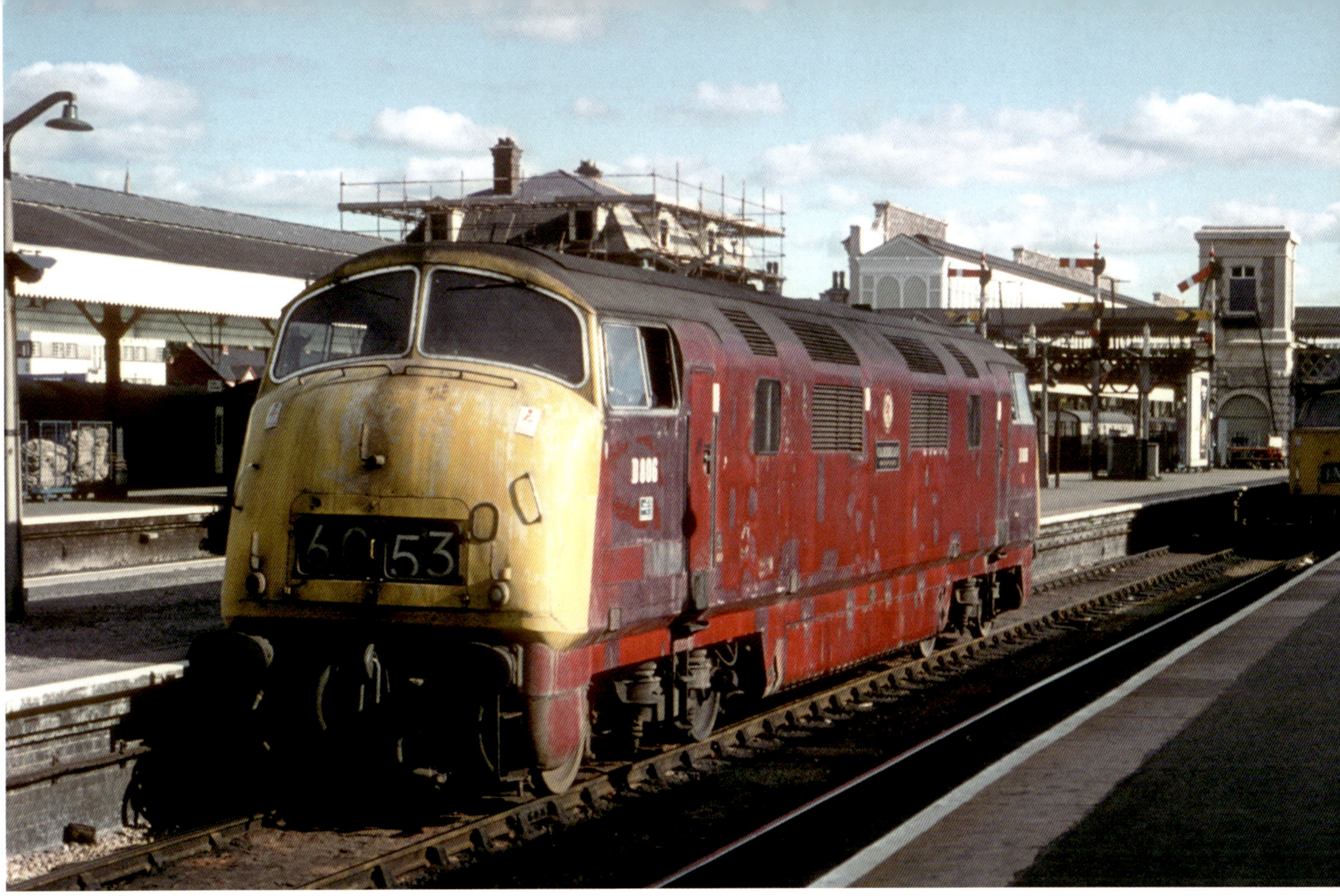

Warships just like the Westerns suffered badly from shabby paintwork, and D806 Cambrian is no exception seen here still in maroon on 9 July 1970. A repaint into blue would take place in early March the following year as one of the last of the class to be overhauled at Swindon Works. ***Jim Binnie***

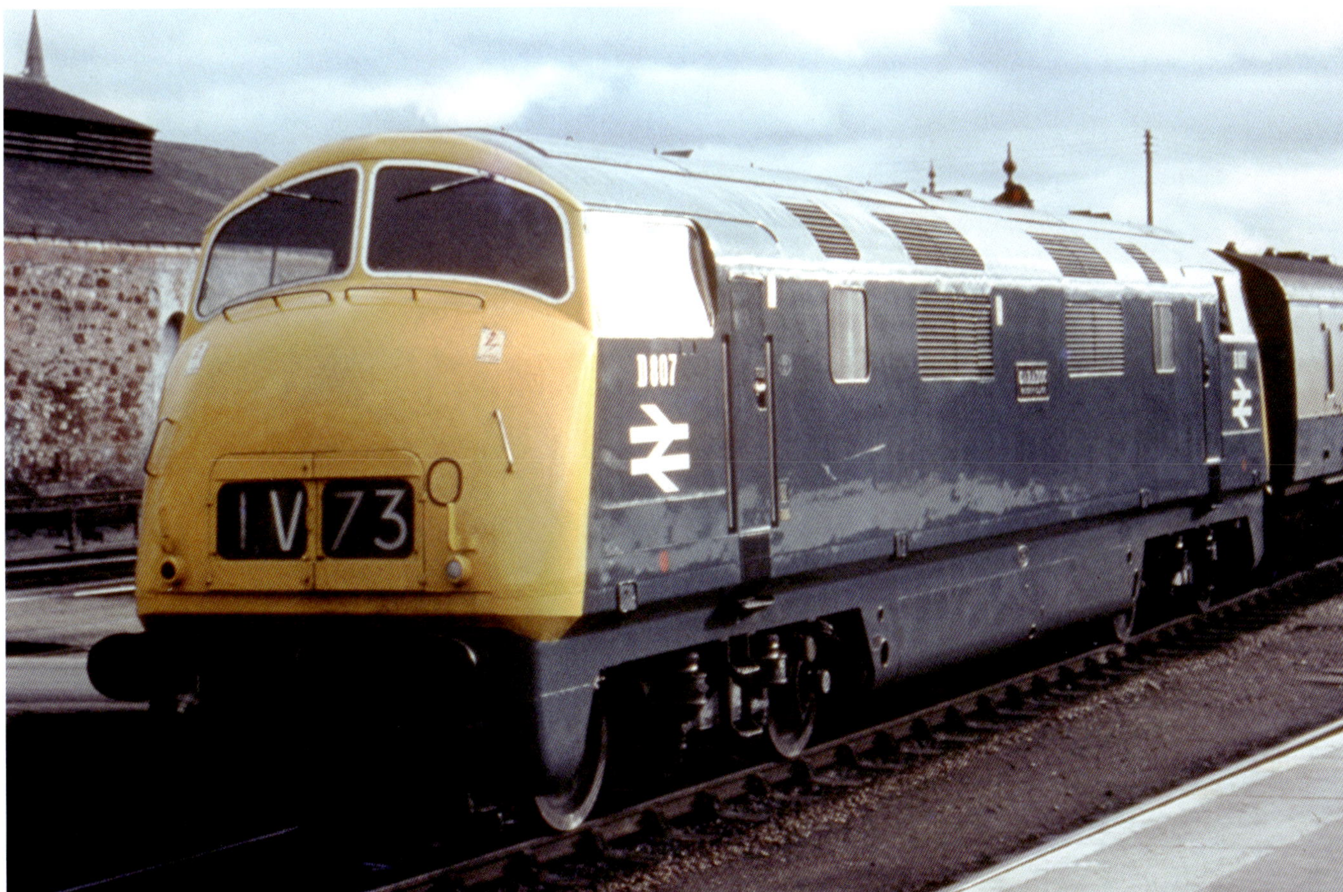

Another early blue repaint was given to D807 Caradoc seen here at Newton Abbot on 11 November 1967 just five days off Swindon Works. ***Exe Rail***

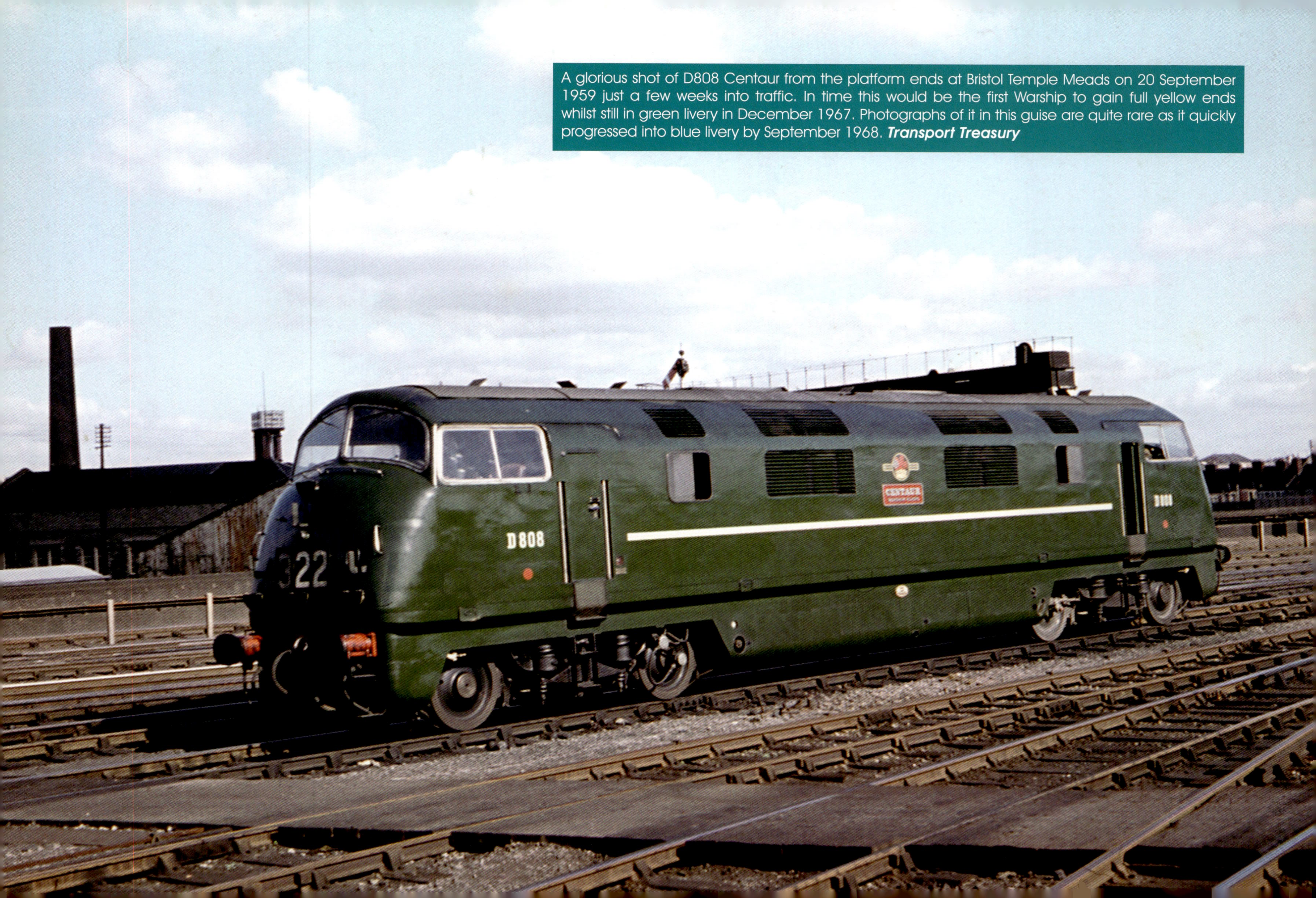

A glorious shot of D808 Centaur from the platform ends at Bristol Temple Meads on 20 September 1959 just a few weeks into traffic. In time this would be the first Warship to gain full yellow ends whilst still in green livery in December 1967. Photographs of it in this guise are quite rare as it quickly progressed into blue livery by September 1968. ***Transport Treasury***

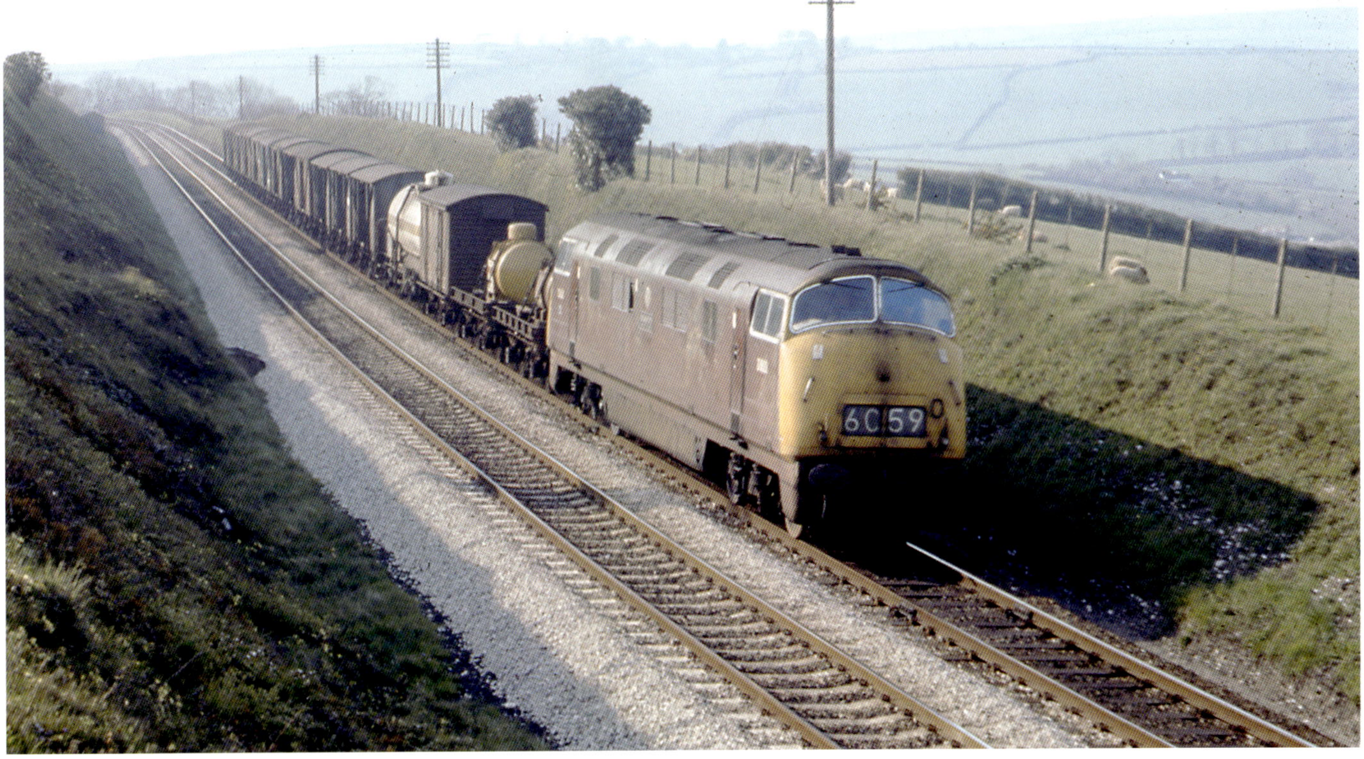

It was not envisaged that the D800 Warships would be used on un-fitted freight work regularly when designed as they were considered too lightweight to have sufficient braking. However they were often sent out to work fitted goods trains in practice as here in April 1971 with D809 Champion trudging along near Moorswater on an up goods. ***Bernard Mills***

The D prefix has been lost now on 810 Cockade recently painted into blue, although along with D808 it was one of only two of the class to gain those full yellow ends whilst still in green livery before they progressed to blue, this view at Exeter was taken on 20 May 1970. ***Jeffrey Lane.***

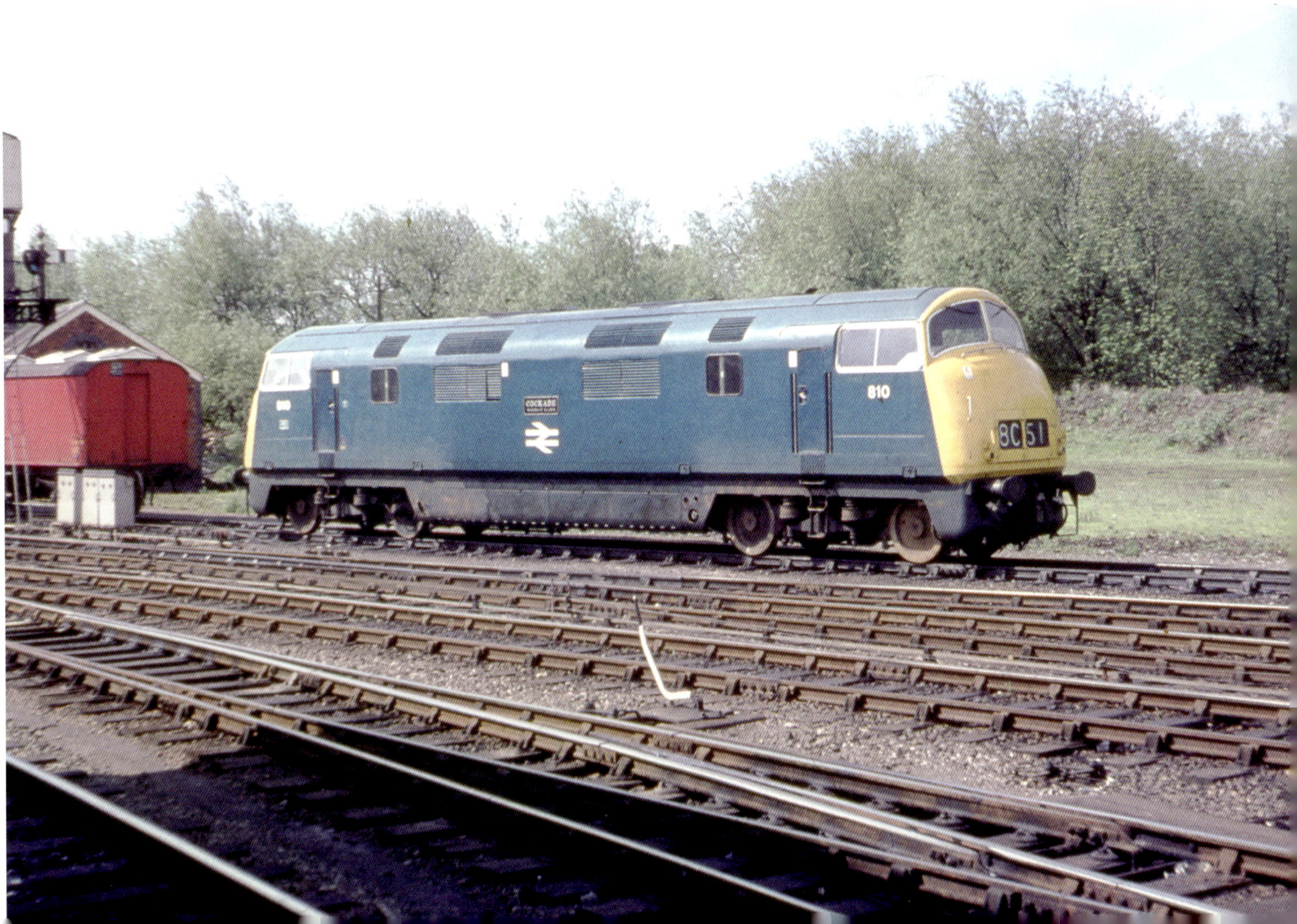

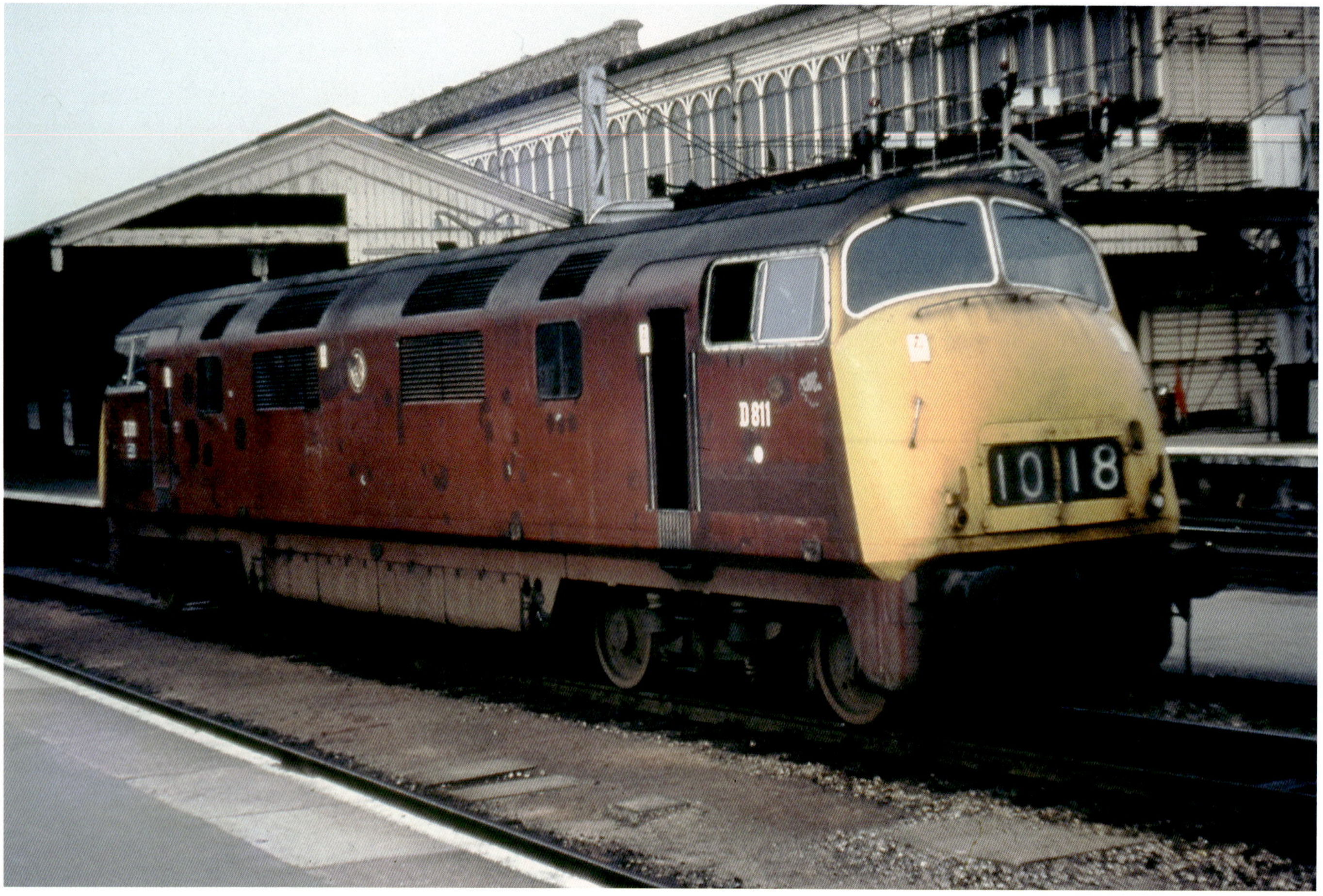

The first of the Swindon built Warships into maroon had been D811 Daring in November 1965, and it would be the first to gain the full yellow ends too, these were added in August 1967, and by 1969 it presented a sorry appearance when seen at Exeter St. Davids with one nameplate missing. A coat of fresh blue paint would have to wait until the start of the following year. ***Exe Rail***

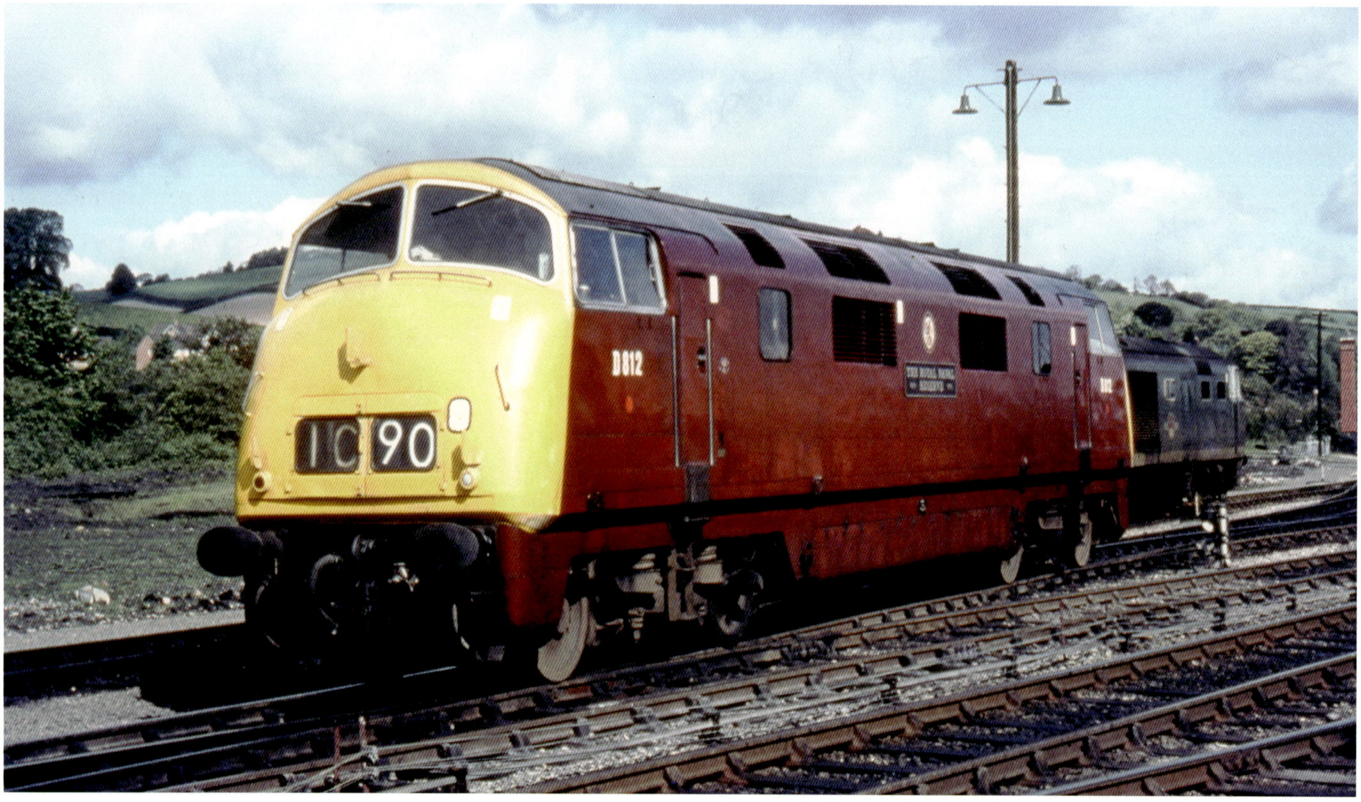

Originally due to carry the name Despatch, D812 was instead to became The Royal Naval Reserve 1859-1959 as its' centenary was being celebrated at the time of the locomotive's introduction. Perhaps suprisingly the next Warship to enter traffic did not take up the name Despatch instead and the whole list of names move down one. When seen at Exeter St. Davids on 18 May 1968, D812 had just been given a full yellow front end and a paintwork spruce up as part of an Intermediate overhaul at Swindon the previous month. ***Exe Rail***

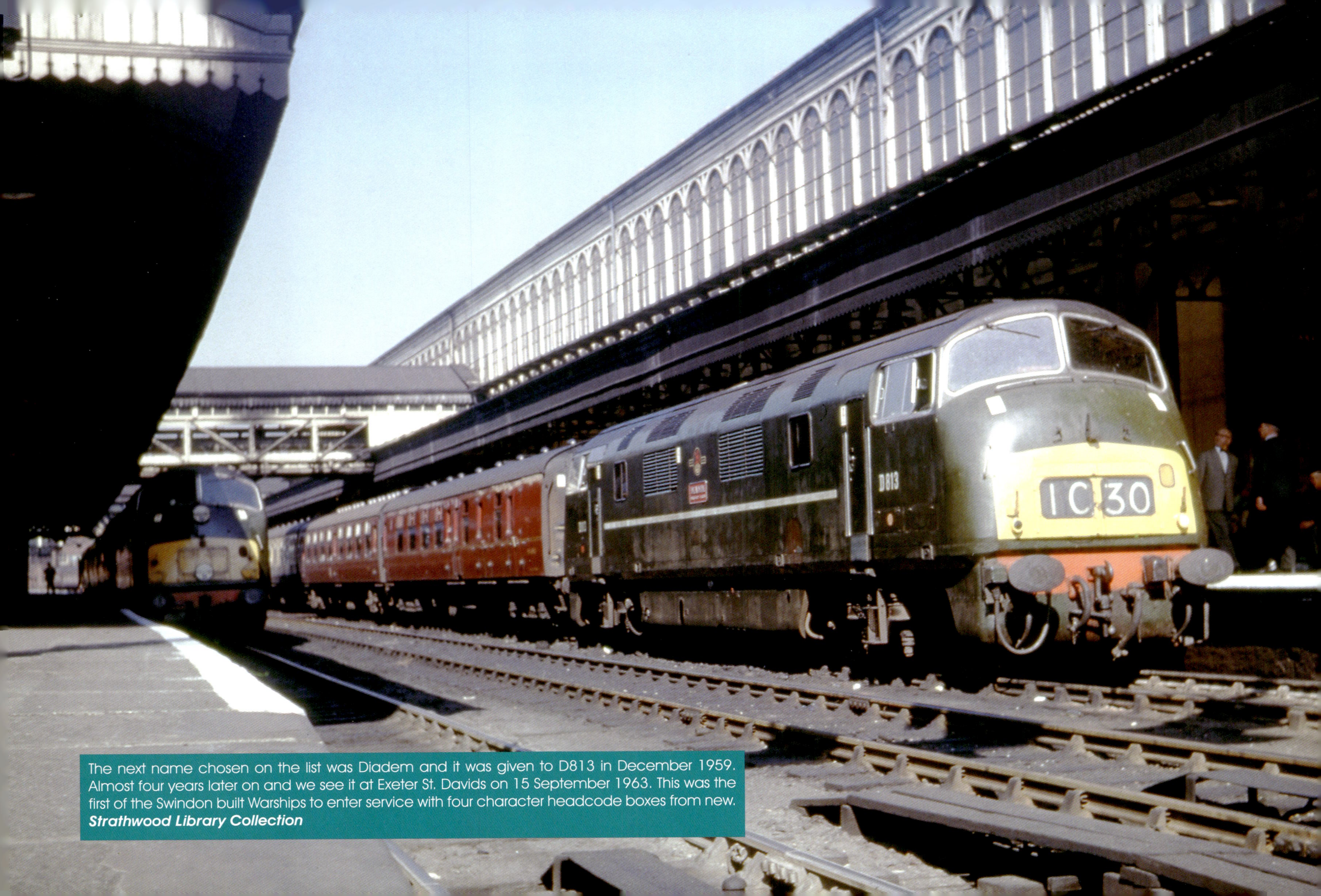

The next name chosen on the list was Diadem and it was given to D813 in December 1959. Almost four years later on and we see it at Exeter St. Davids on 15 September 1963. This was the first of the Swindon built Warships to enter service with four character headcode boxes from new. ***Strathwood Library Collection***

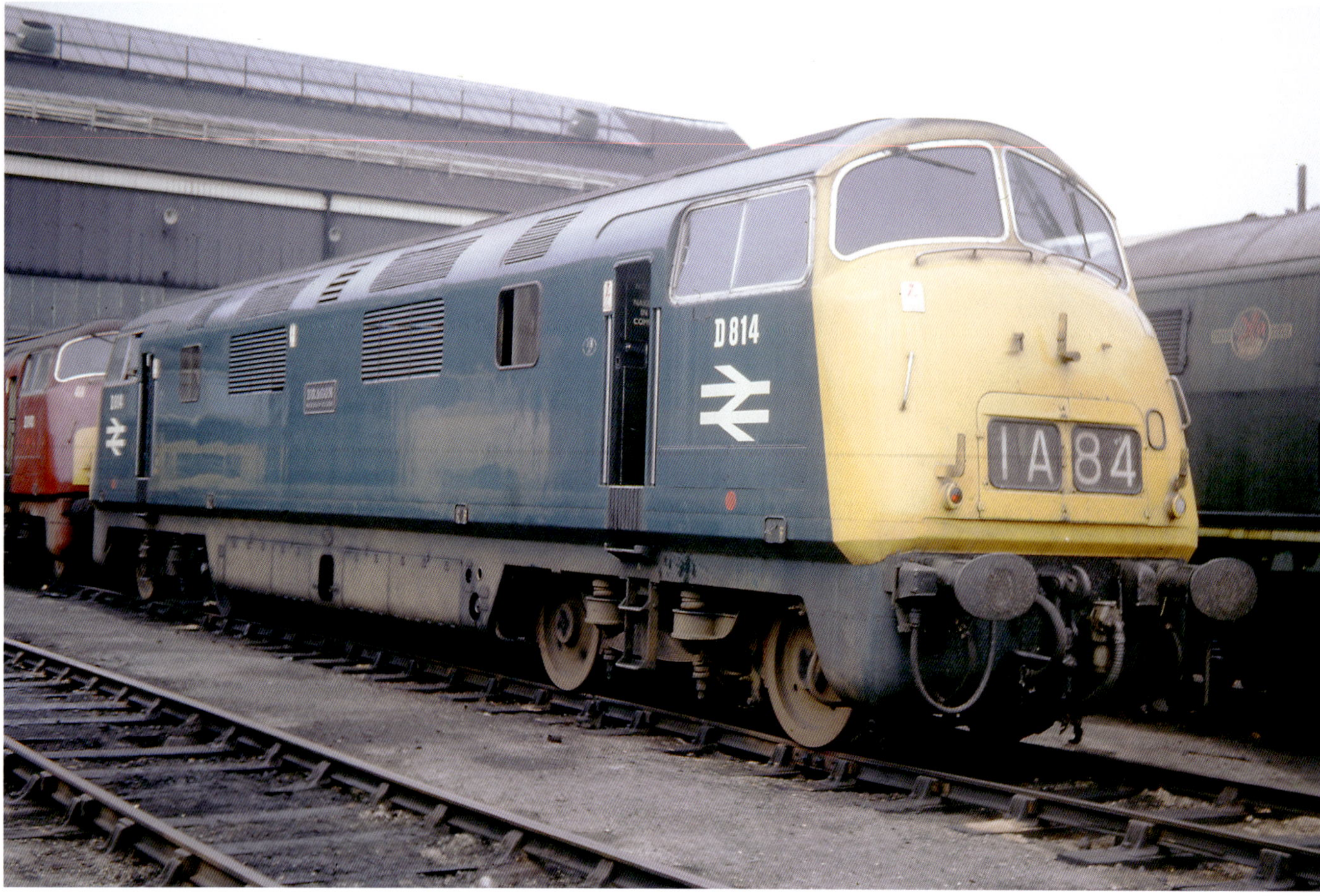

The ventilation louvres above the nameplates on all four Warships in this spread were provided on one side only to assist the cooling of the Stone Vapor steam heating boilers as fitted to locomotives D813 to D865. This is D814 Dragon at Old Oak Common in June 1968, this would be one of the last to be cut up in Febraury 1974. ***Derek Everson***

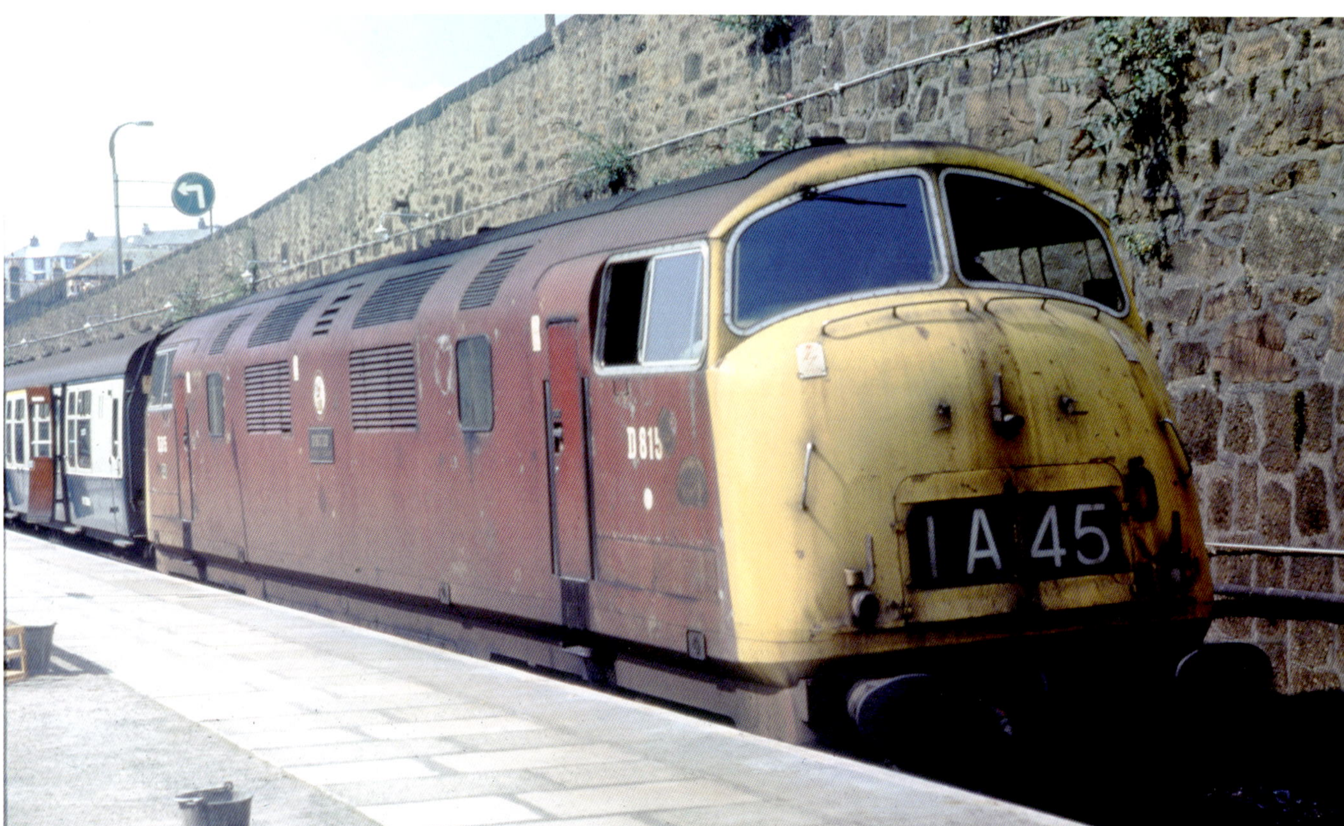

The last of the Swindon built Warships to go into maroon livery before the adoption of blue would be D815 Druid, released to traffic from Swindon Works on 17 October 1966. The full yellow ends were applied in late January 1968 and it would remain in this condition as seen at Penzance, until it was scrapped as we will see on page 93. ***Strathwood Library Collection***

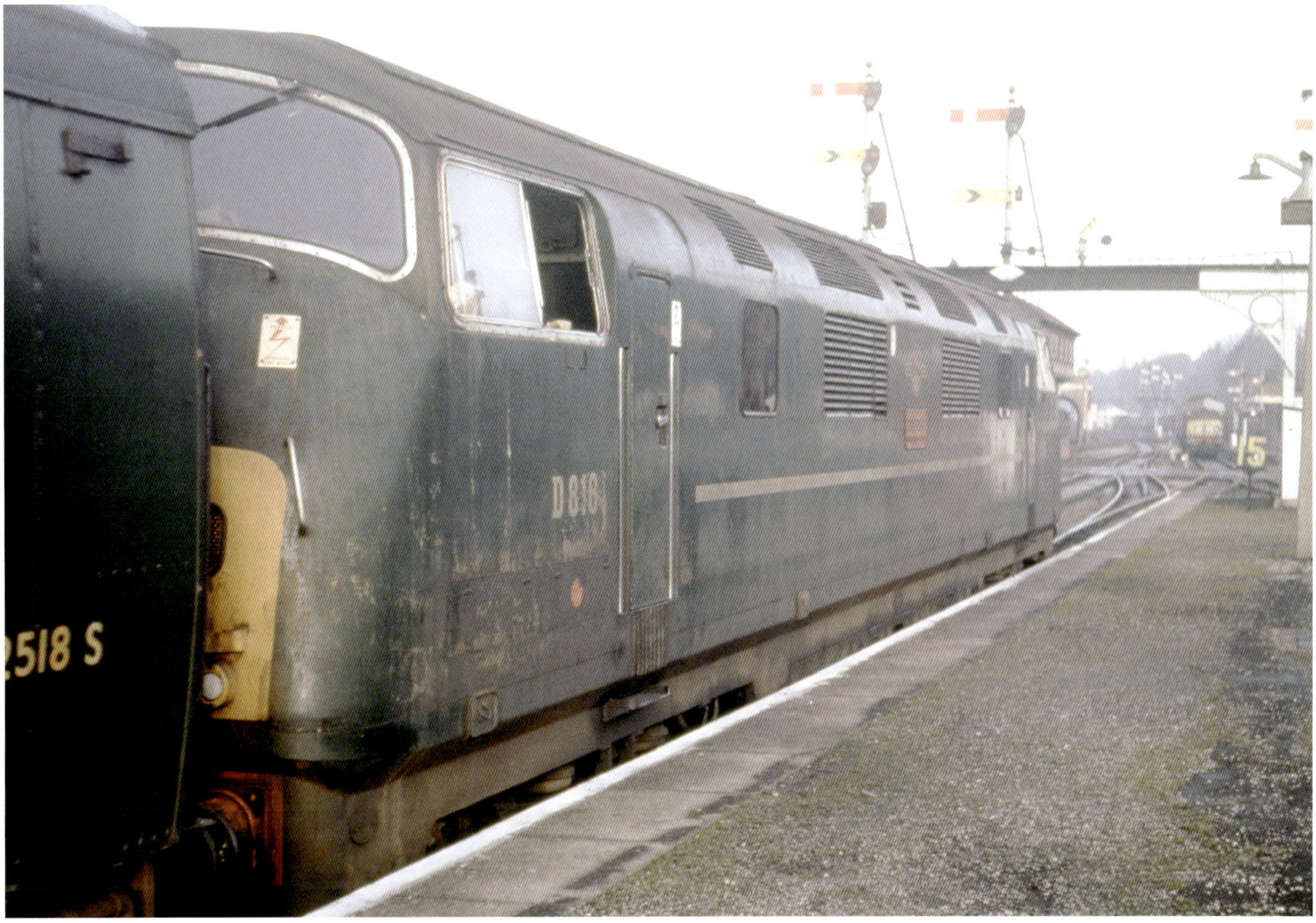

The other type of steam heating boilers fitted to D800 to D812 and D866 to D870, were Spanner Mk 1s which did not require the extra ventilation in service. Among the Warships to go straight to blue from the green livery was D816 Eclipse at the head of some Southern Region stock at Exeter St. Davids. ***Strathwood Library Collection***

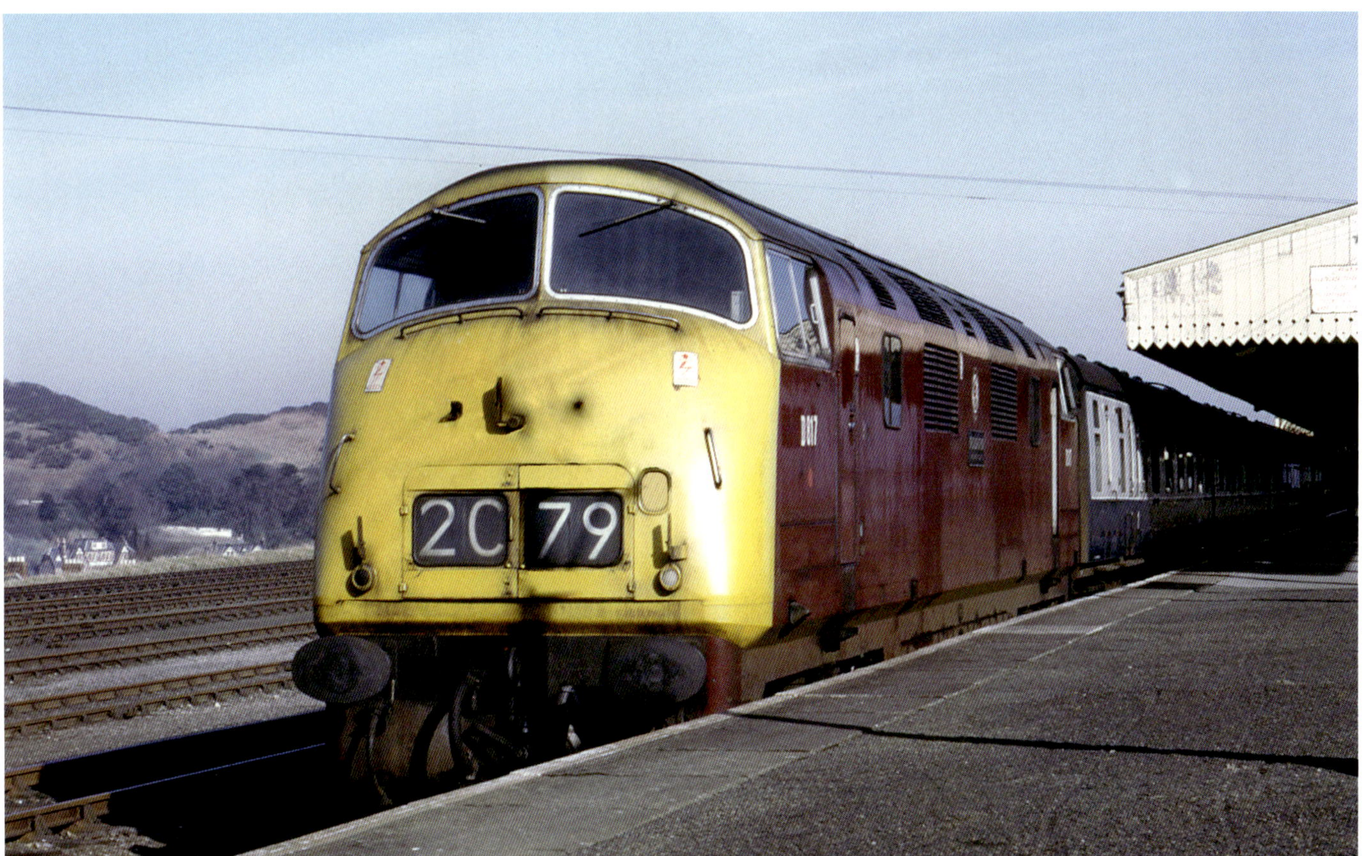

Another turn onto Southern metals for D817 Foxhound as it awaits departure from Ilfracombe with a four coach stopping service back to Exeter in March 1969. The storage sidings in the background once full of stock on summer saturdays lay empty, and will not see much use in the coming season either. ***John A.Vaughan/Rail Photoprints***

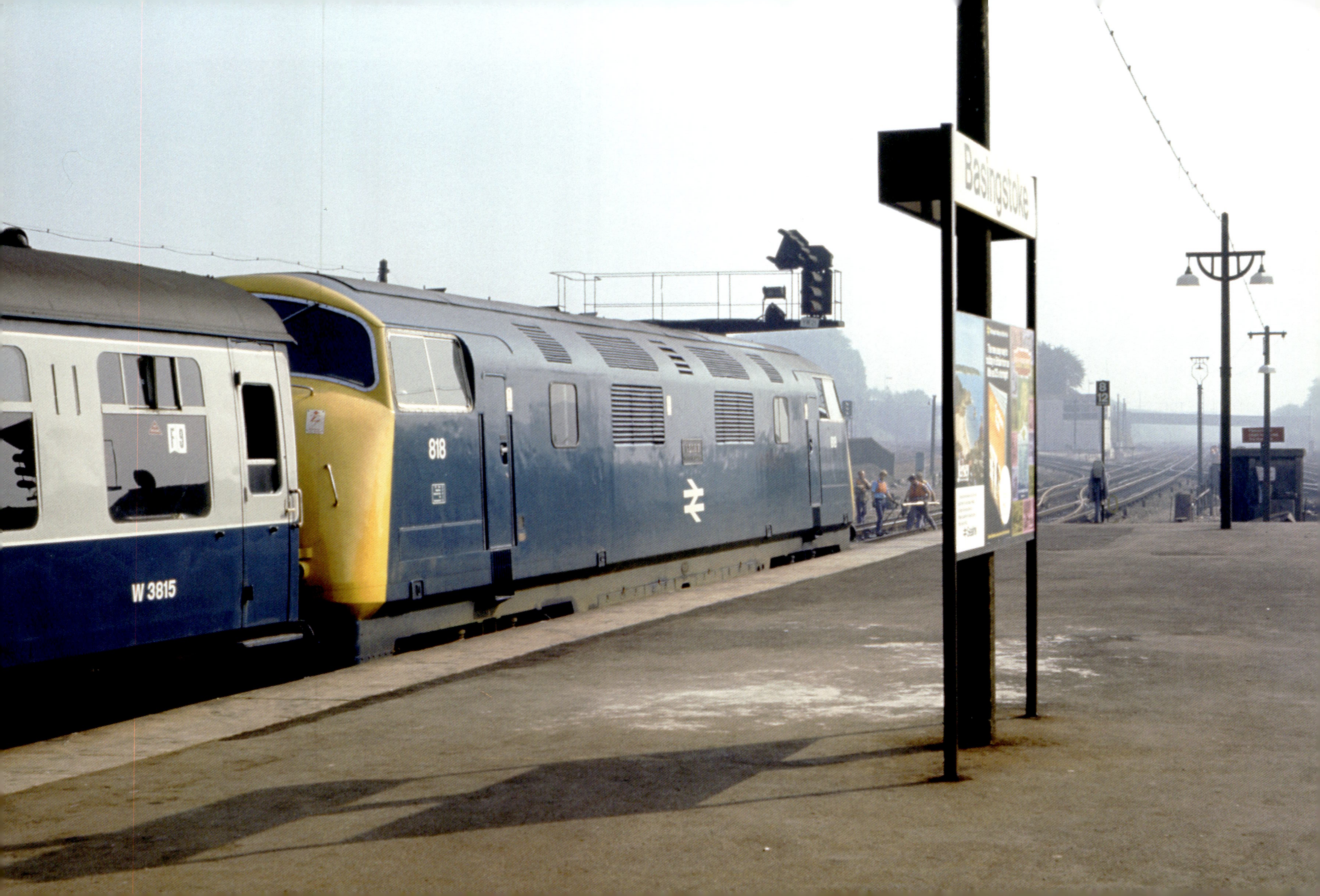
Basingstoke
818
W 3815

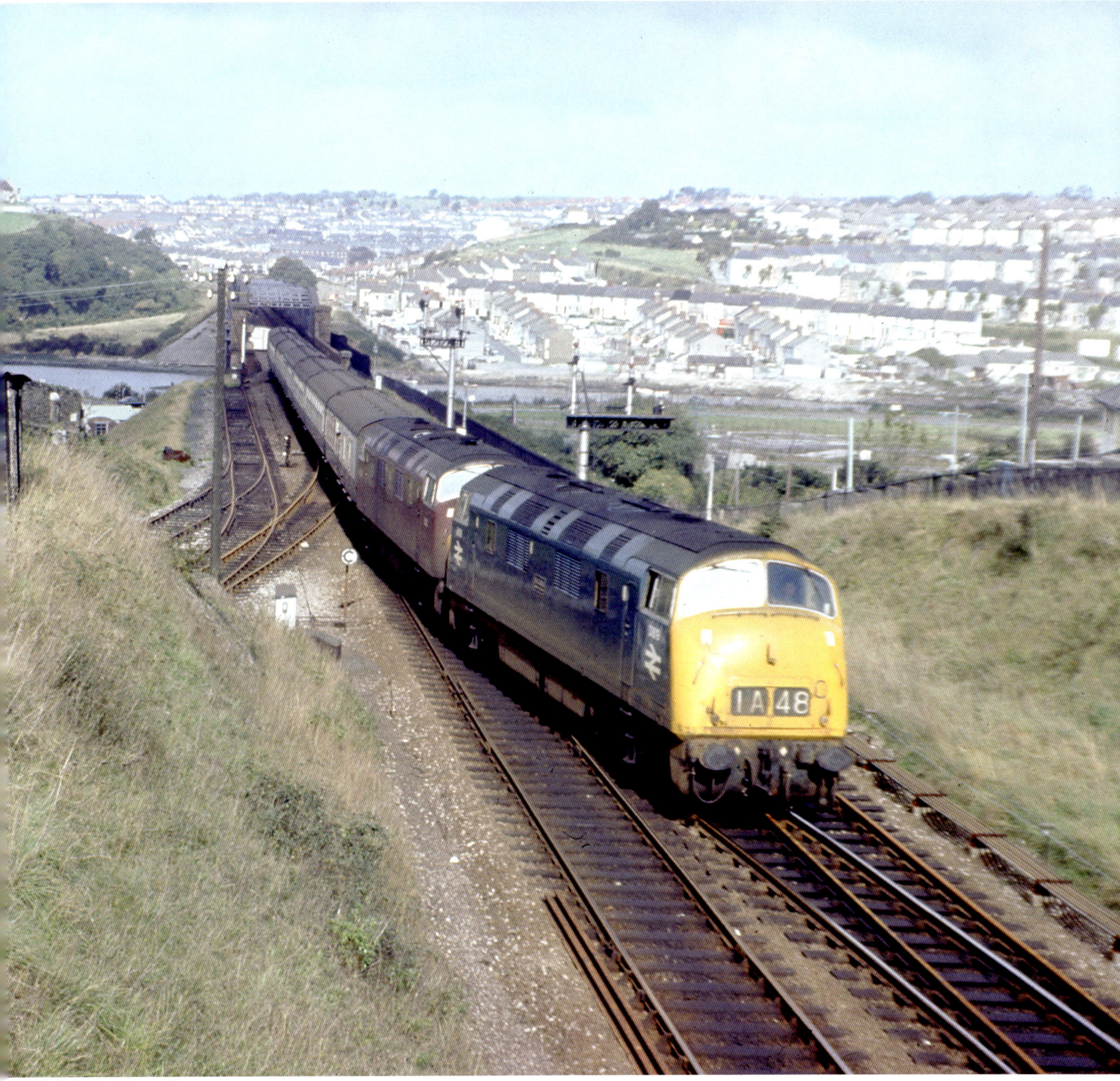

Page left: Making the Basingstoke stop on 25 August 1971 was 818 Glory, later on in another chapter we will see four other Class 42s at work on the Waterloo to Exeter route on this same day. Sadly Glory would become the last Warship to be cut up, after lingering around Swindon Works in a sort of preserved state for a number of years, sometimes being used as an exercise for apprentice painters to practice their skills on from time to time, until the Works was posted for closure and the locomotive scrapped in 1985. Thankfully a number of spares were salvaged for the benefit of D821 Greyhound in preservation. ***Bernard Mills***

Above: Paired with D832 Onslaught it is D819 Goliath that is up front in this Warship duet at Weston Mill in 1968. With the use of two locomotives for the Paddington to Plymouth and Penzance expresses for the summer timetable during this year journey times and reliability issues were much improved. However the experiment was short lived, as it was to be single Class 52 Westerns that took over most of the trains for the following summer. ***Bernard Mills***

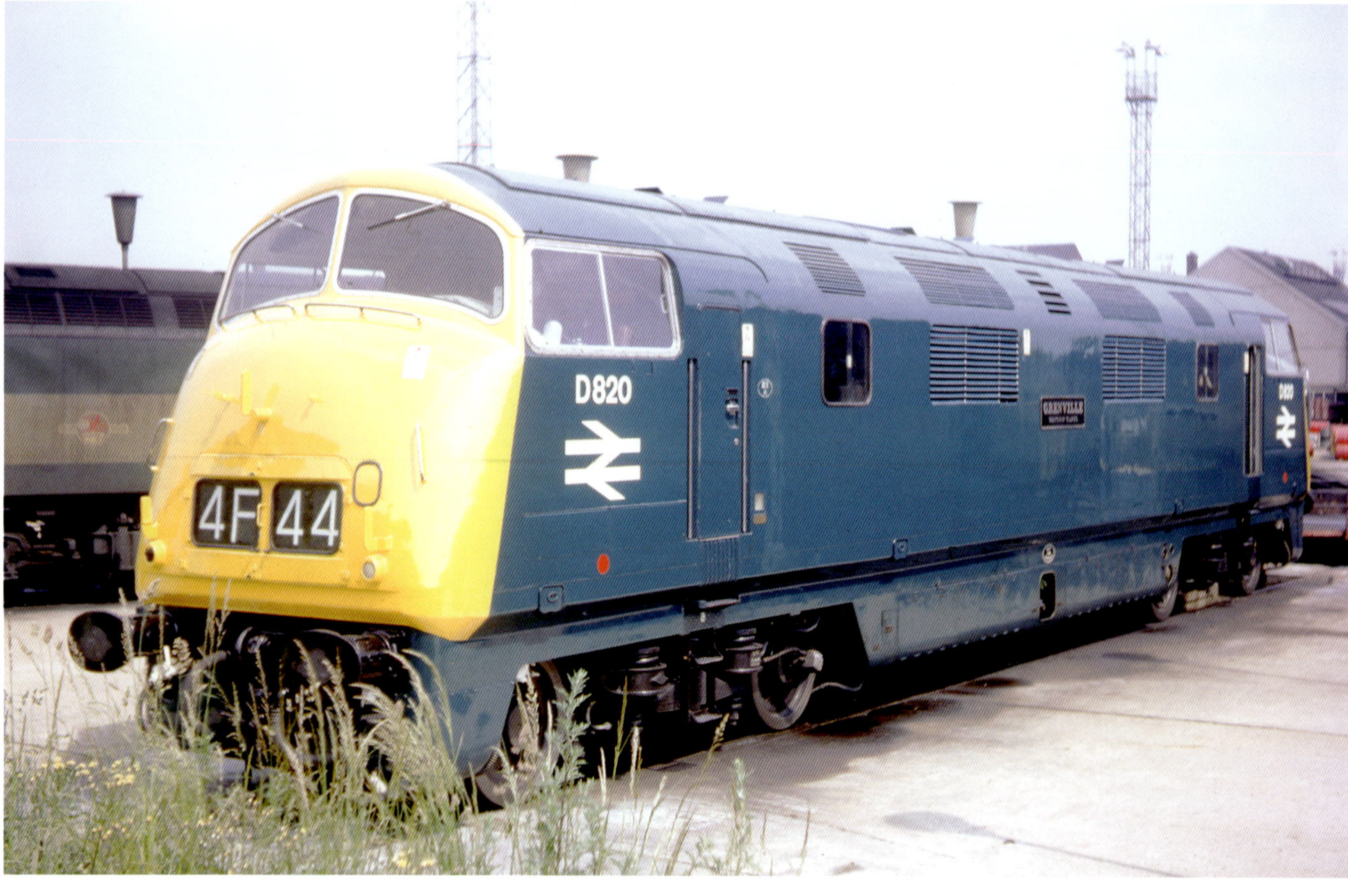

This example had first been painted into the new blue livery with Serif style numbering during the summer of 1967, however when D820 Grenville was recorded on one of Old Oak Common's turntable roads in late May 1968 we can see that Gill Sans numbering has now been applied by Swindon along with a fresh coat of blue paint once again. ***Derek Everson***

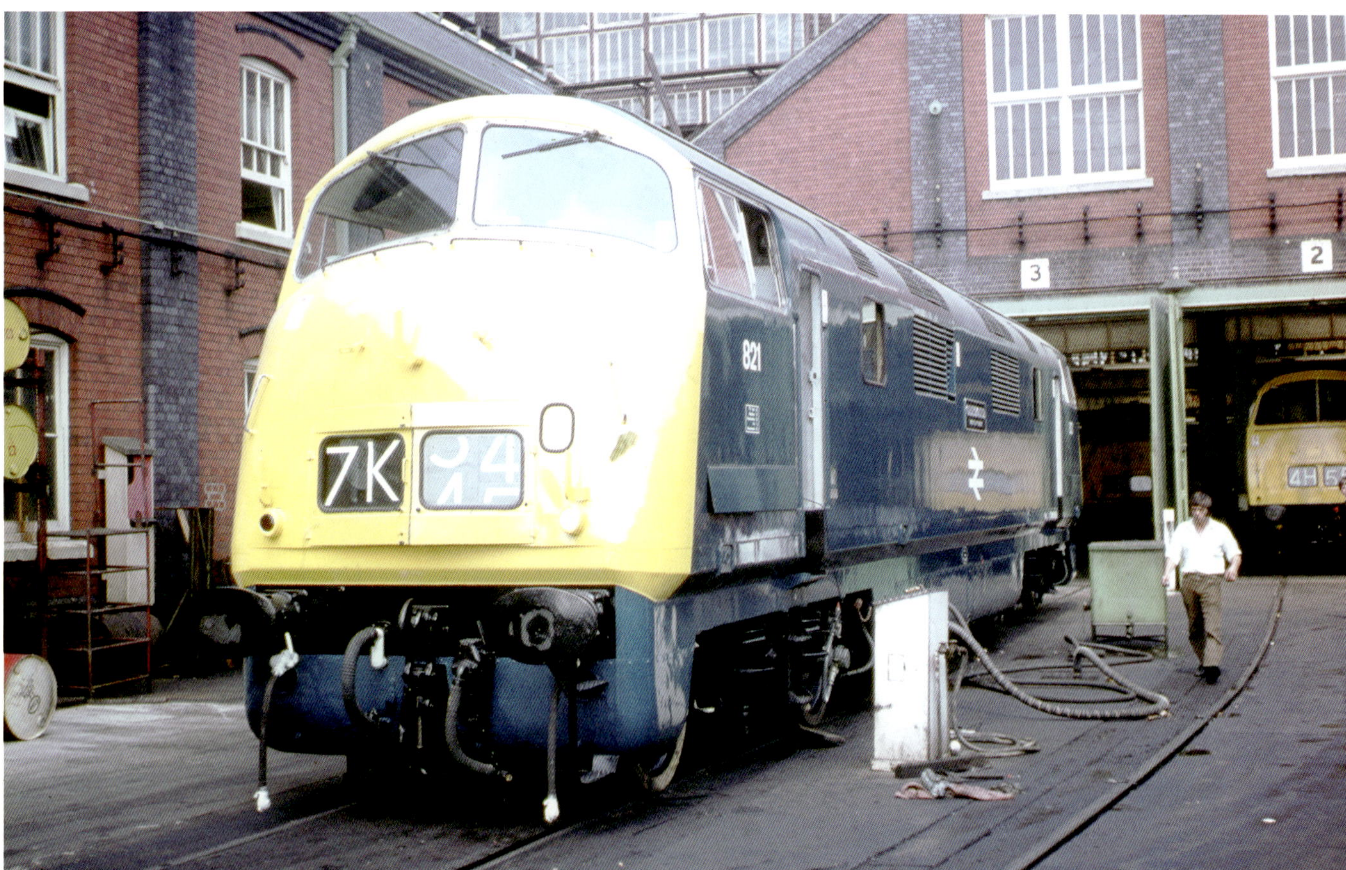

Almost ready to depart Swindon Works, or so it seems on 6 July 1971 was 821 Greyhound, in the event it was to return to traffic on 18 August 1971, a few days after the works open day. When withdrawal came on 3 December 1972 it returned to Swindon Works for storage firstly and would become the first privately preserved mainline diesel locomotive in the country. ***Jeffrey Lane***

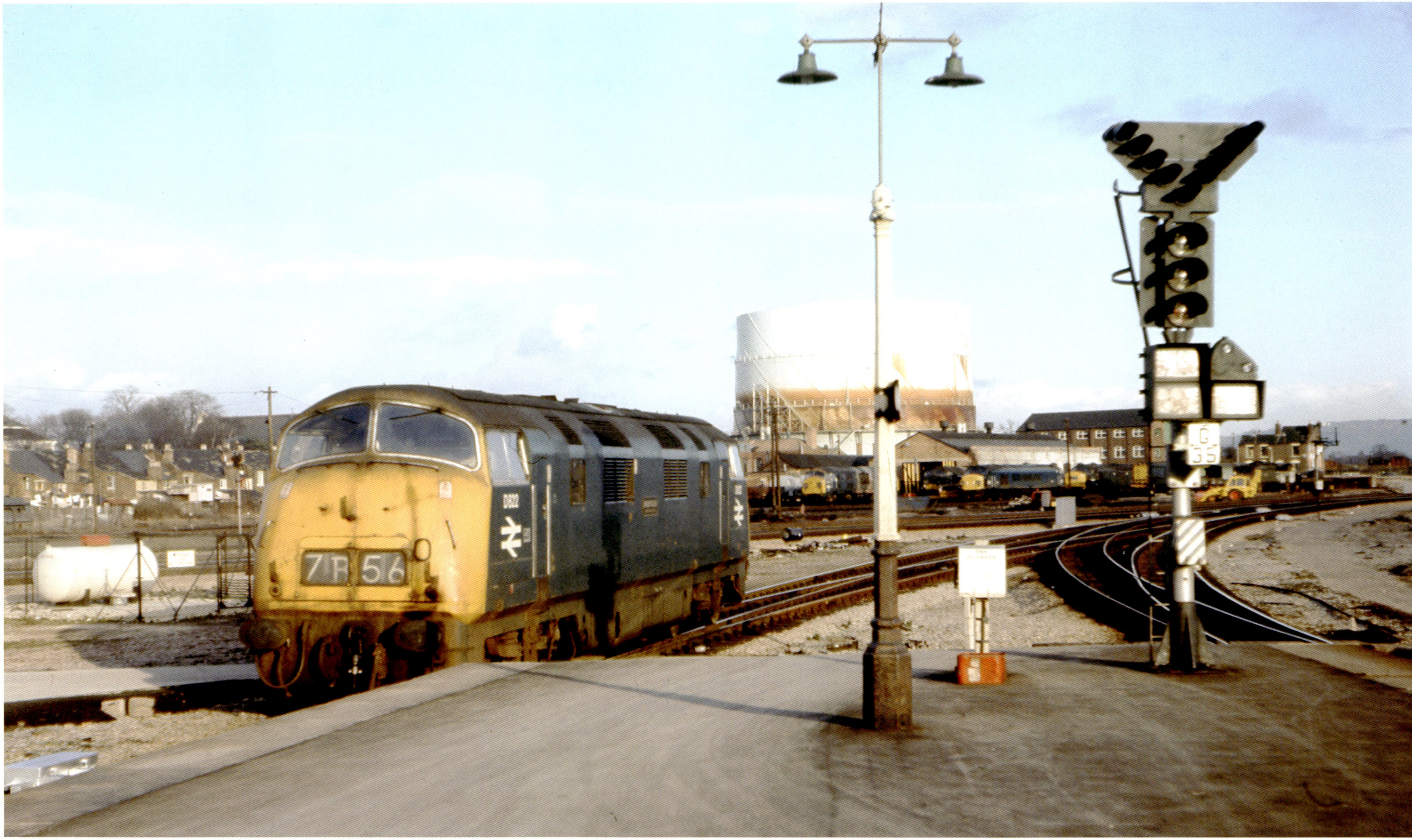

Although it is D822 Hercules that is the subject for this photograph at Gloucester's Eastgate station, one cannot help looking to the background and the locomotives stabled on Gloucester Horton Road as well on 24 February 1970. Although most through workings to the London Midland Region and the north had been given over to Peaks by this time, it was only a few years before this that Warships could often be found further north at Bescot and Crewe. Indeed if only a few more cameramen of the time had focussed on Warships at Crewe rather than the last gasps of Duchesses on the WCML six years previously. ***Bernard Mills***

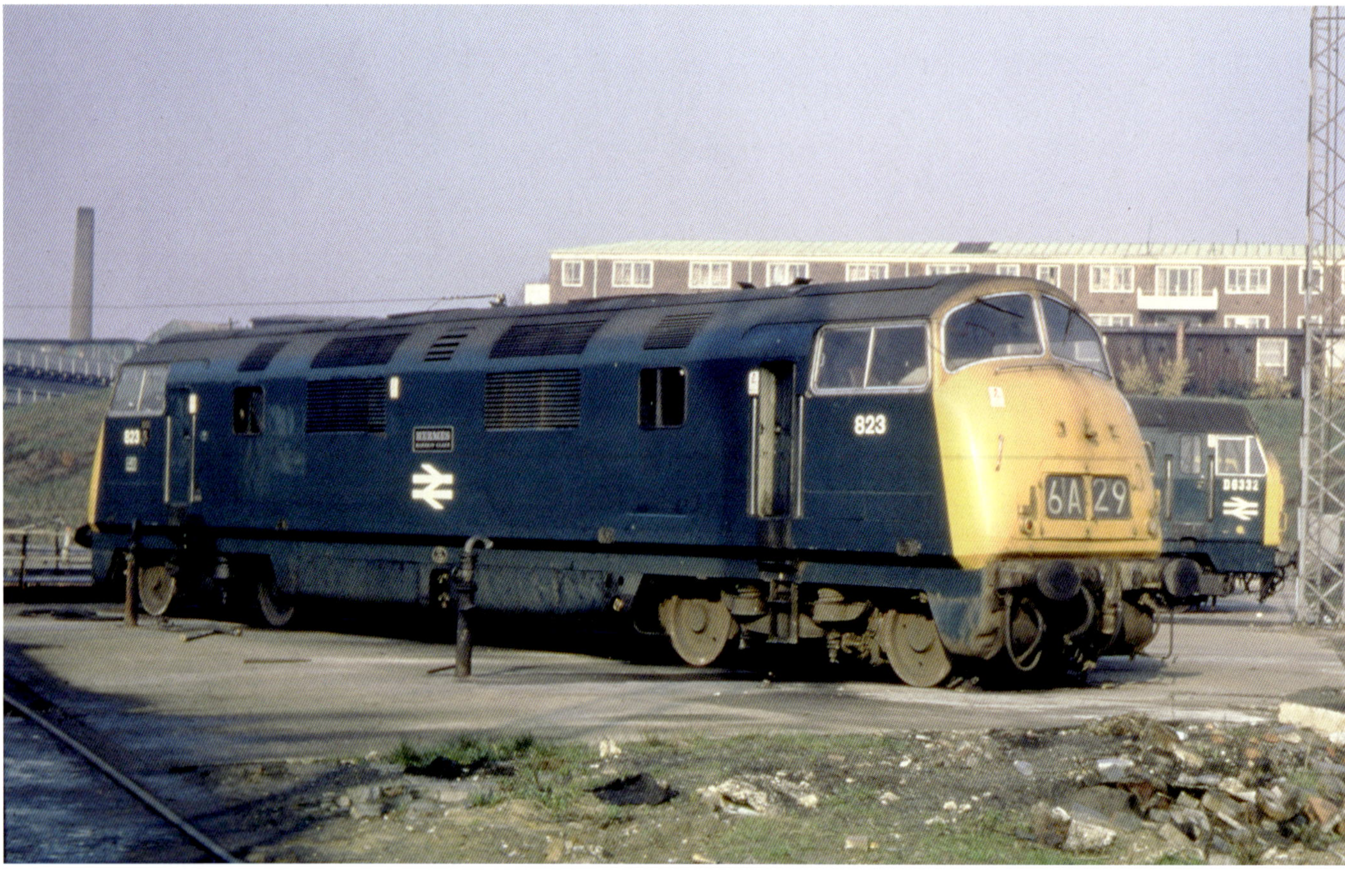

The badge linking 823 Hermes with the Royal Navy's warship of the same name can be seen affixed to the far cab in this view of the locomotive whilst stabled on one of Old Oak Common's famous turntable roads on 11 April 1970. Two badges were fitted in October 1965, one to each end of the Warship on the driver's side under the cab windows. ***Strathwood Library Collection***

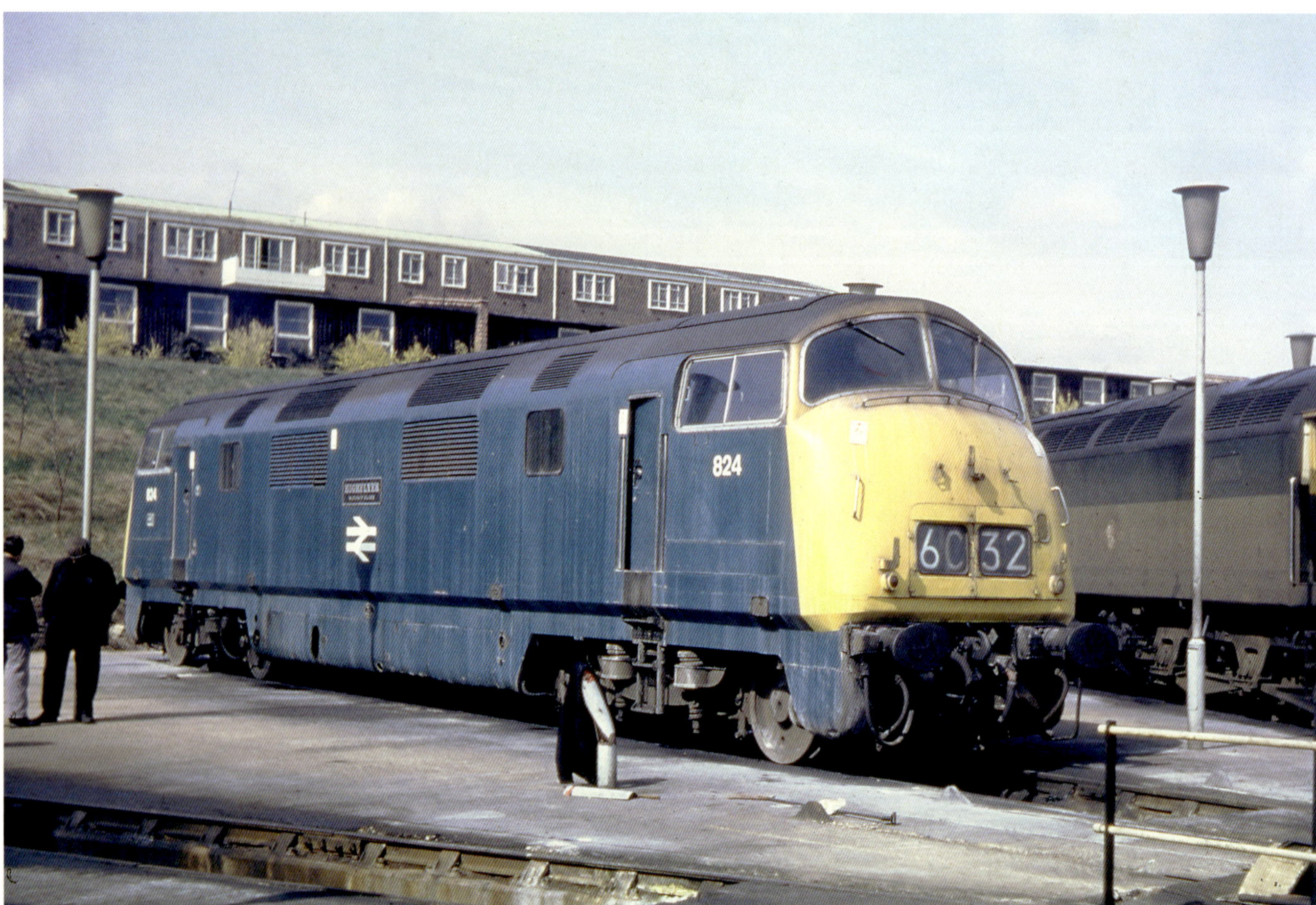

Many readers will recall walking down from Old Oak Lane and into the depot to be greeted by an array of hydraulics during this period, on 5 April 1970 it would be 824 Highflyer that would be among the first into your notebook today. ***Strathwood Library Collection***

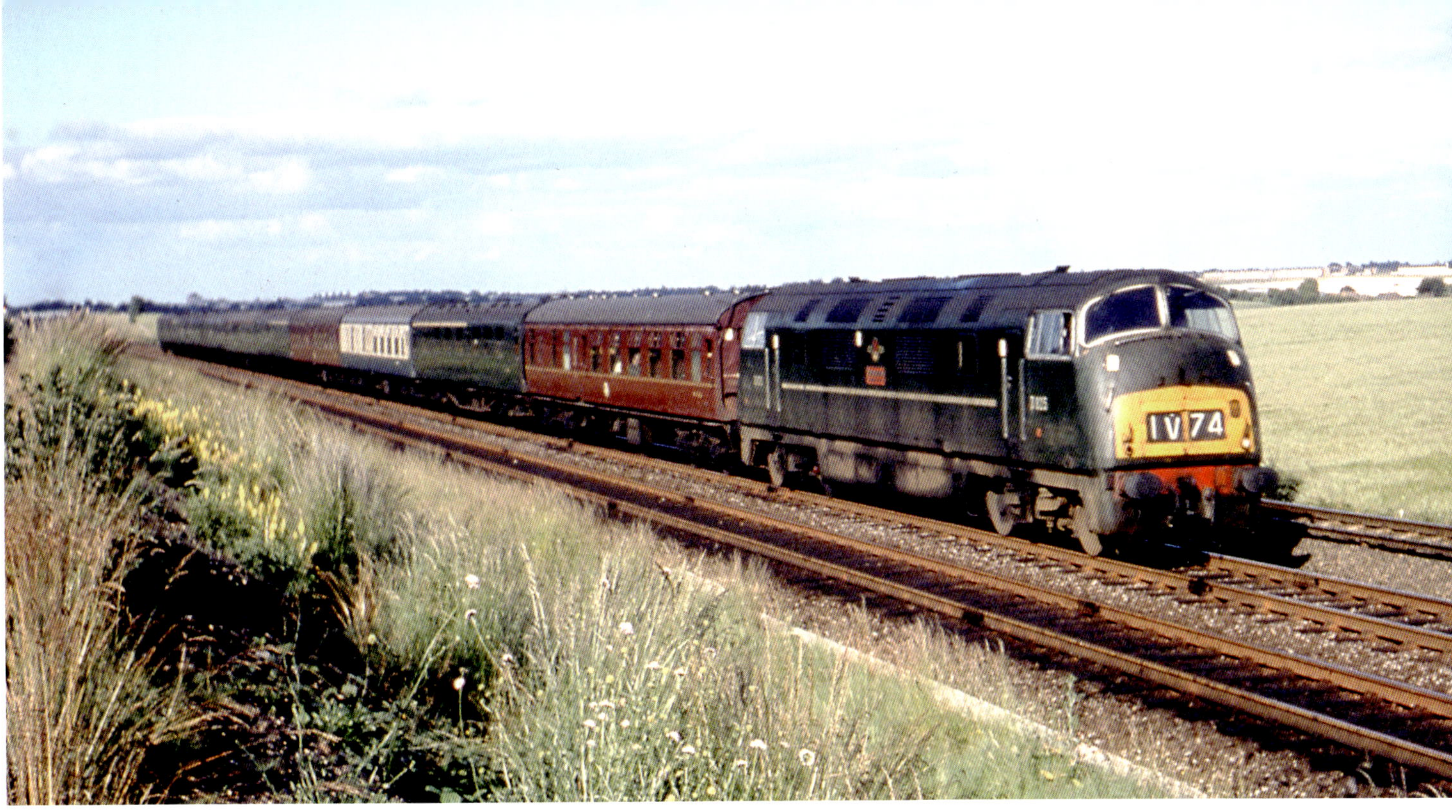

As steam gave way to diesel and electric services on the Southern Region in the summer of 1967, it was not unusual to see mixed liveries within the rakes of coaches making up services, such as this Salisbury train at Battledown behind D825 Intrepid. ***Strathwood Library Collection***

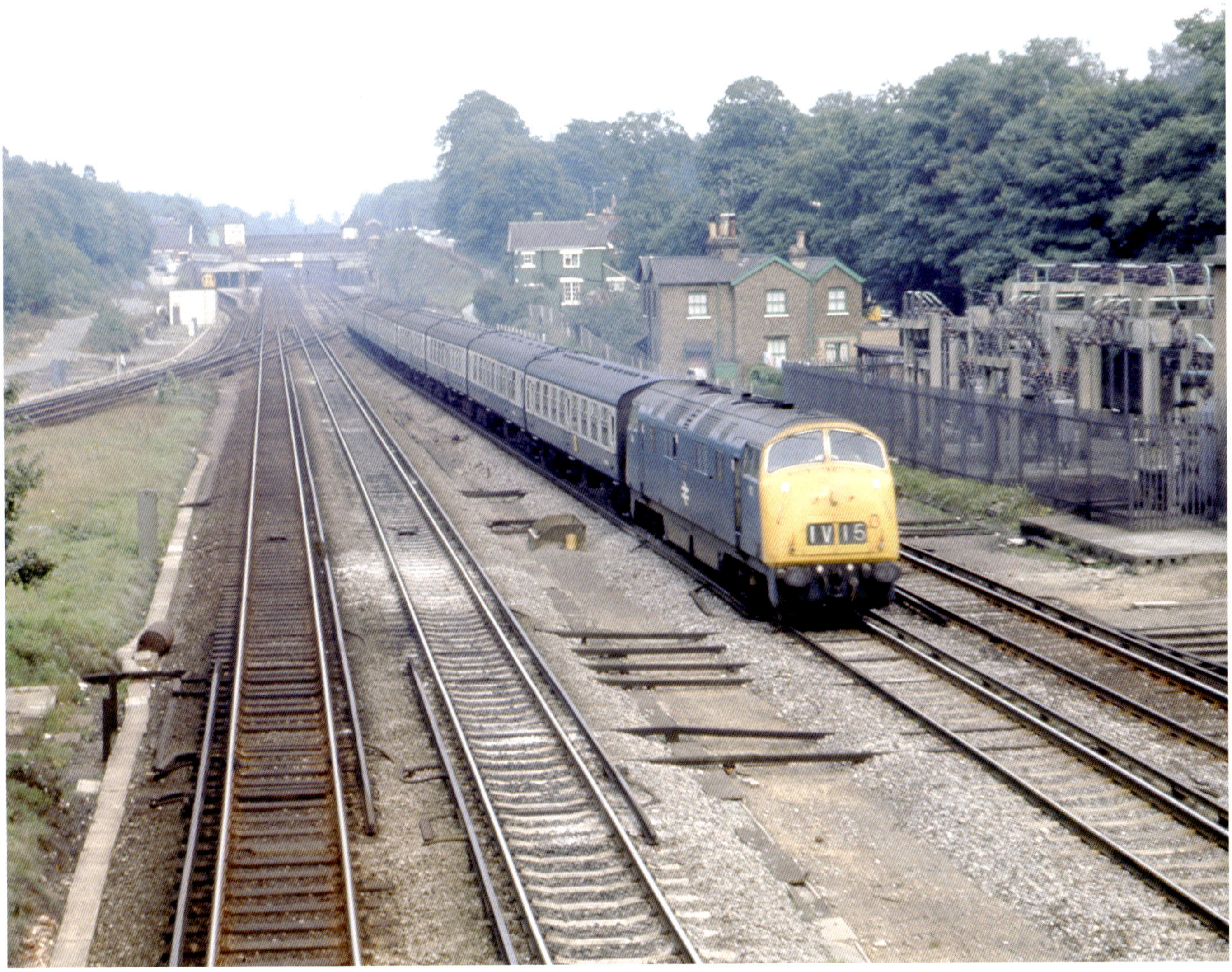

However by 22 September 1971 when D826 Jupiter was heading westwards away from Weybridge with an Exeter line express, all the Southern Region's green stock had all but dissappeared. ***Bernard Mills***

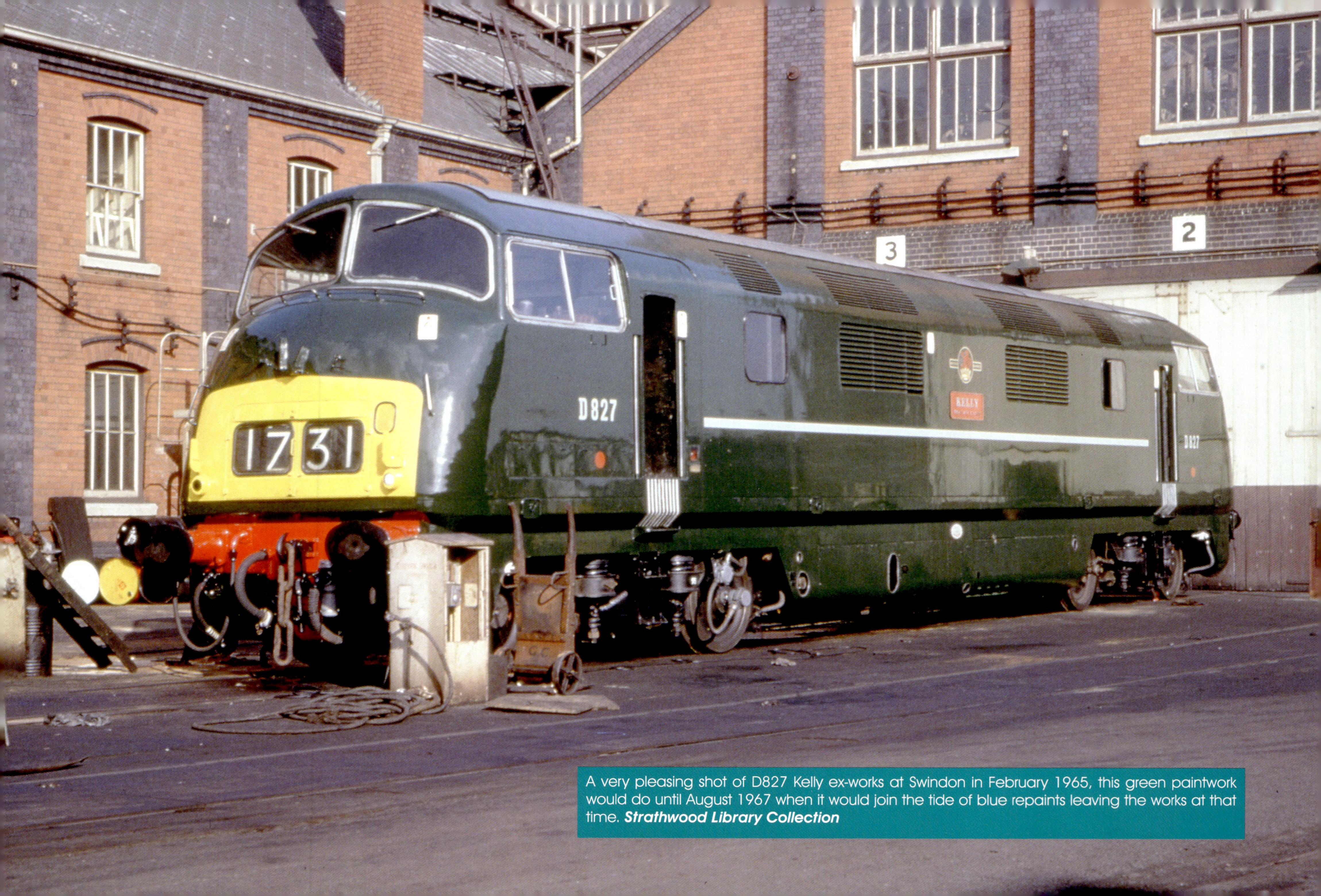

A very pleasing shot of D827 Kelly ex-works at Swindon in February 1965, this green paintwork would do until August 1967 when it would join the tide of blue repaints leaving the works at that time. ***Strathwood Library Collection***

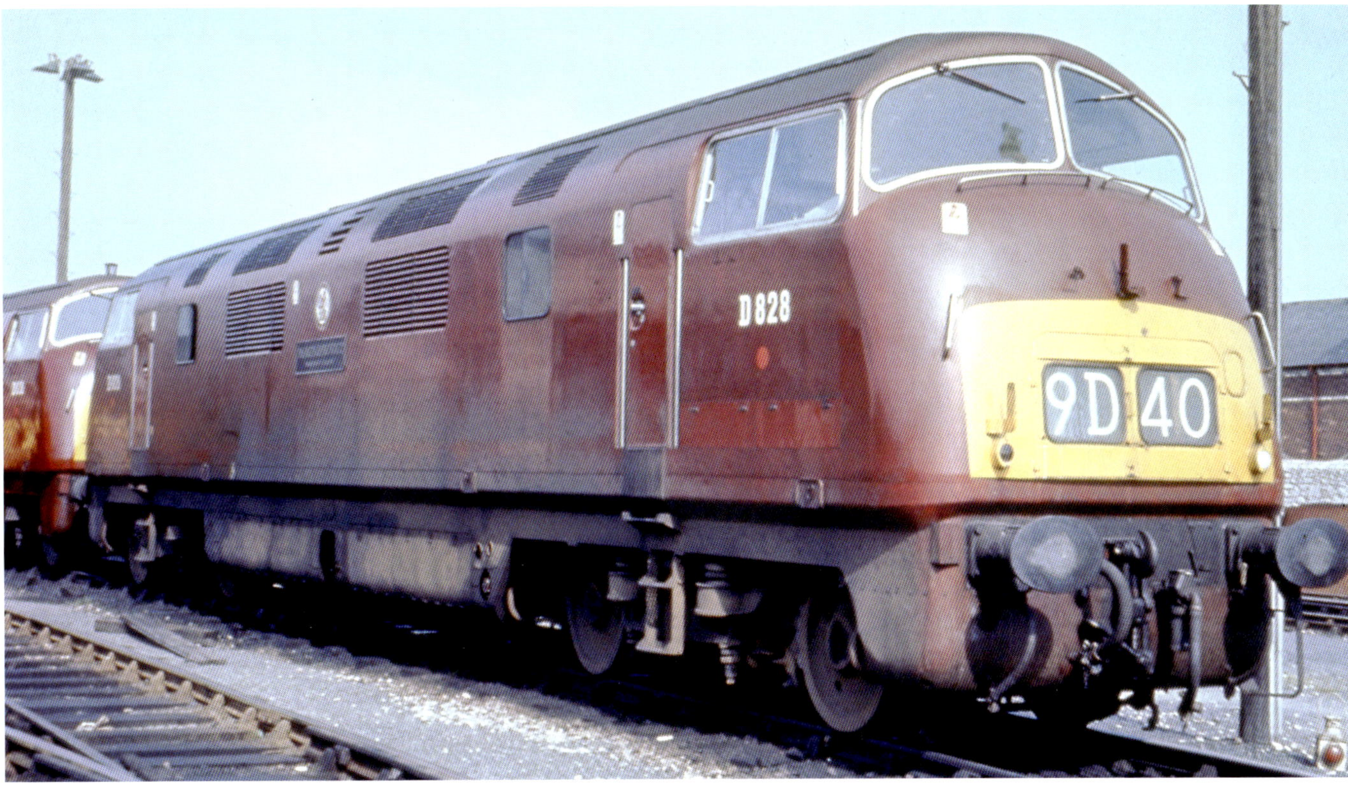

Although it may have been named Magnificent, D828 seen here at Newton Abbot on 18 September 1966, it was after the warship and certainly not for its condition a lot of the time, as your author recalls it was often seen in a less than perfect state at the time. ***Strathwood Library Collection***

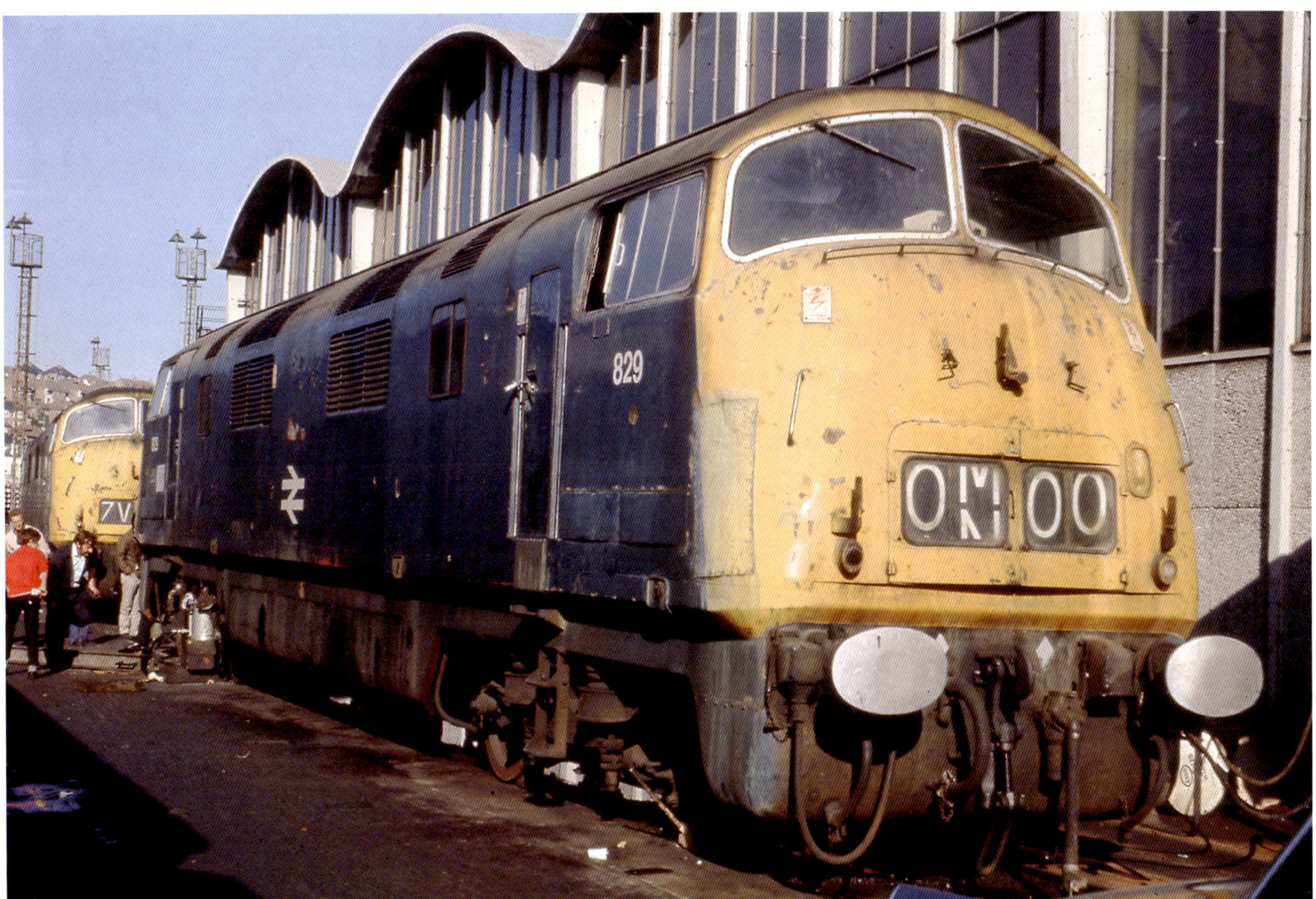

As the BBC's television programme of the same name had adopted 60532 Blue Peter, ITV's Magpie children's show made mention of 829 in the early seventies as well. However it was not to do so well, as the Warship had been withdrawn on 26 August 1972, after being laid up here at Laira for a few weeks beforehand. This shot was taken during an open day on 23 September 1972, and along with 825 Intrepid seen in the background they were to be used for re-railing exercises. Although Magpie remained at Swindon Works afterwards whilst others were cut up, it fell to the cutters in late January 1974. ***Bernard Mills***

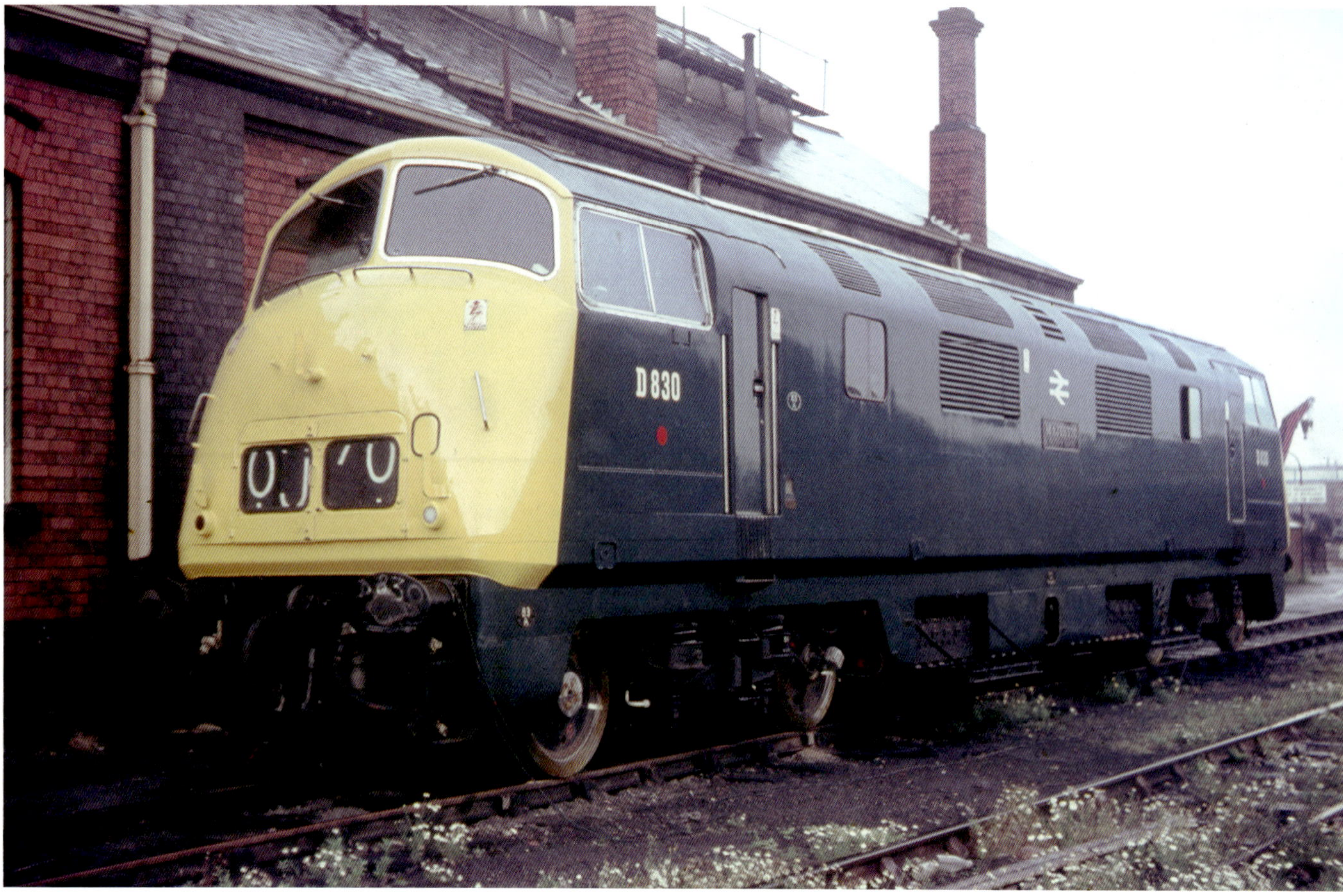

Back at Swindon once again for another blue repaint in August 1967 was the unique Paxman engined Warship D830 Majestic. Seen here with it's battery doors hanging down as the last preparations are made for it to depart the works. The first blue scheme for Majestic can be seen on page 67 with a half yellow front which it gained in December 1966. ***Derek Everson***

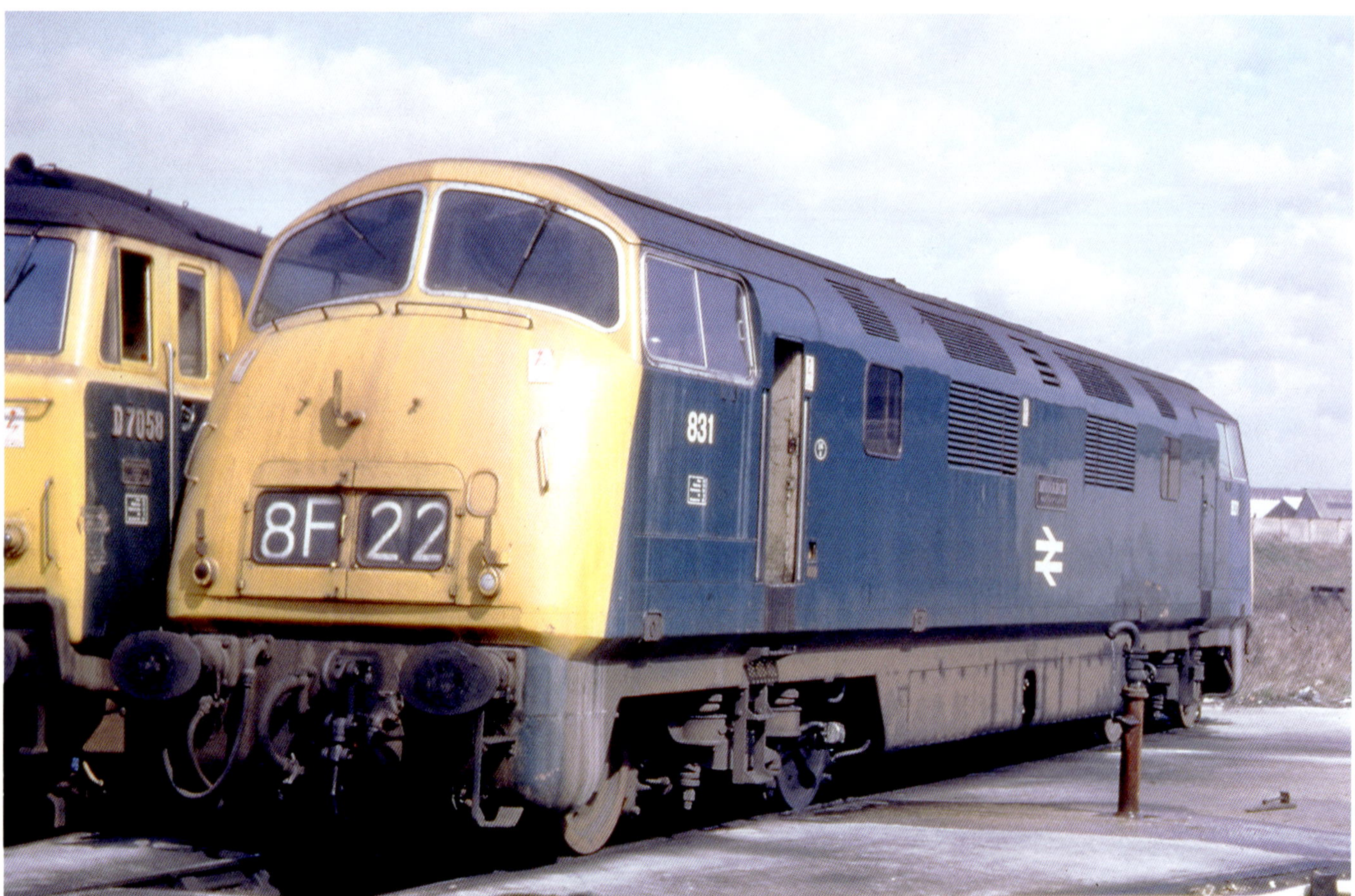

Likewise the earlier version of blue livery for 831 Monarch can also be seen on the same page. Whilst on 5 April 1970 it was just another Warship to be seen around the turntable at Old Oak Common. ***Strathwood Library Collection***

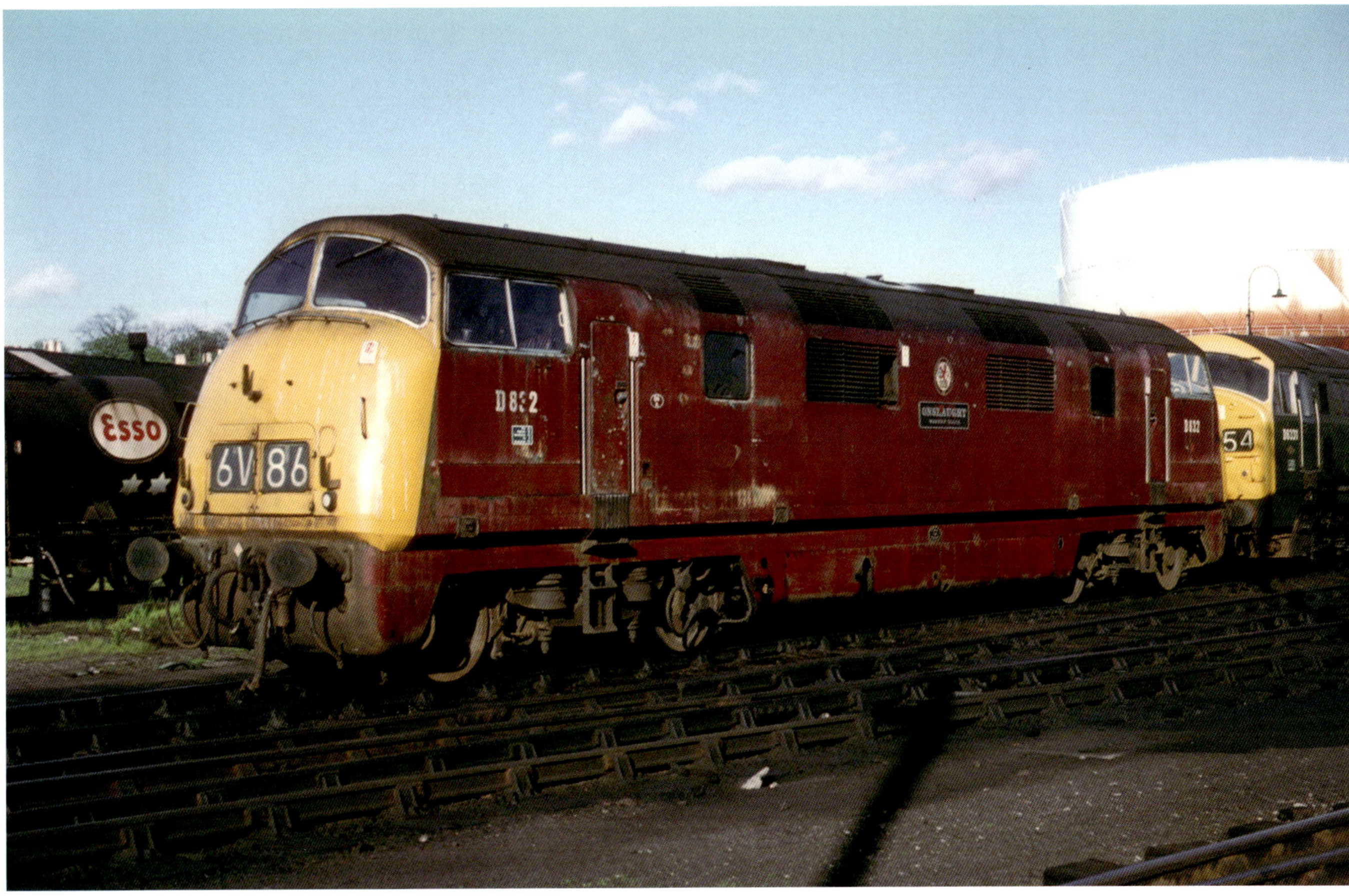

It appears that it was D832 Onslaught that was the last of the maroon Warships to gain the full yellow ends treatment in early 1969. On 29 April 1970 it was to be found at Gloucester Horton Road among other hydraulic brethren. ***Jim Binnie***

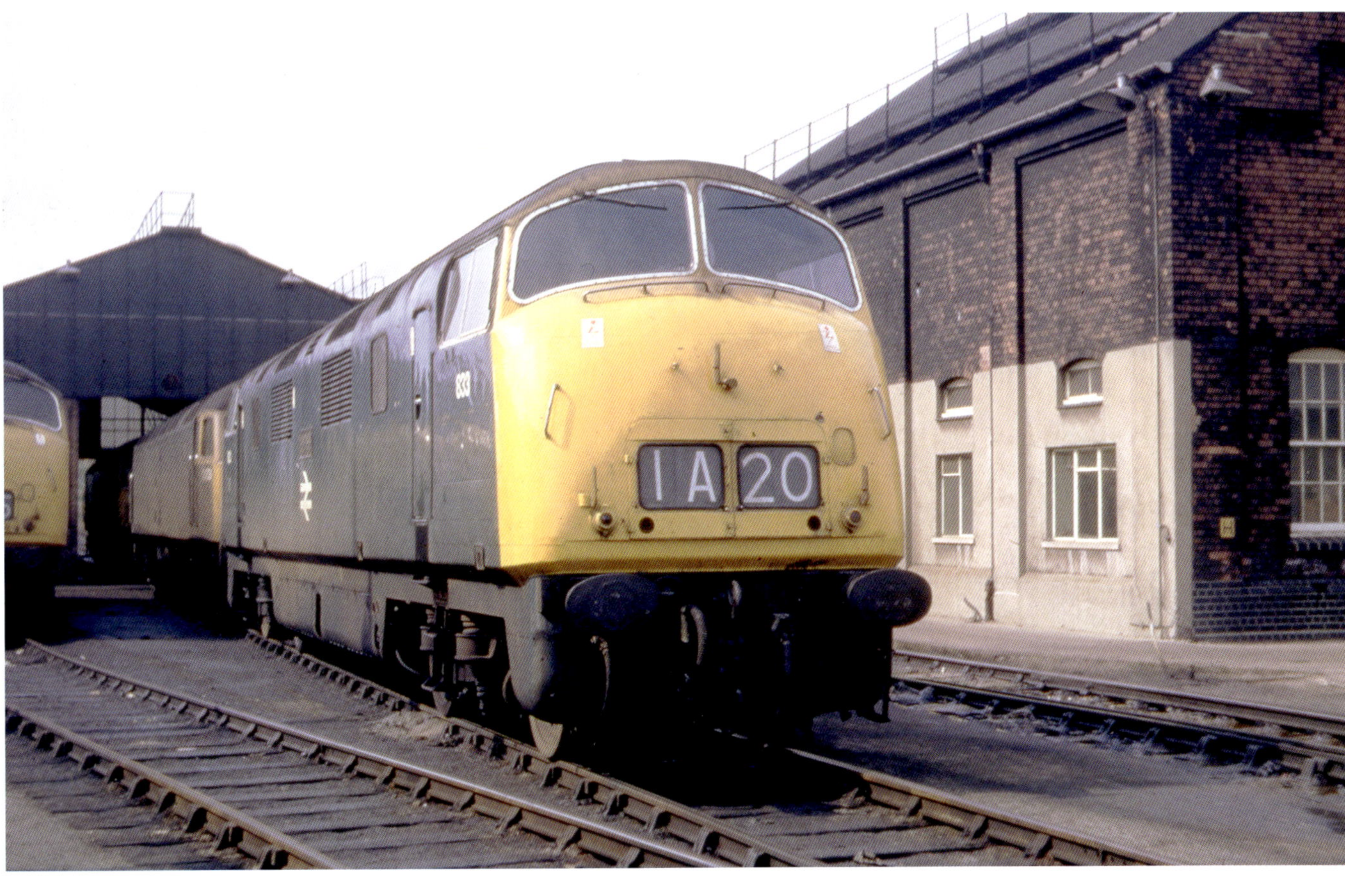

As we now take a look at the North British built Warships from Glasgow later to become Class 43. We start with 833 Panther at Old Oak Common in 1970. We can also begin studying the various positions and styles of extra ventilation grilles fitted here at 81A to attempt to relieve the problems of engine fumes building up in the cabs of NBL locomotives, this led to Old Oak crews nicknaming these Warships as Iron Lungs. ***Strathwood Library Collection***

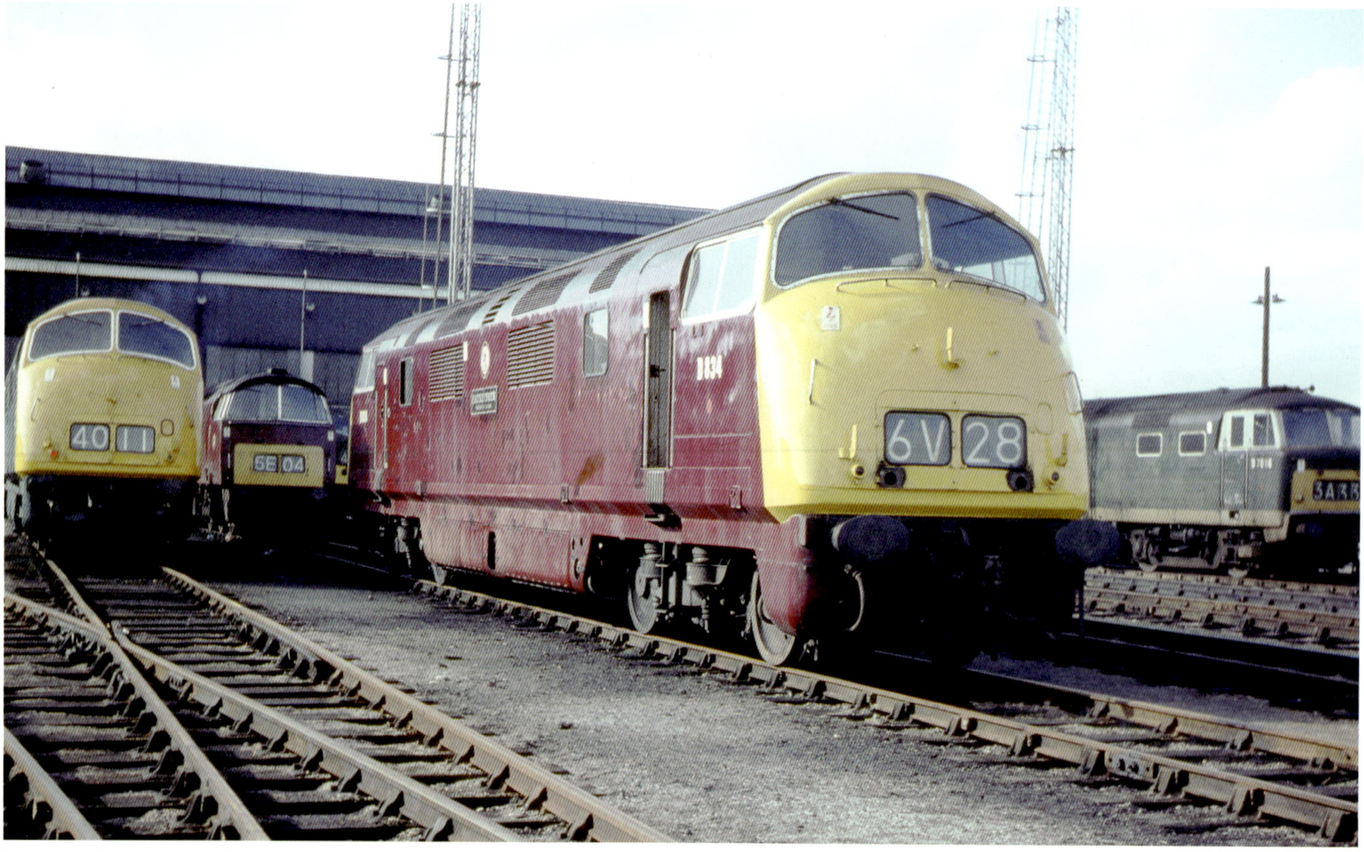

The freshly applied full yellow front end paintwork has suffered as the fitting staff at Old Oak Common have used an oxy-acetylene torch to burn the holes first before fitting the grilles to D834 Pathfinder in February 1968. ***The Late Robert Jenkins, courtesy of the Railway Club of Wales***

An ex-works 835 Pegasus has had smaller vents fiited below its headcode boxes when seen at Gloucester Horton Road on 30 April 1970, this Warship would be among the big cull of North British built machines withdrawn on 3 October 1971. ***Jim Binnie***

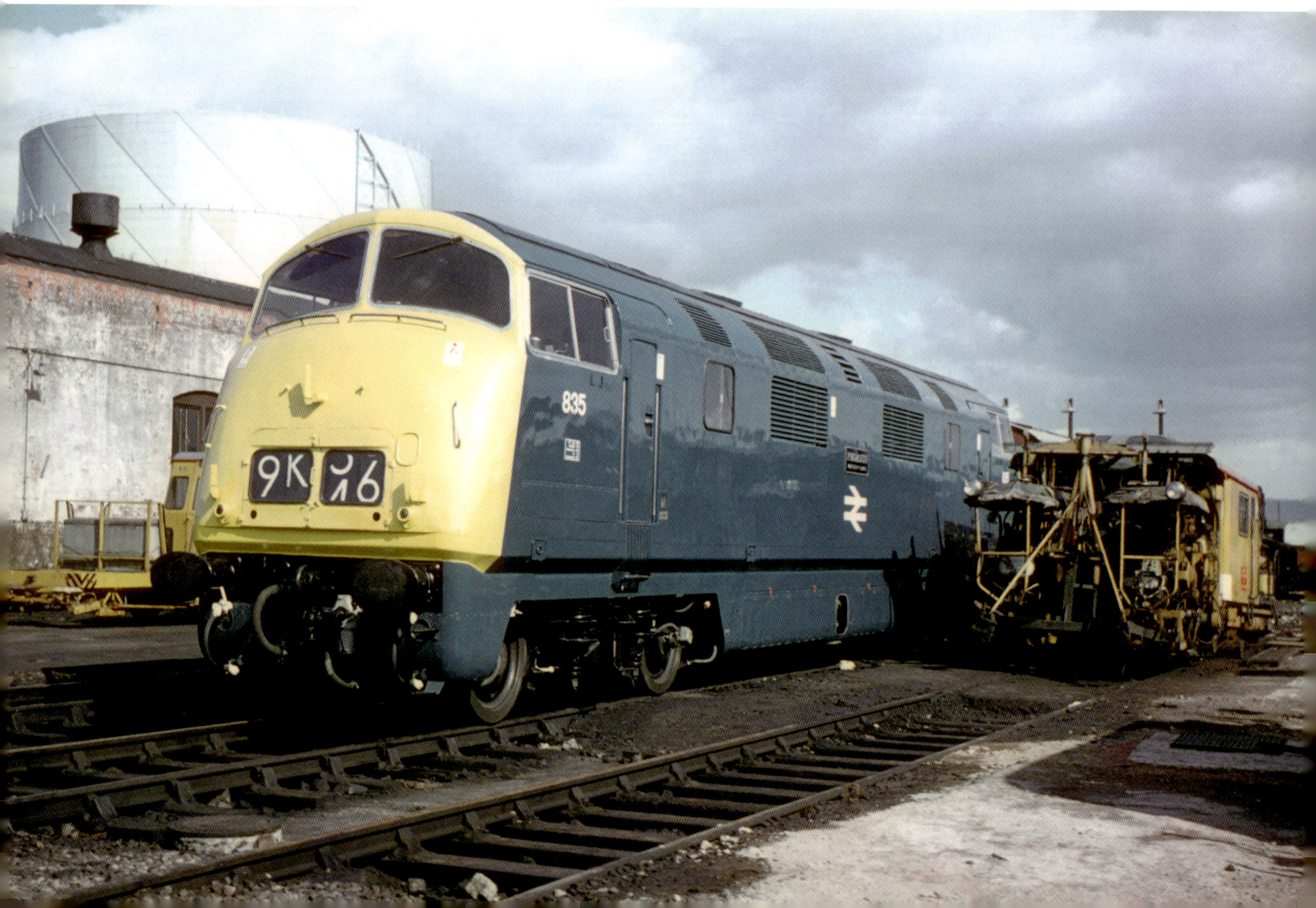

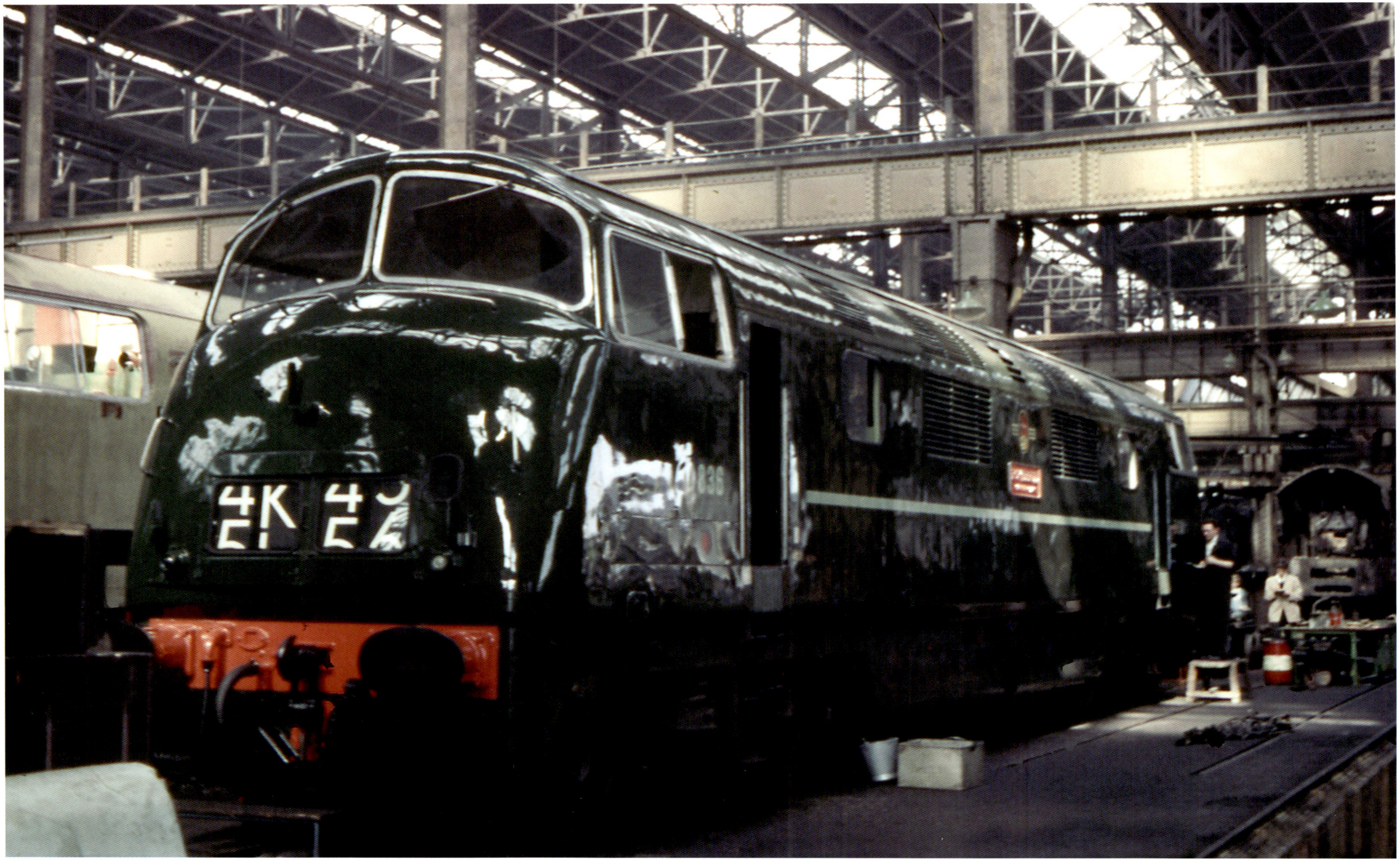

Inside Swindon Works for acceptance checks in September 1960 was D836 Powerful freshly delivered from North British in Glasgow. Now for the eagle eyed the Scottish built Warships had their numbers and side stripes painted slightly lower on their bodysides than the Swindon variety. ***Transport Treasury***

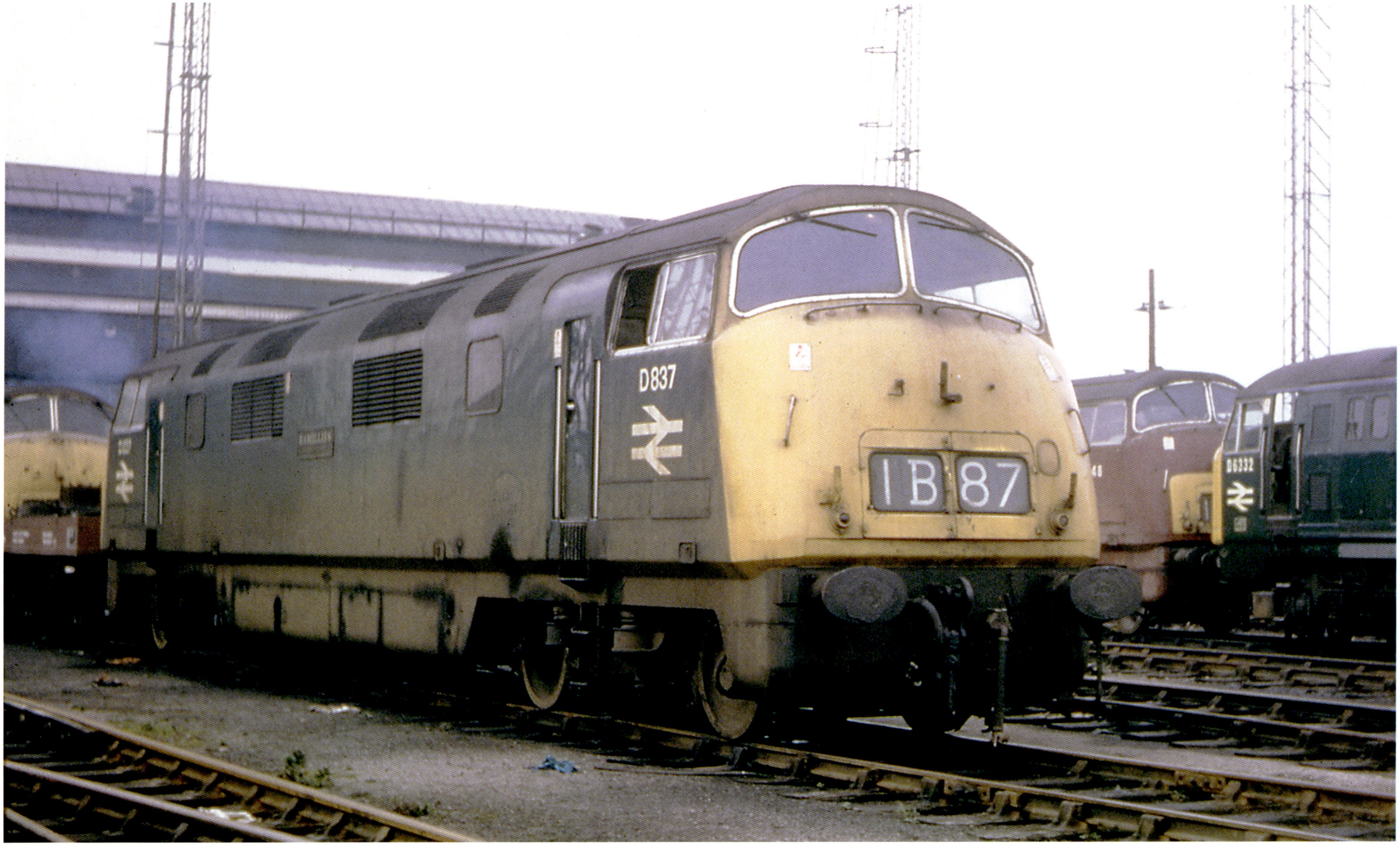

This shows that D837 Ramilies missed out on these extra front vents when seen laid up at Old Oak Common on 15 March 1970. Perhaps the locomotive must have been troublesome as this unfortunate Warship went into storage at Newton Abbot the following month, and was withdrawn on 22 May a short while later. ***Strathwood Library Collection***

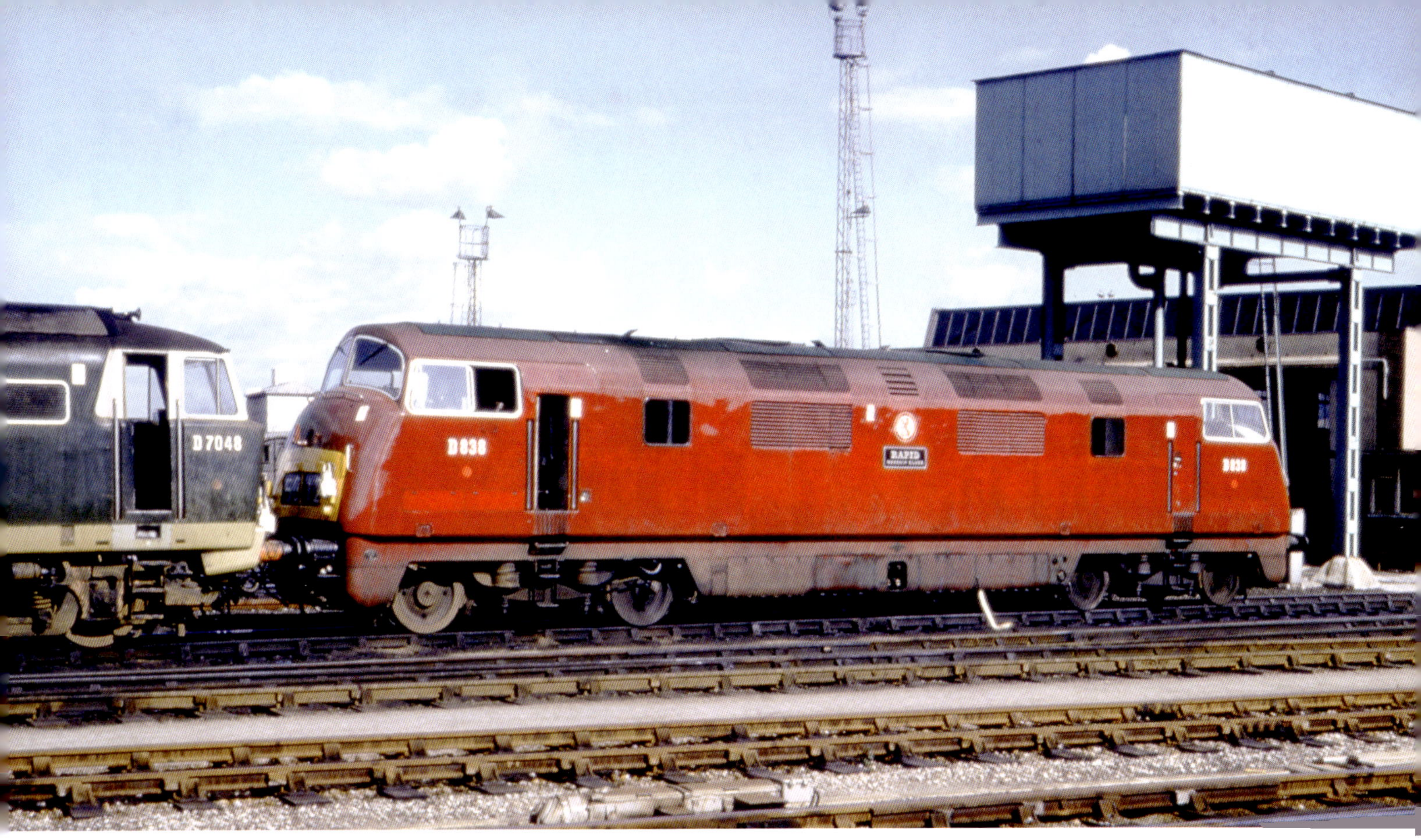

It has been muted that D838 Rapid was used for a livery experiment using four of the round carriage style emblems, one on each cabside with the numbers under the cabside windows. Although this view of D838 Rapid at Bristol Bath Road in 1966 shows it in service in the standard version of maroon livery, not long after recieving new livery. ***Strathwood Library Collection***

Another of the rarer finds within anyone's photographic collections is sure to be D839 Relentless captured here in August 1968 at Moreton-in-the-Marsh with the 11.15 Paddington to Worcester. ***Bernard Mills***

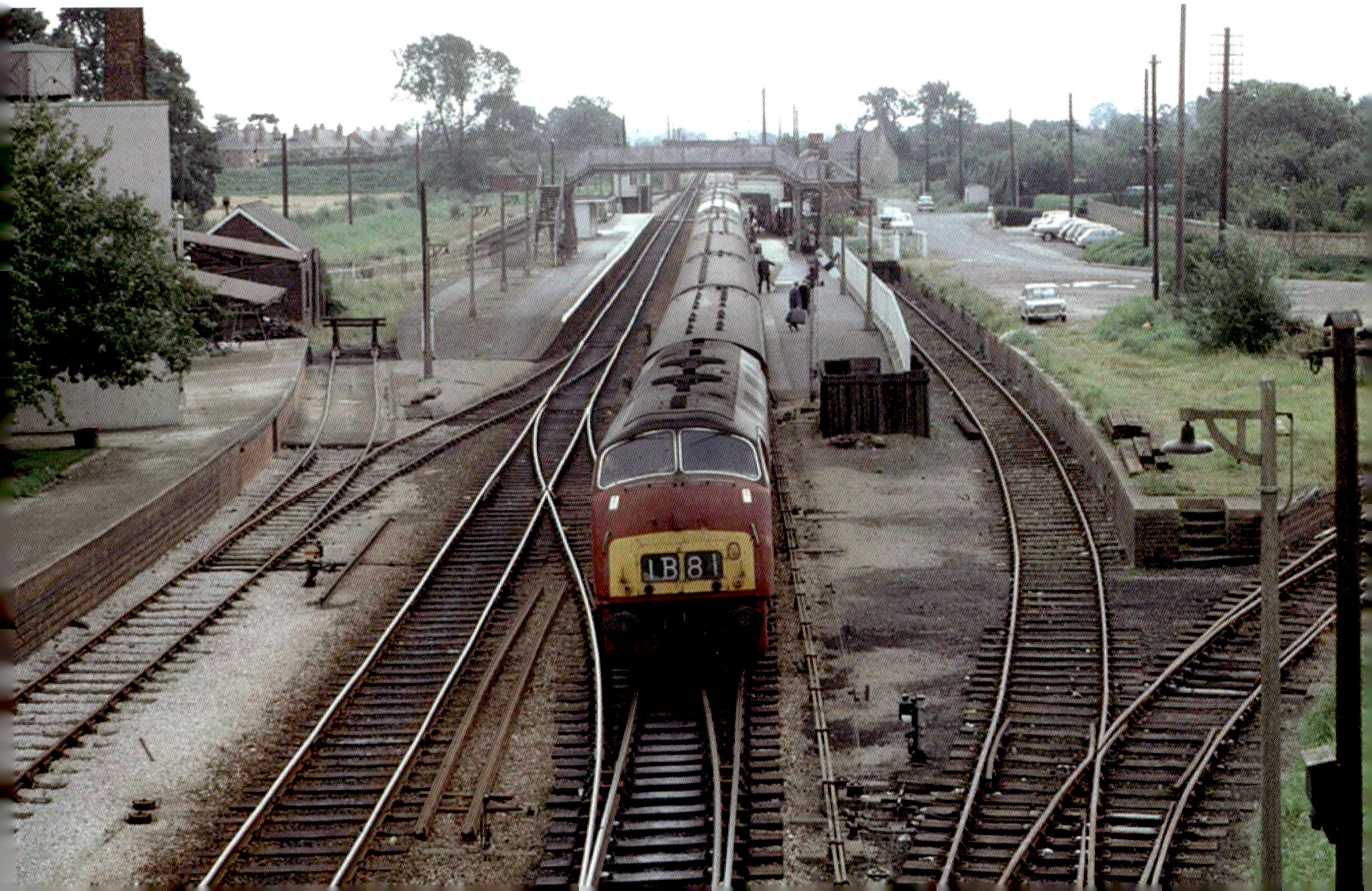

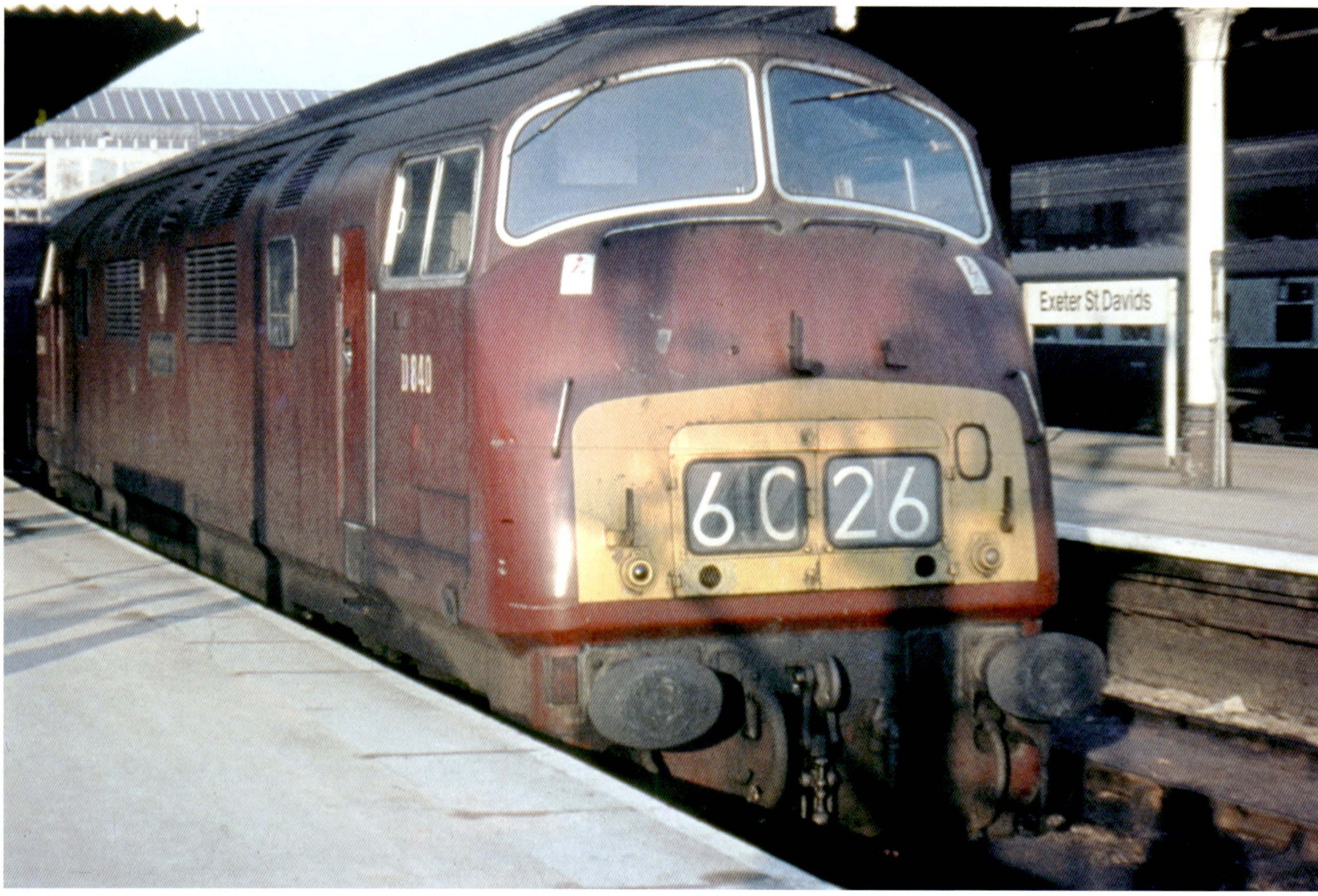

Fate would decree that D840 Resistance seen here at Exeter St. Davids would be the very last Warship to be outshopped in maroon livery leaving Swindon Works three days after D815 Druid on 20 October 1966, although it is thought that D838 Rapid was the last to actually be painted into maroon. It would be D840 Resistance though that would not last long enough to gain full yellow ends, as it joined D848 Sultan at Old Oak Common as a source of spares in April 1969. ***Exe Rail***

Observers will note those additional front vents on D841 Roebuck are unusual in being oblong in shape as we see it stabled at Old Oak Common in June 1968. Another observation pertaining to the larger bodyside grilles shows that D800 to D812 had just the one central vertical bar on the larger bodyside grille. Whilst the rest of the Warships had two. However the water filling grille was the same on all of both the classes with two vertical bars. Whilst D800 to D812 and D866 to D870 also had different roof sections to access their boiler compartments as well. ***Derek Everson***

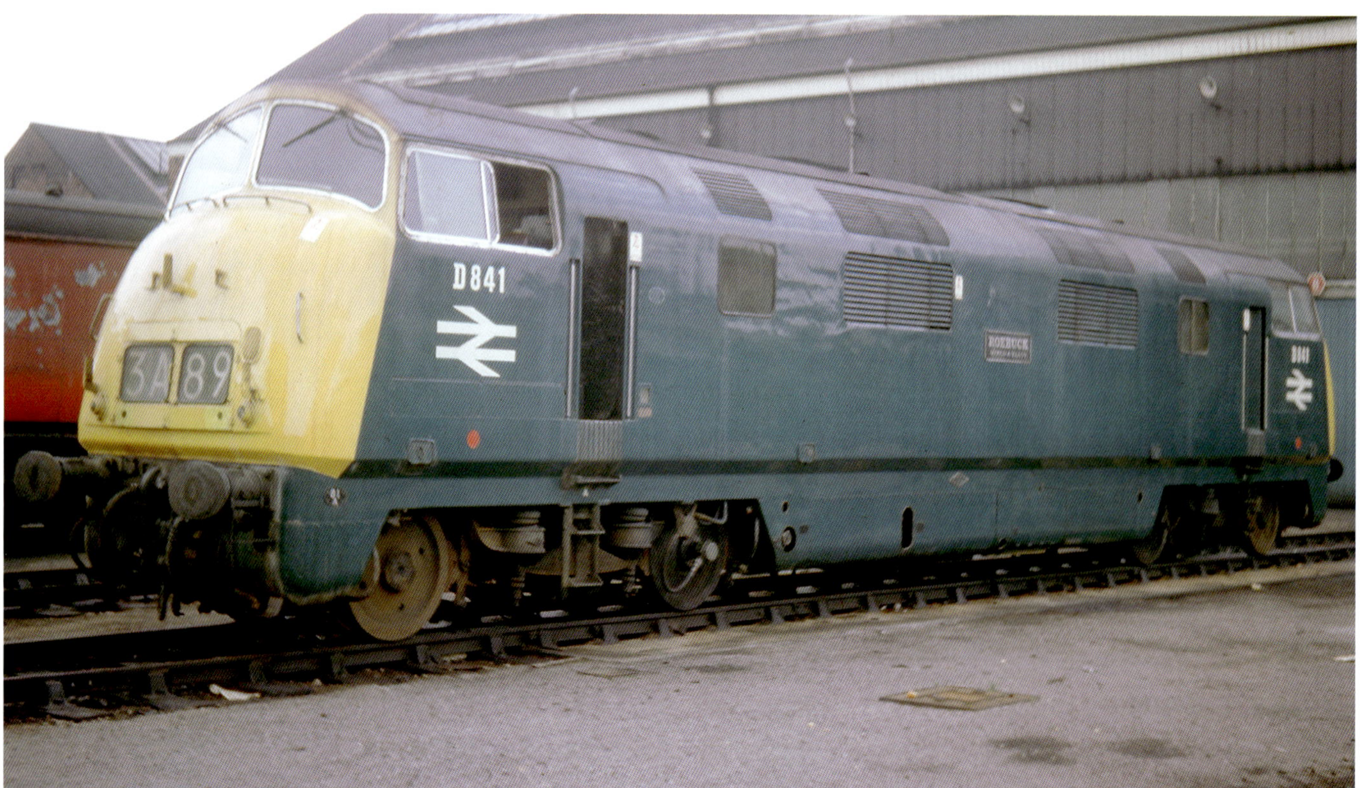

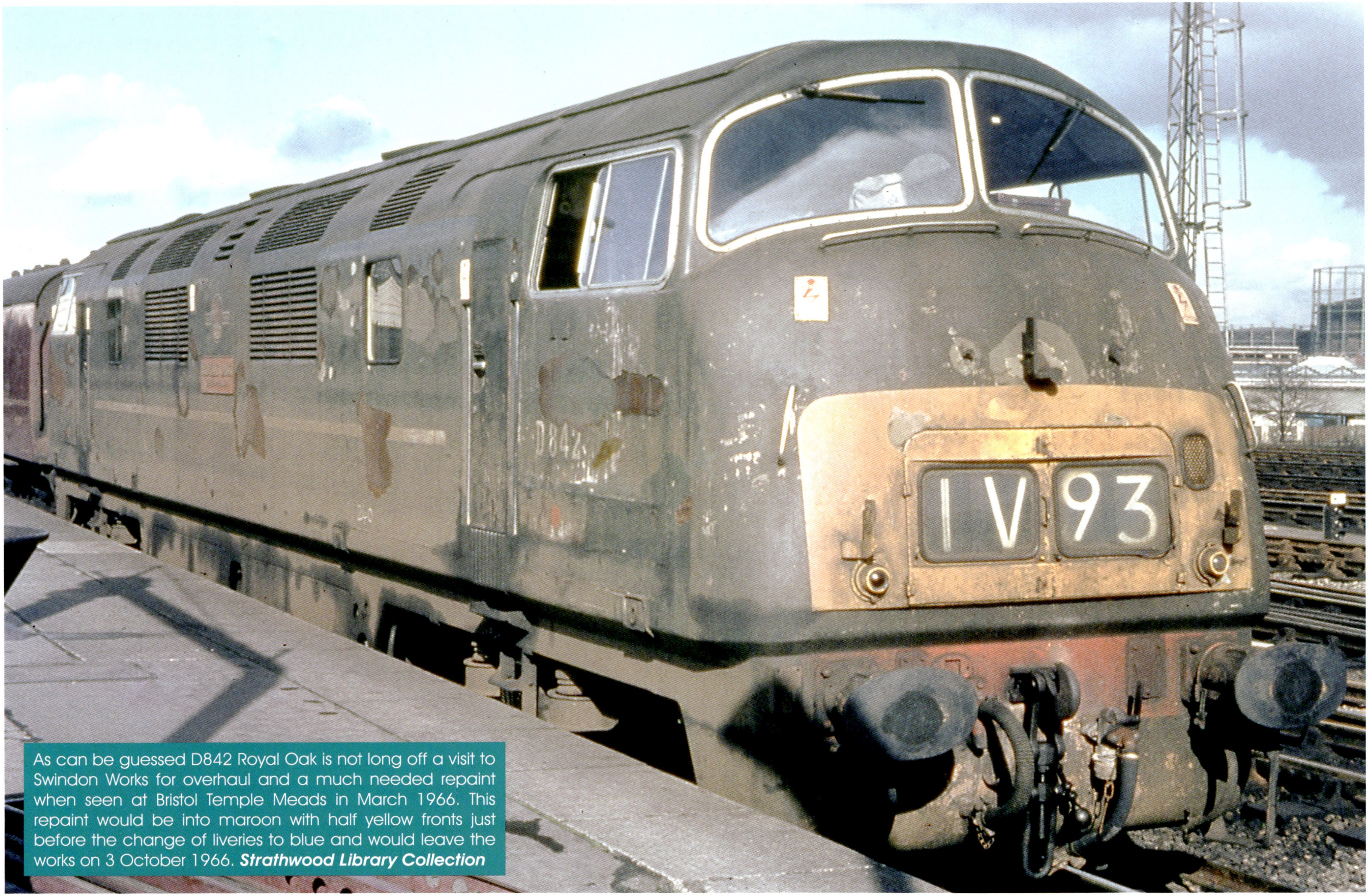

As can be guessed D842 Royal Oak is not long off a visit to Swindon Works for overhaul and a much needed repaint when seen at Bristol Temple Meads in March 1966. This repaint would be into maroon with half yellow fronts just before the change of liveries to blue and would leave the works on 3 October 1966. ***Strathwood Library Collection***

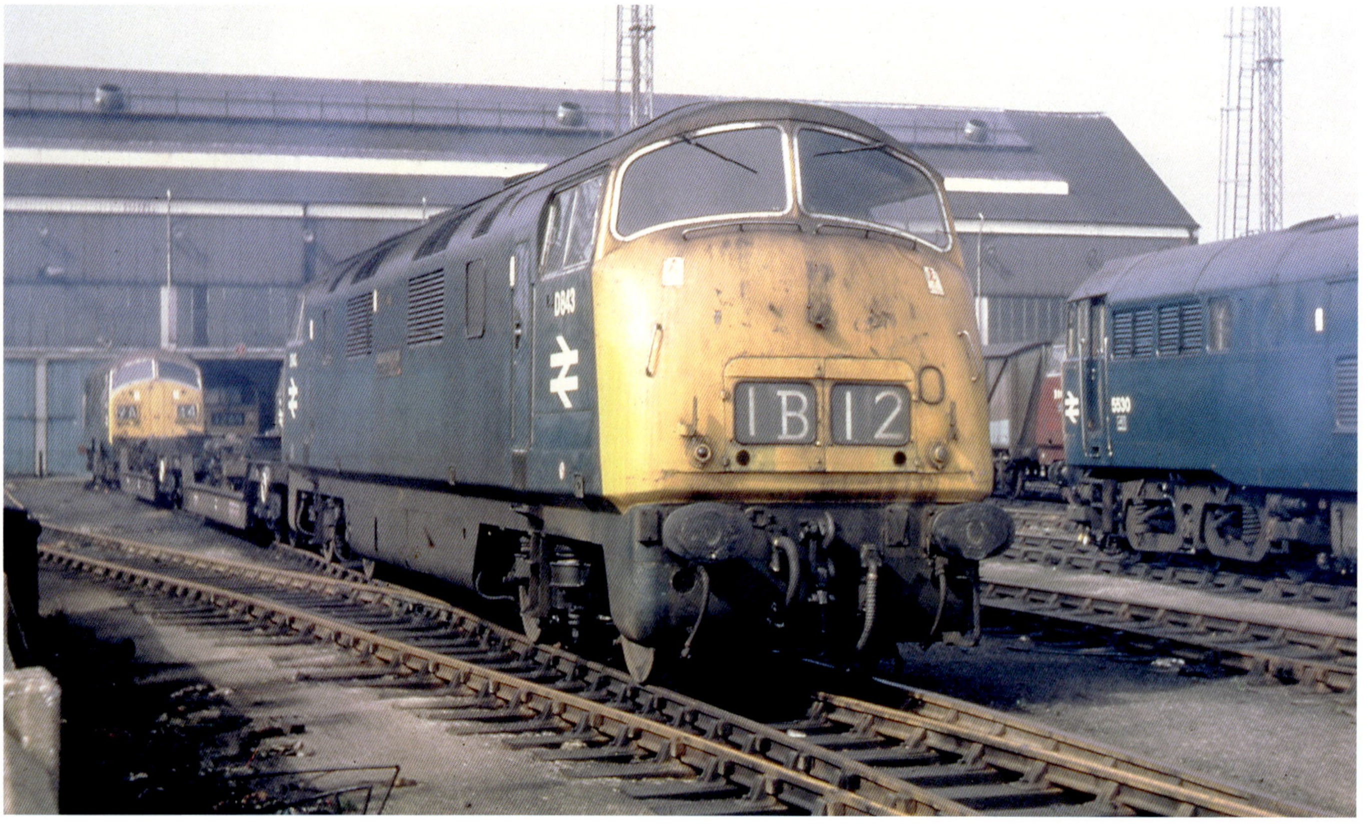

Another of the first wave of North British Class 43 Warship withdrawals in May 1971 would remove D843 Sharpshooter, whilst all seemed to be okay when seen at Old Oak Common in March 1970. The Class 43 Warships built in Glasgow were specified with a small mounting bracket on the bufferbeams for affixing a cast iron or cast alluminium shedplate, although they were not often used after the mid sixties as seen here on Sharpshooter. ***Strathwood Library Collection***

Below: The hinged opening side body grille for boiler water refills can be seen left ajar in this profile view of D844 Spartan stabled at Newton Abbot on 19 September 1967. After withdrawal on 3 October 1971 it spent almost two months as a temporary train heating boiler at Worcester before going for scrap at Swindon. **Exe Rail**

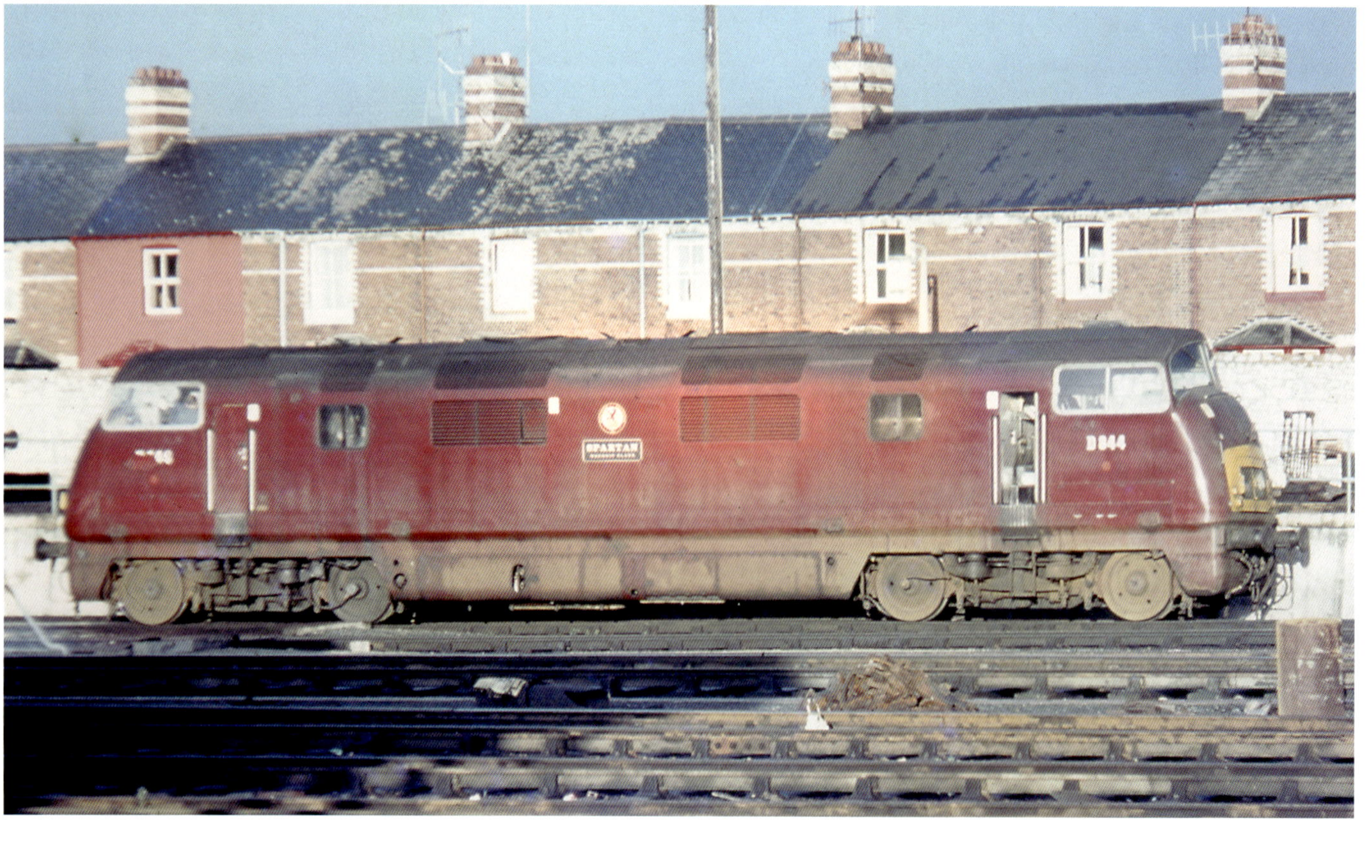

Page opposite: Among the last of the repaints from green into blue livery was 845 Sprightly in early 1970, we catch up with it at Gloucester Horton Road on 18 March a few weeks later. ***Jim Binnie***

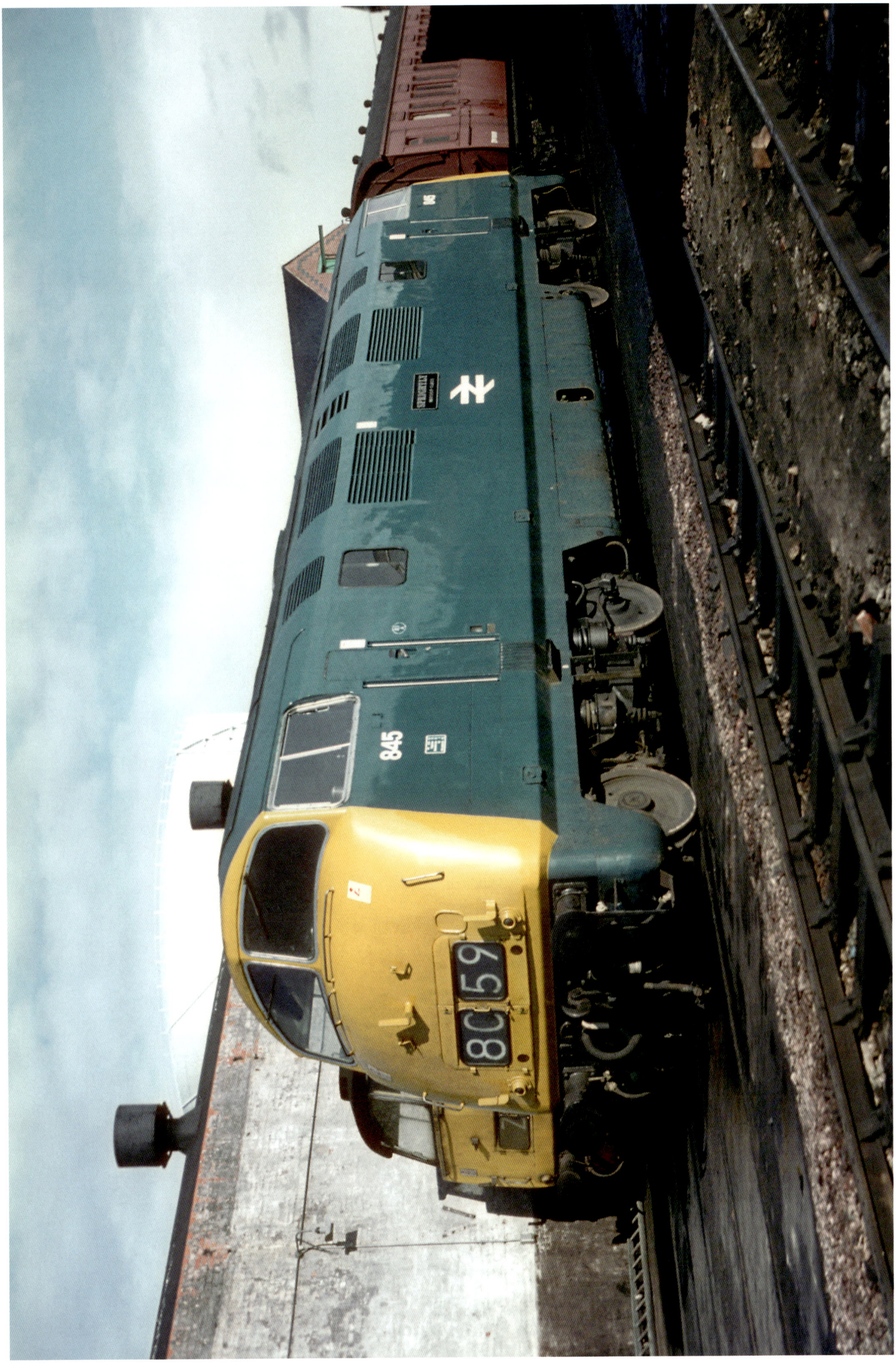
845
8C59

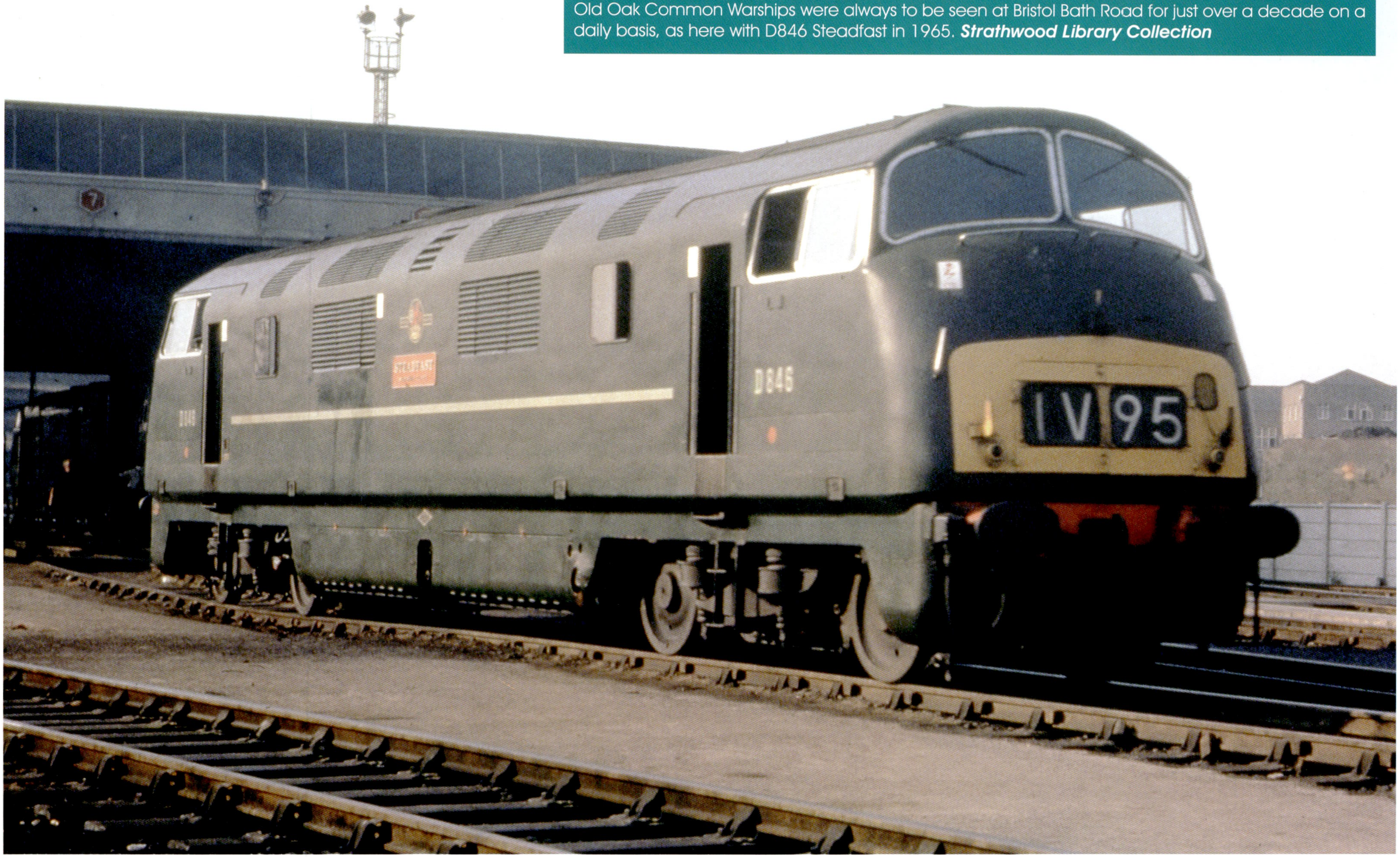

Although the main responsibilty for Warship maintenance would be with Laira, Newton Abbot and Old Oak Common Warships were always to be seen at Bristol Bath Road for just over a decade on a daily basis, as here with D846 Steadfast in 1965. ***Strathwood Library Collection***

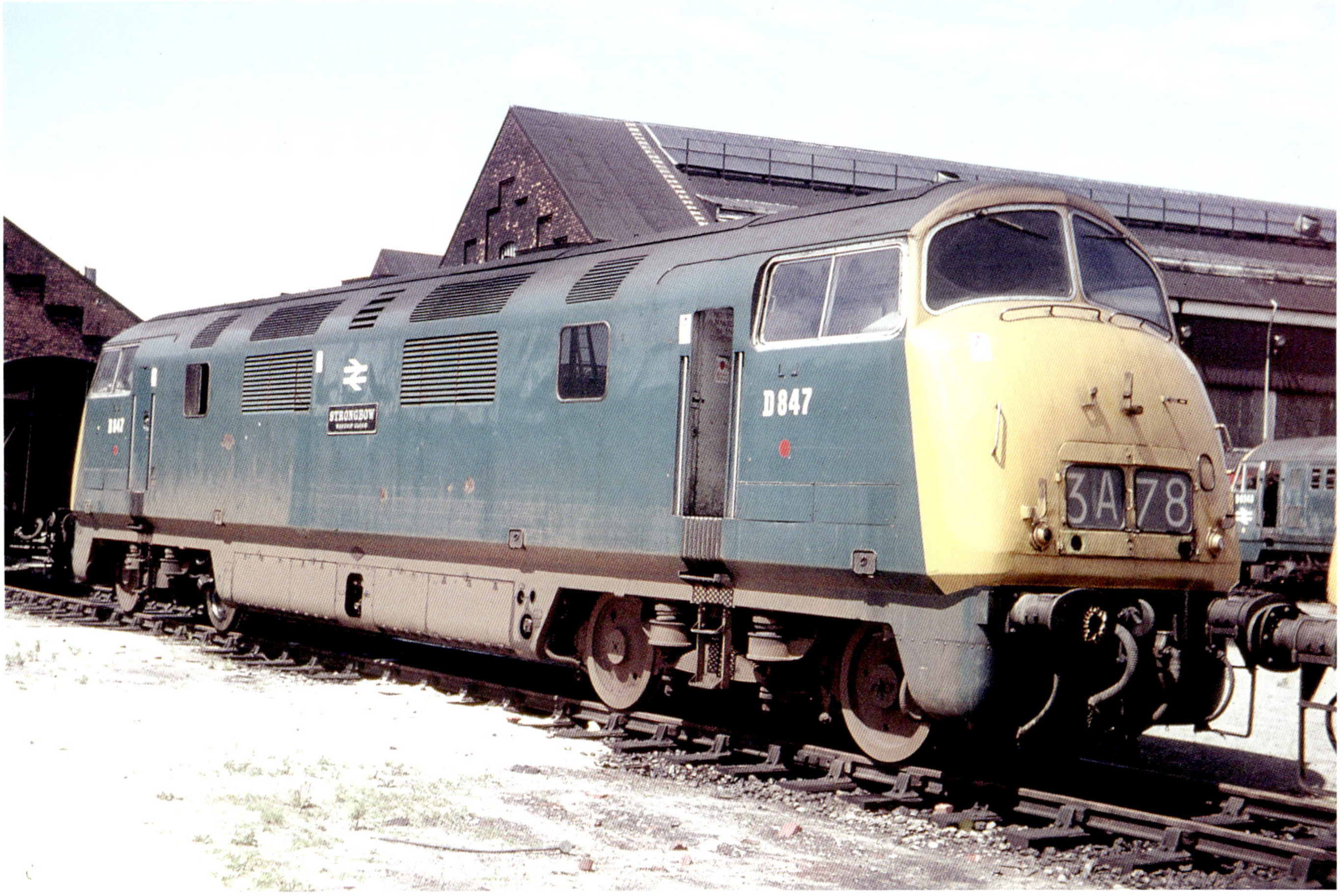

The driver's name brackets were affixed slightly lower under the driver's cabside window on the North British built locomotives as seen here at Old Oak Common in June 1968 on D847 Strongbow. ***Derek Everson***

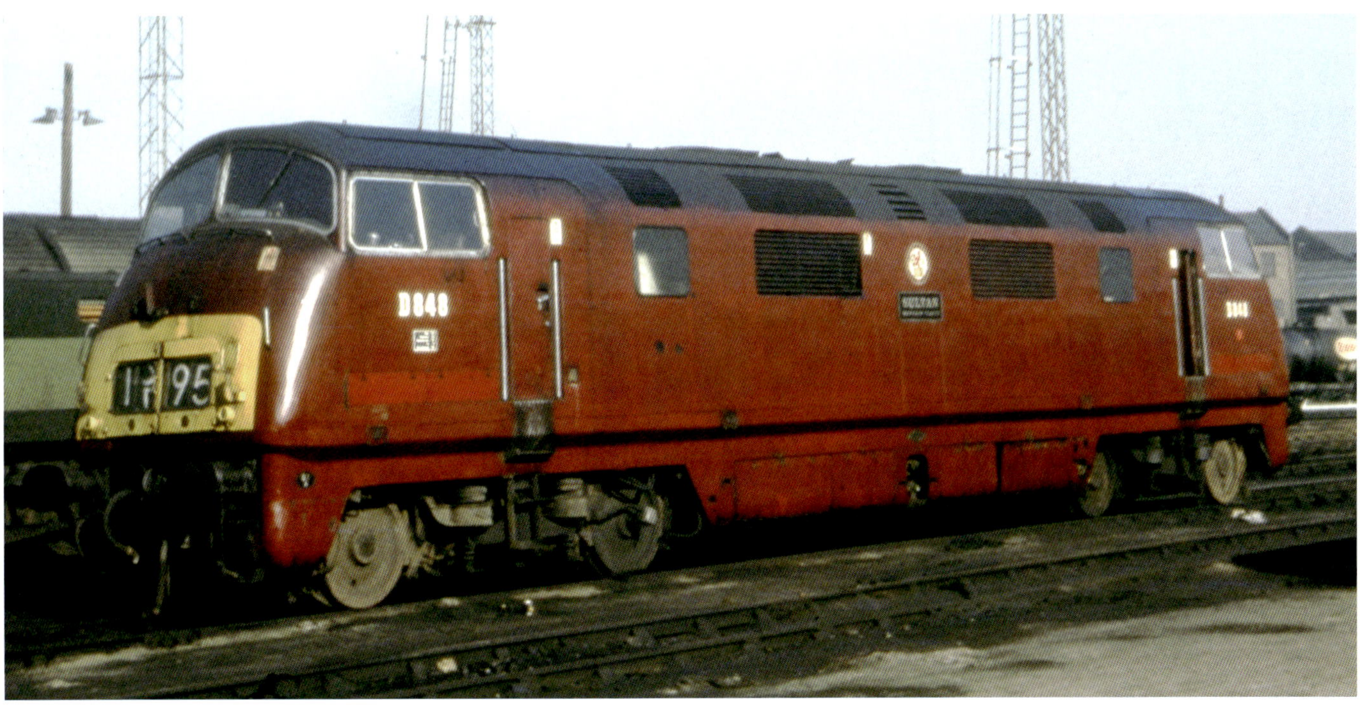

Another exception to the rule for repaints in maroon would be D848 Sultan which was seen at Swindon Works after an Intemediate repair in it's new coat of paint, but still with red backed nameplates in June 1966. By February 1969 it was parked up here at Old Oak Common for storage, this view was taken a few weeks later on 8 March. The locomotive would be withdrawn officially on 26 March 1969 and would linger here for thirteen further months being robbed as needed for spares to keep other North British built Warships on the move. Once sent to Swindon Works the cutters made swift work of it although the cabs were still to be seen as late as November 1970. ***Strathwood Library Collection***

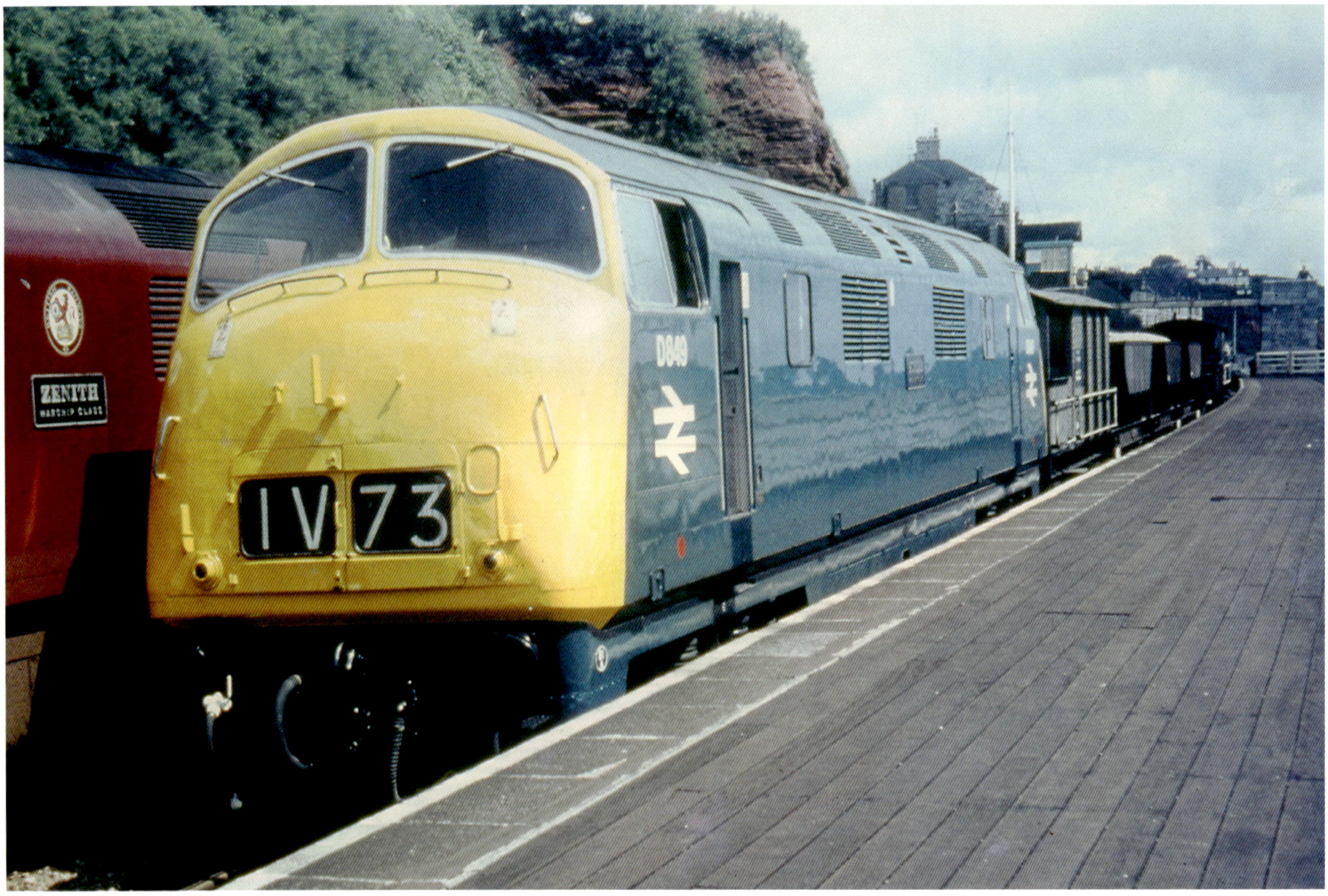

Light duties for an ex-works D849 Superb at Dawlish on 23 June 1968, we can just pick out the oblong vents below the headcode which have certainly been restricted by the fresh coat of yellow paint applied at Swindon Works. ***Exe Rail***

Below: Whereas the coarser mesh on those fitted to D850 Swift at Old Oak Common in May 1968 looks to be less affected by the attentions of Swindon's painters. ***Derek Everson***

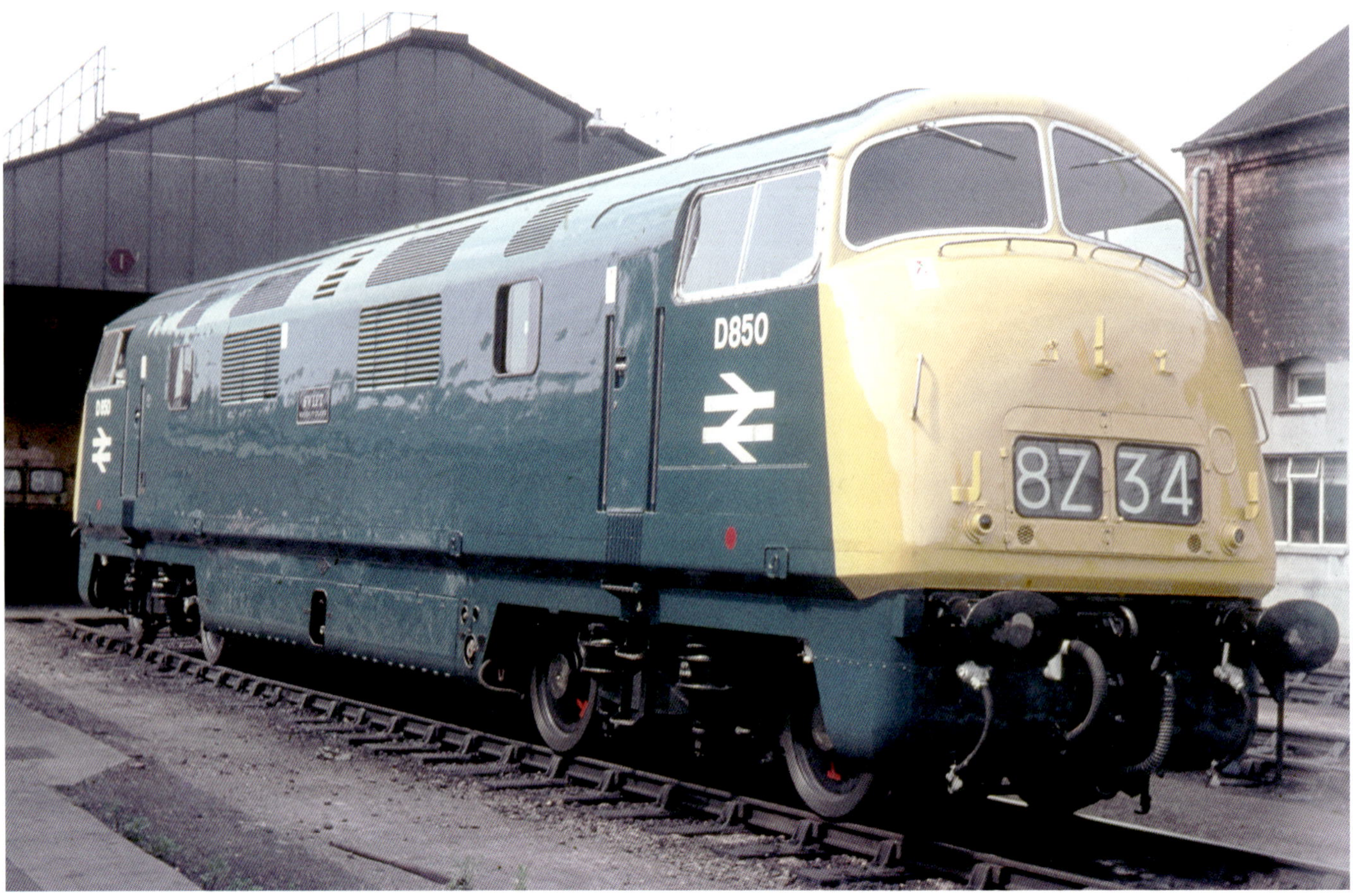

Page opposite: Another Old Oak Common regular was D851 Temeraire again seen on that same visit to 81A on 5 April 1970 by the turntable, ah happy 70s spotting days! ***Strathwood Library Collection***

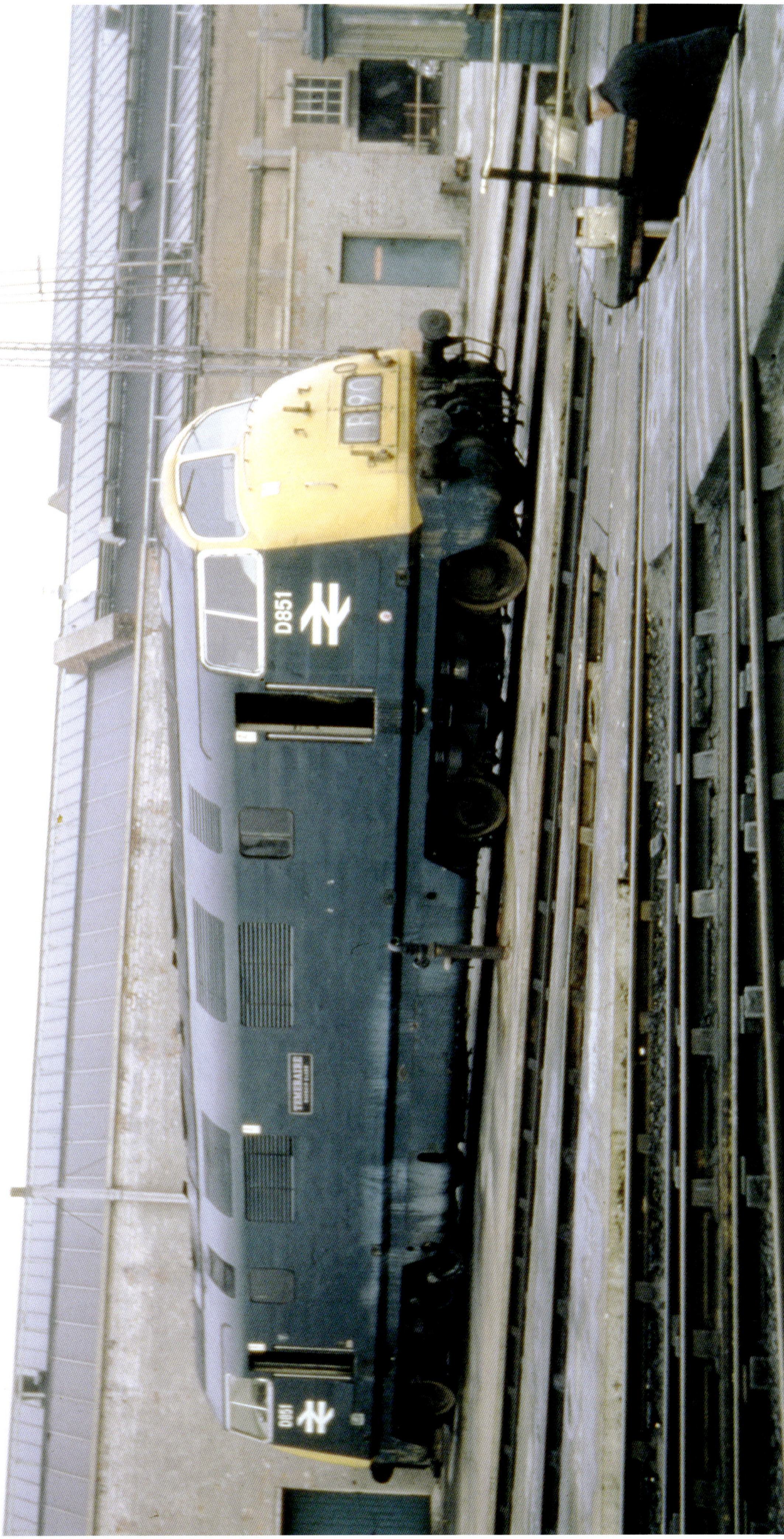
D851

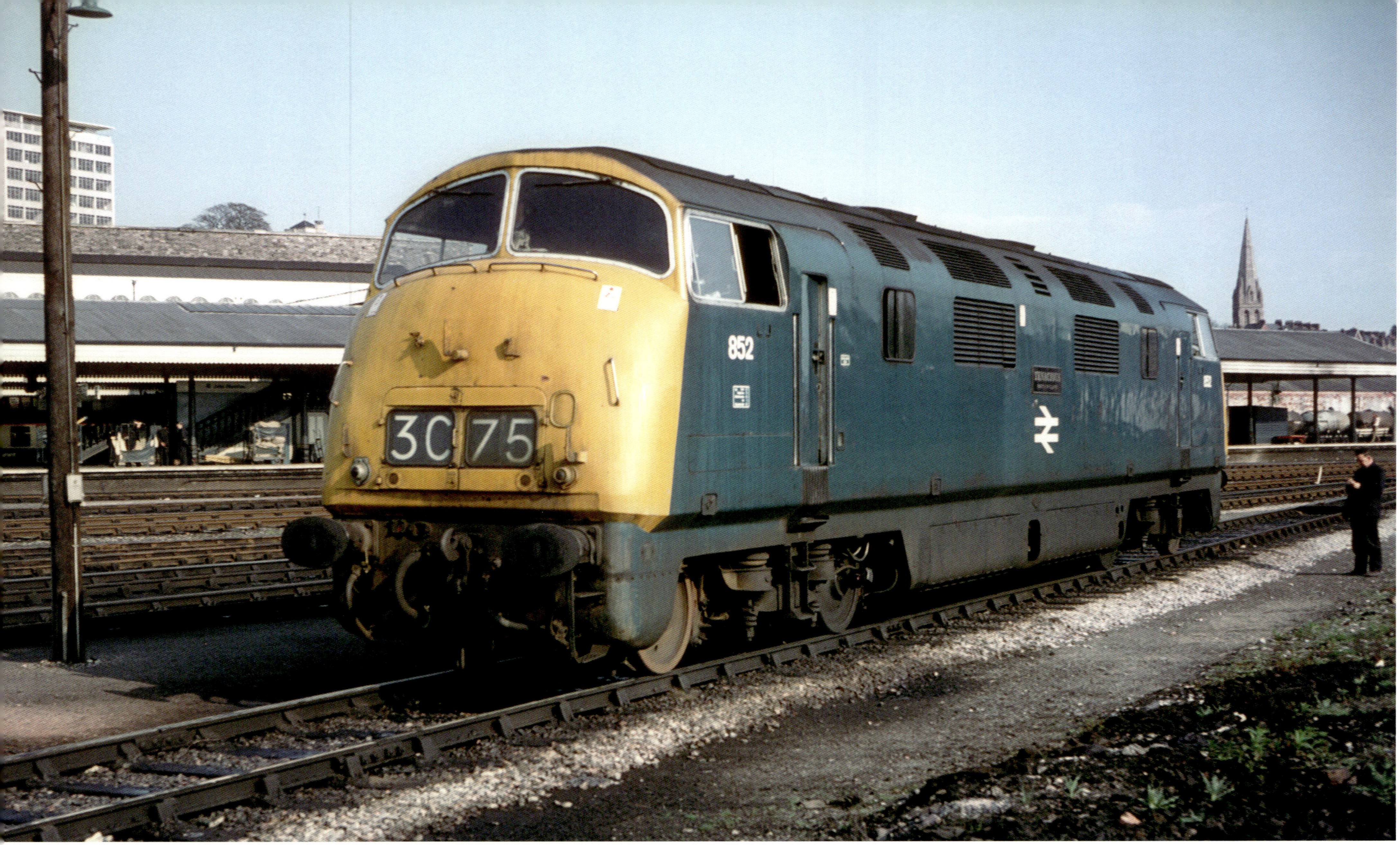

It seems that 852 Tenacious lost its D prefix even before this repaint into blue took place from green livery, with it being painted over before it went to Swindon Works for overhaul in September 1969. It had been in store at Newton Abbot from May of 1969 beforehand. This is the locomotive still at work on 1 May 1971 at Exeter between duties. By September it would be back in store this time at Old Oak Common to be officially withdrawn on 3 October 1971. It would leave 81A for the last time shortly afterwards to be dumped in the rows of Warships and Class 22s assembling at Swindon Works for scrapping. The final act would take place in late May and early June 1972. ***Jim Binnie***

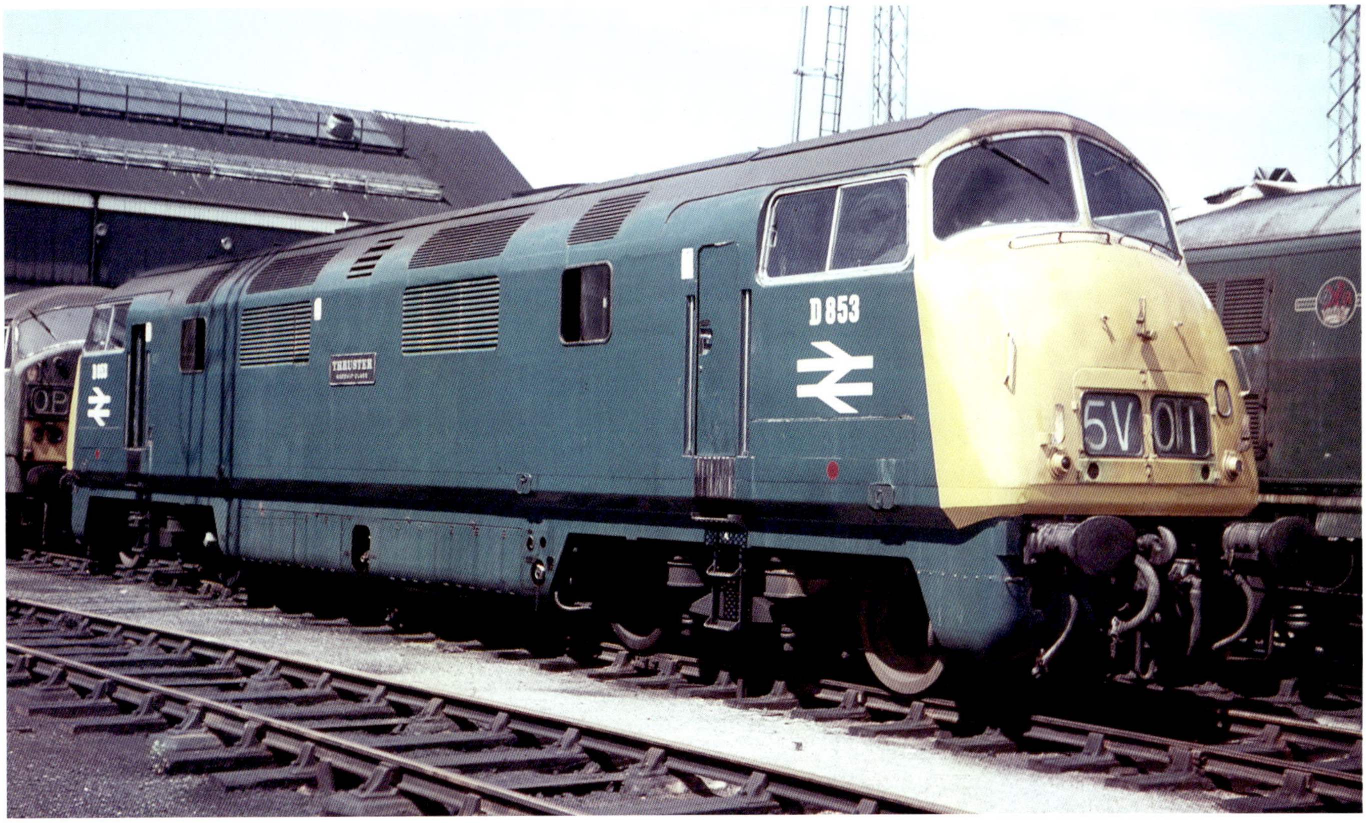

The front vents fitted to D853 Thruster, whilst stopped with a major oil leak as seen at Old Oak Common in June 1968 appear to be larger and not have any form of mesh fitted to them at this point. ***Derek Everson***

Another longer term green Warship was 854 Tiger once again seen at 81A, this time on 15 March 1970, having been released from Swindon in this livery only three months beforehand. ***Strathwood Library Collection***

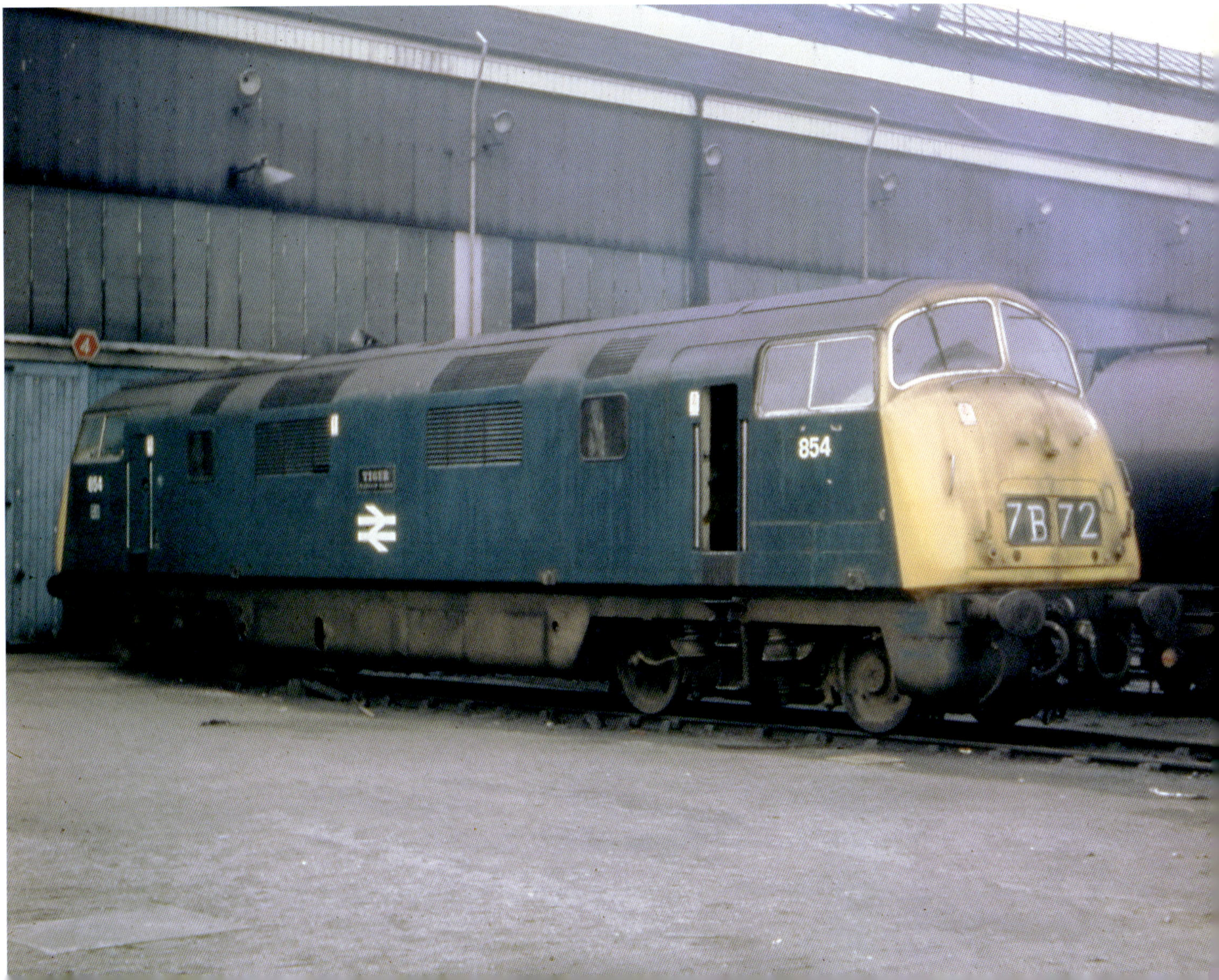

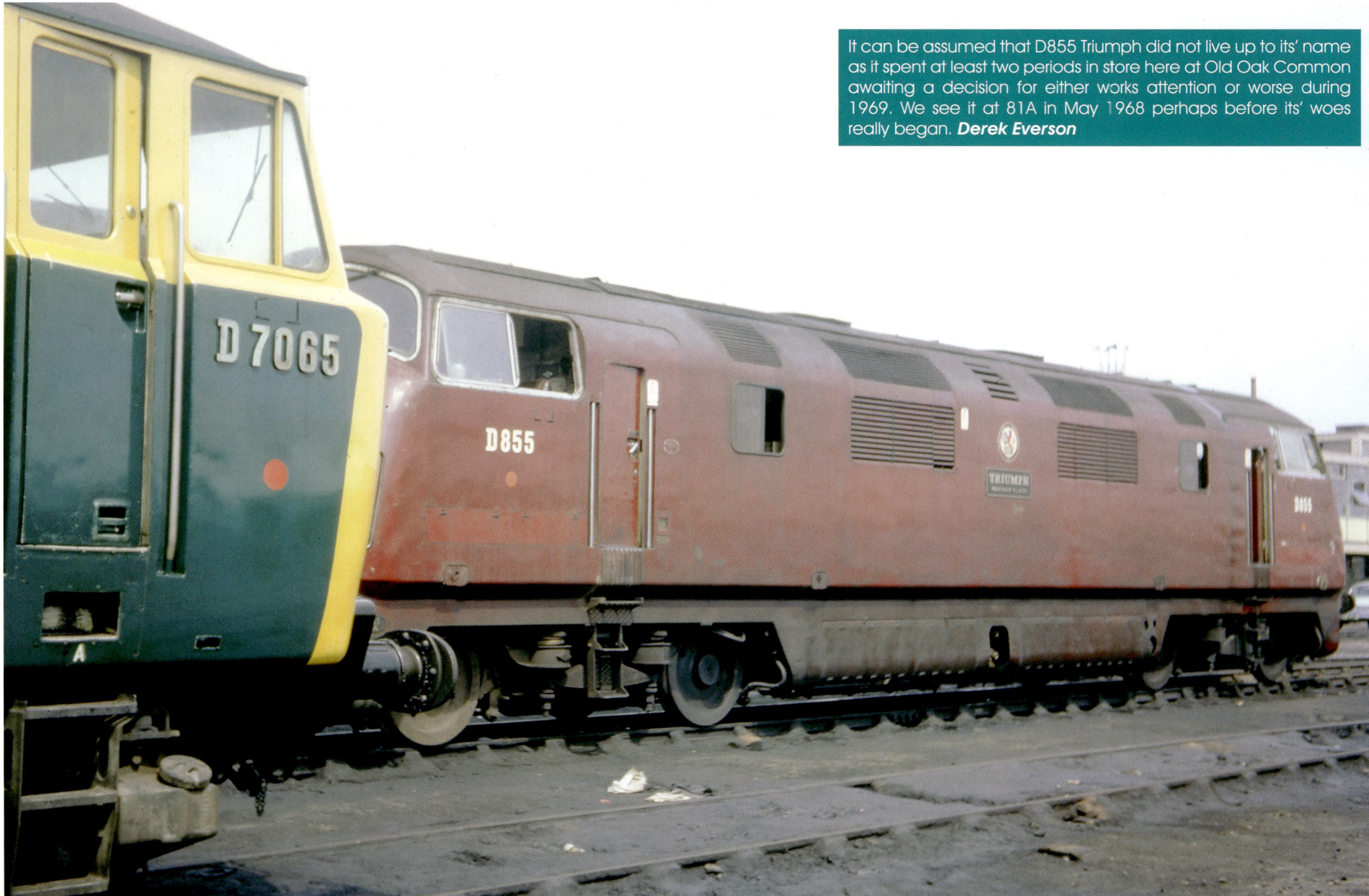

It can be assumed that D855 Triumph did not live up to its' name as it spent at least two periods in store here at Old Oak Common awaiting a decision for either works attention or worse during 1969. We see it at 81A in May 1968 perhaps before its' woes really began. ***Derek Everson***

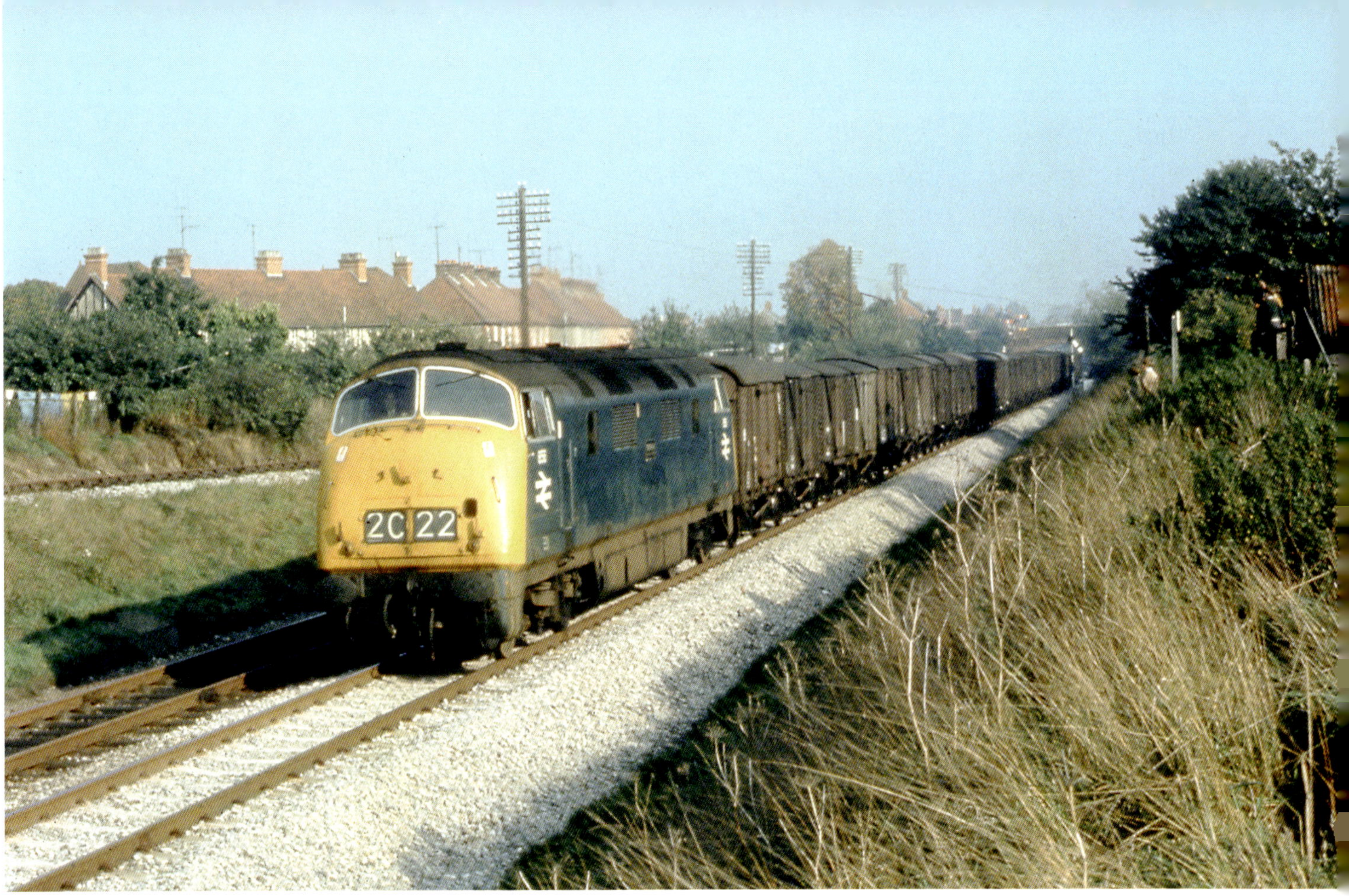

As we have seen already the original larger front ventilation grille on the Warships nose was often plated over and painted yellow with the rubber seals often being painted as well. However as 856 Trojan approaches the cameraman near Newbury this vent shows up very dark, is it still in place at all, as other shots we have seen show it to be painted over with the black rubber seal un-painted? ***Transport Topics***

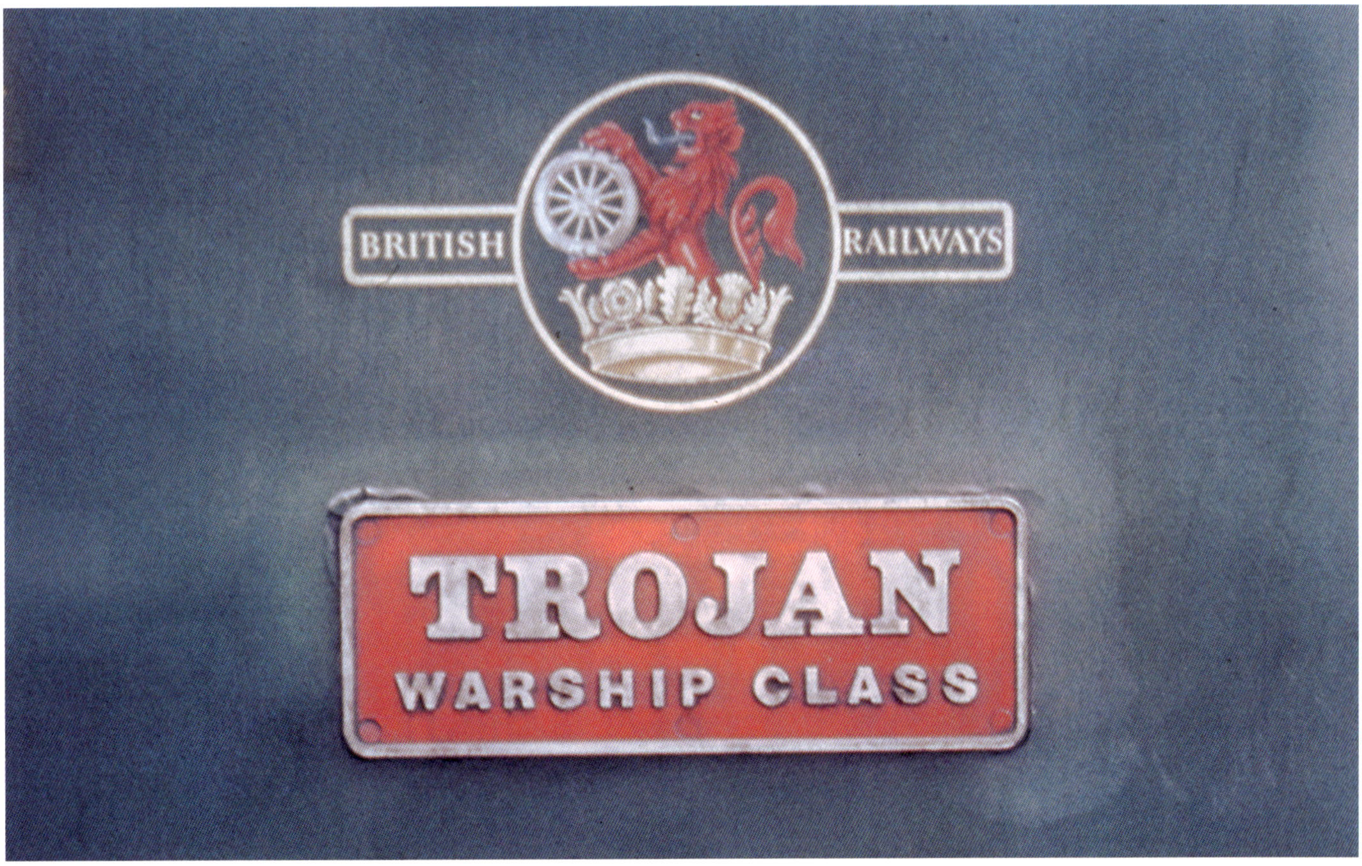

The Warship nameplates were picked out in red whilst they were in green livery, this being changed to black backgrounds upon the moves to either maroon or blue liveries. Along with Swindon built D803 Albion, North British built D856 Trojan would be the final two Warships to recieve their half yellow warning panels with the latter being the very last in May 1965. ***Exe Rail***

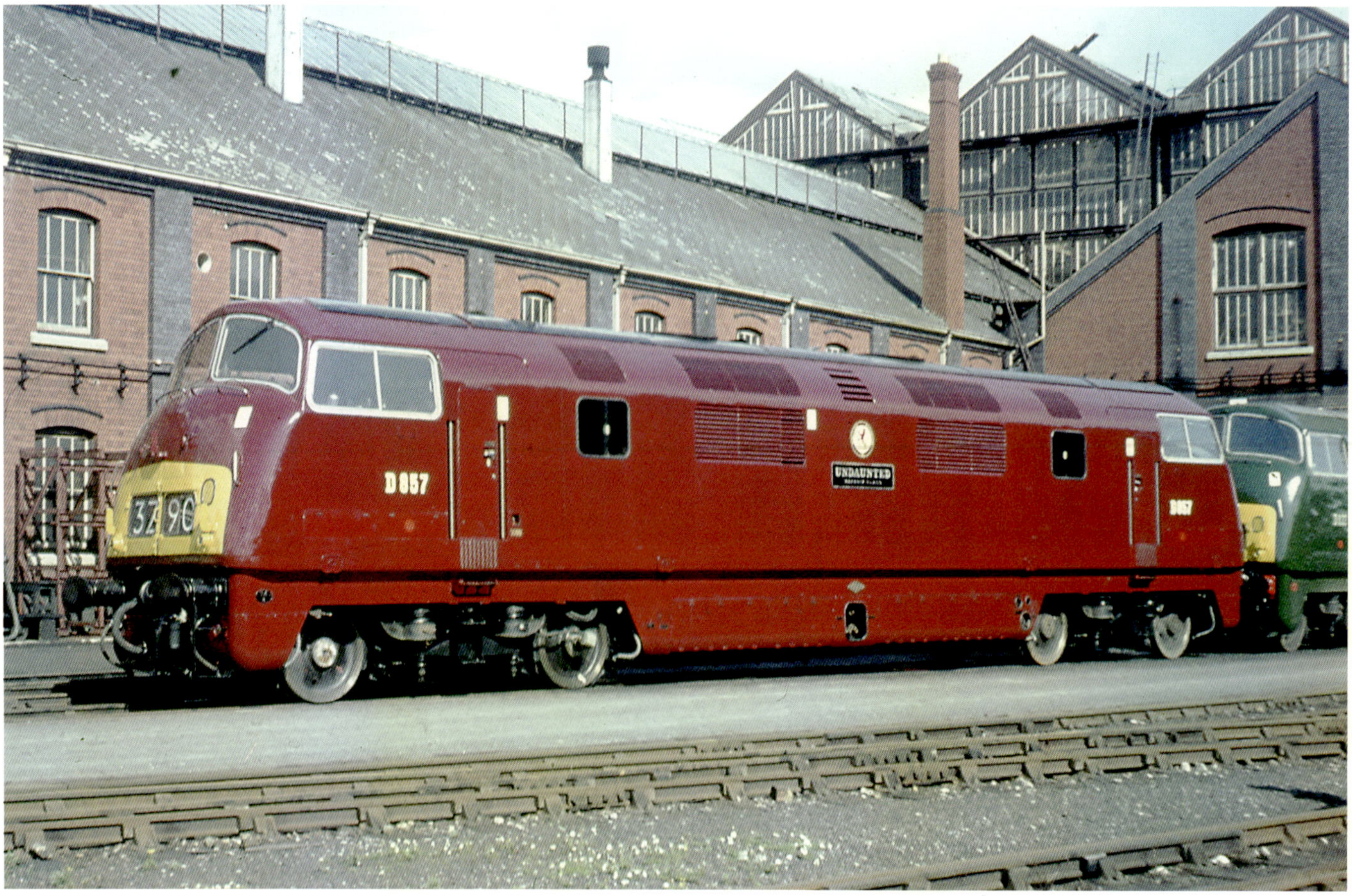

The first Warship to be painted into maroon livery would be D857 Undaunted which was in Swindon Works for an Intermediate repair from the end of May until 22 September 1965. We see this camera shy locomotive awaiting its return to use once more in the Indian summer sunshine. It should also be noted that its numbers have been repainted in the same position as if it were still green, in line where the stripe used to be. ***Strathwood Library Collection***

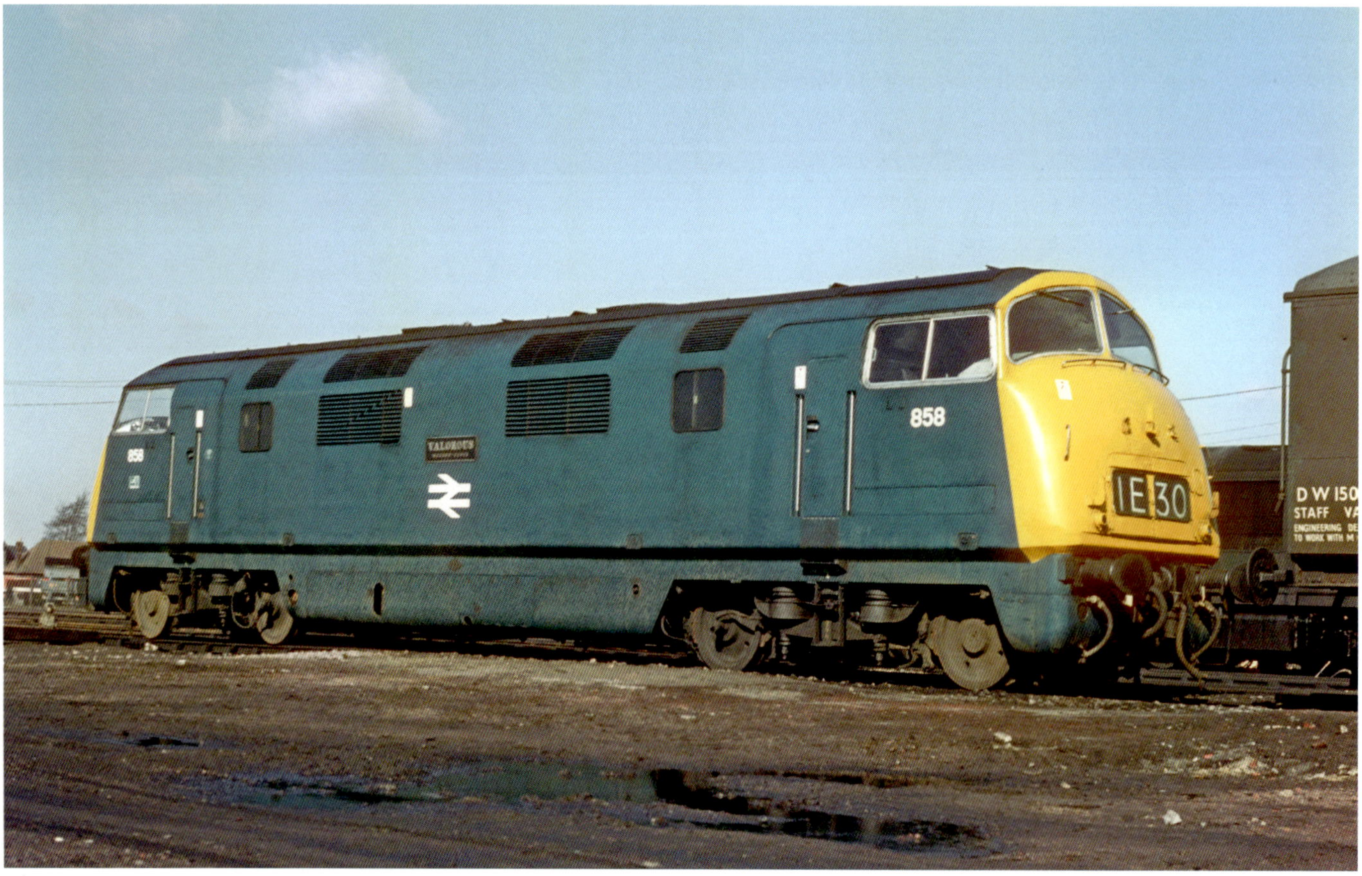

As we have already seen Gloucester Horton Road depot was always a good spot to photograph Warships during their latter service years, and we can enjoy this time 858 Valorous laid over in the sunshine on 5 March 1970. ***Jim Binnie***

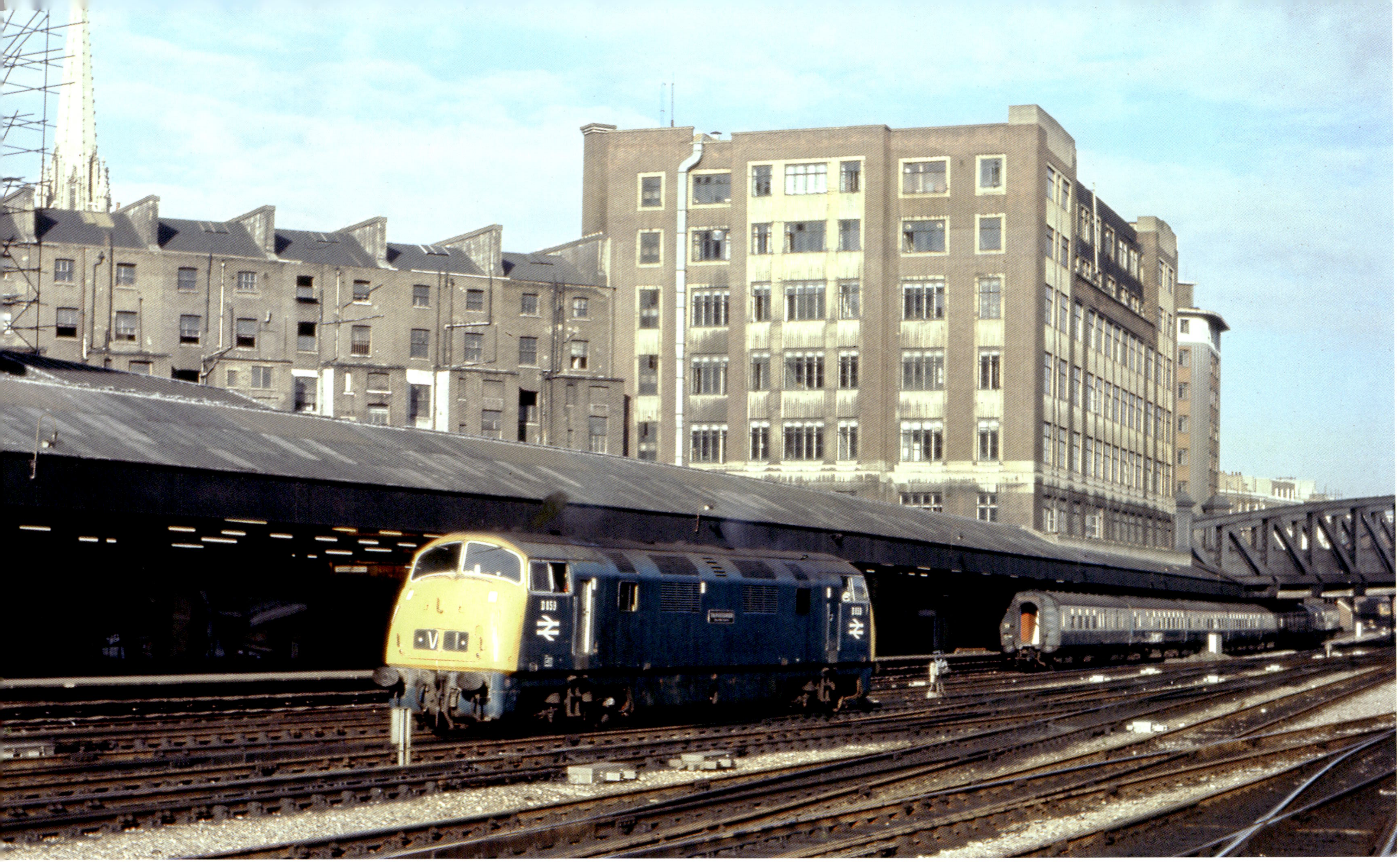

Another rarer Warship to the cameramen seems to be D859 Vanquisher, seen here light engine in the station throat at Paddington on 10 July 1970. This locomotive was the first Warship to gain a half yellow warning panel when it entered service on 9 January 1962, it was closely followed by D834 which Swindon turned out after repairs on 16 January 1962. The first Swindon built Warship to gain the yellow warning panels would be D822 Hercules ten days later. ***Bernard Mills***

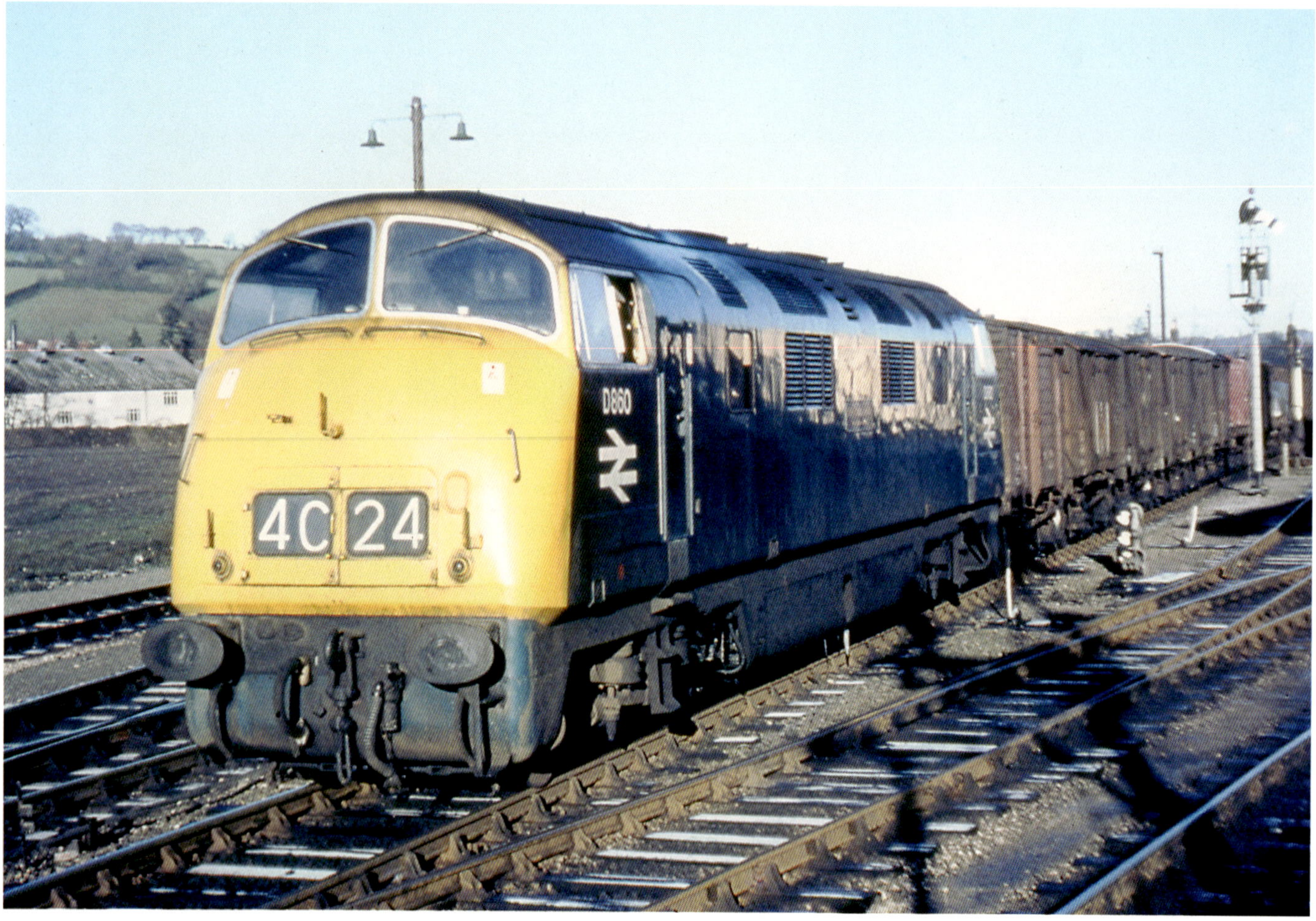

It will be a fitted freight for today's duty away from Exeter St. Davids for D860 Victorious in the winter of 1968. It was sent when new to Laira in January 1962 before the new diesel depot opened there in September 1963, and it became a Newton Abbot engine from July 1965 until it was withdrawn in March 1971. ***Exe Rail***

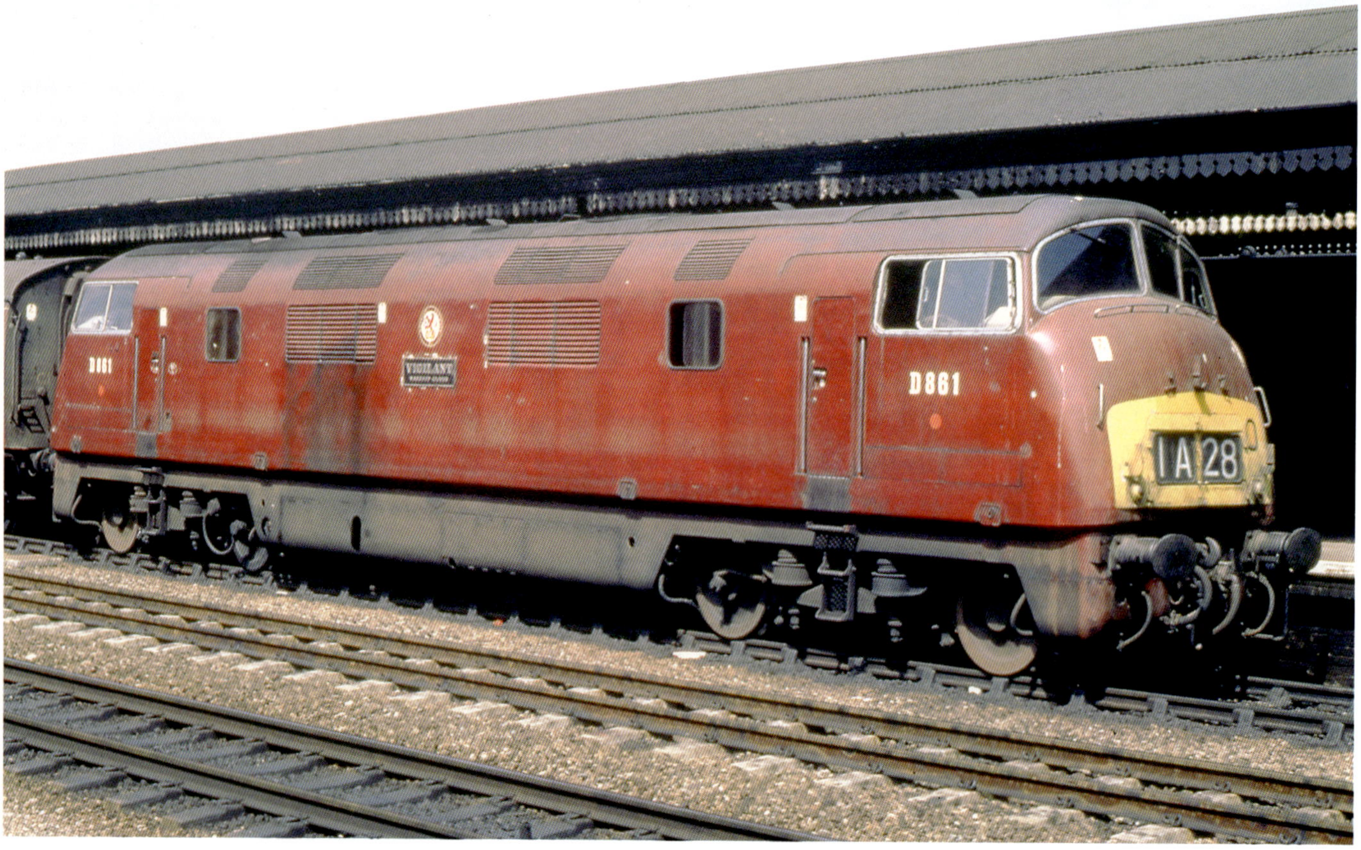

Clearly the inset of the battery boxes and the inside frame bogies is beyond the effective cleaning power of the automated washing plants as seen on D861 Vigilant as it waits at Reading General with an up express in July 1968. ***Strathwood Library Collection***

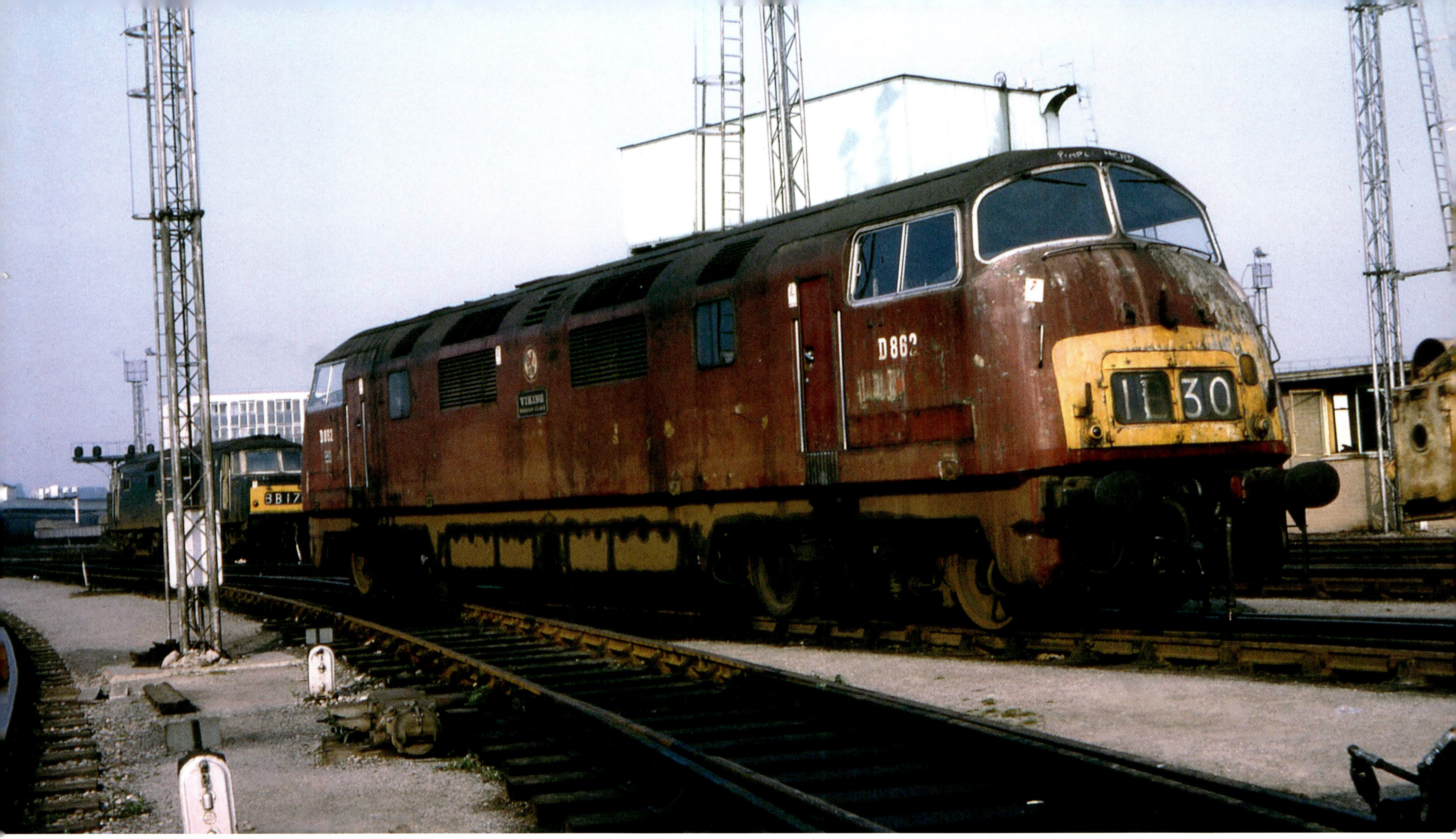

One feels however that no amount of cleaning will bring D862 Viking back to its' glory without the use of a paintbrush when it was seen at Bristol Bath Road during the open day on 18 October 1969. Thankfully that repaint would come and Viking would emerge from Swindon Works in April 1970 in pristine blue livery with the Inter City arrows placed under the nameplates, and Gill Sans numbering without the D prefix. Viking would however be among the last survivors of the Class 43 Warships being withdrawn on 3 October 1971. ***Michael Ellis***

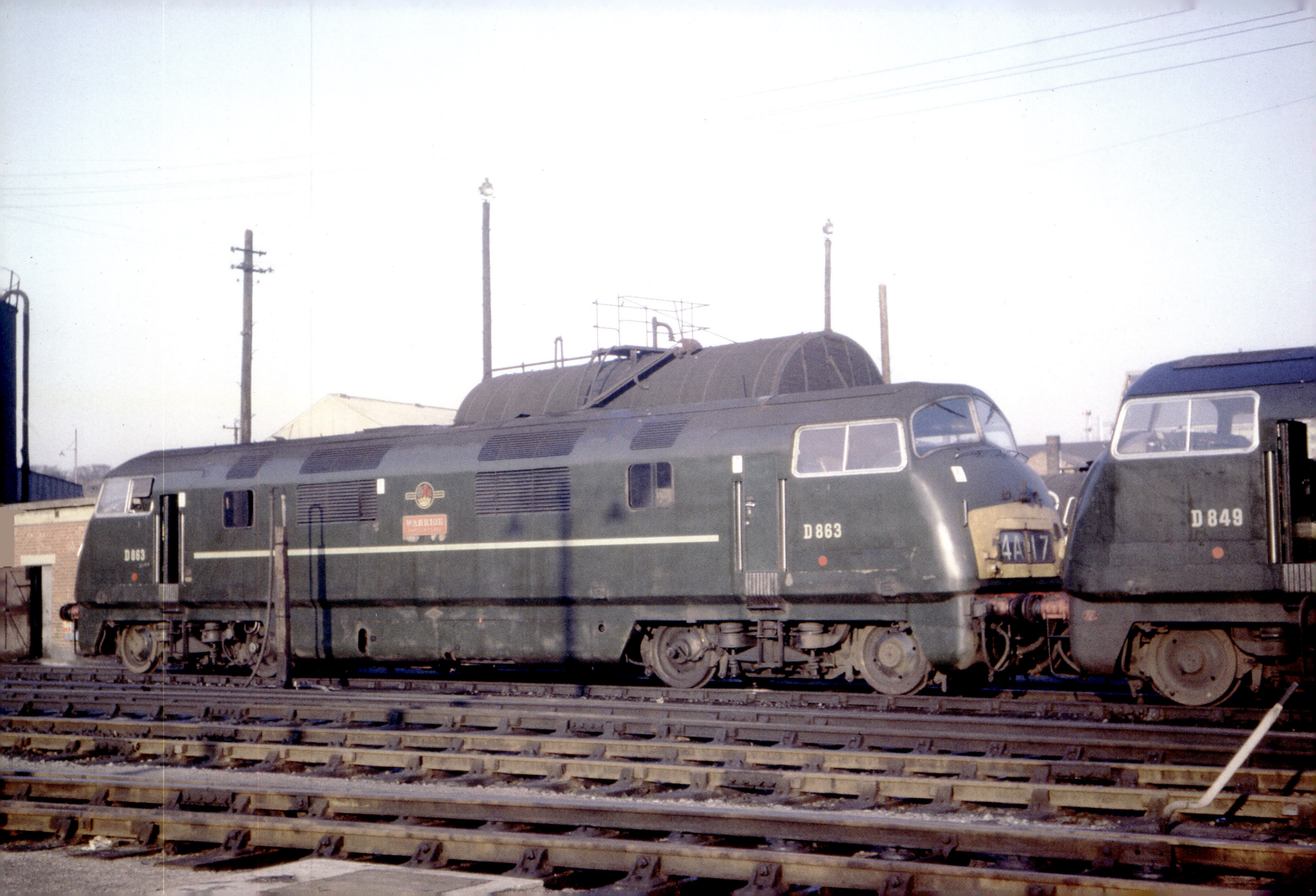
D863
WARRIOR
D863
4A17
D849

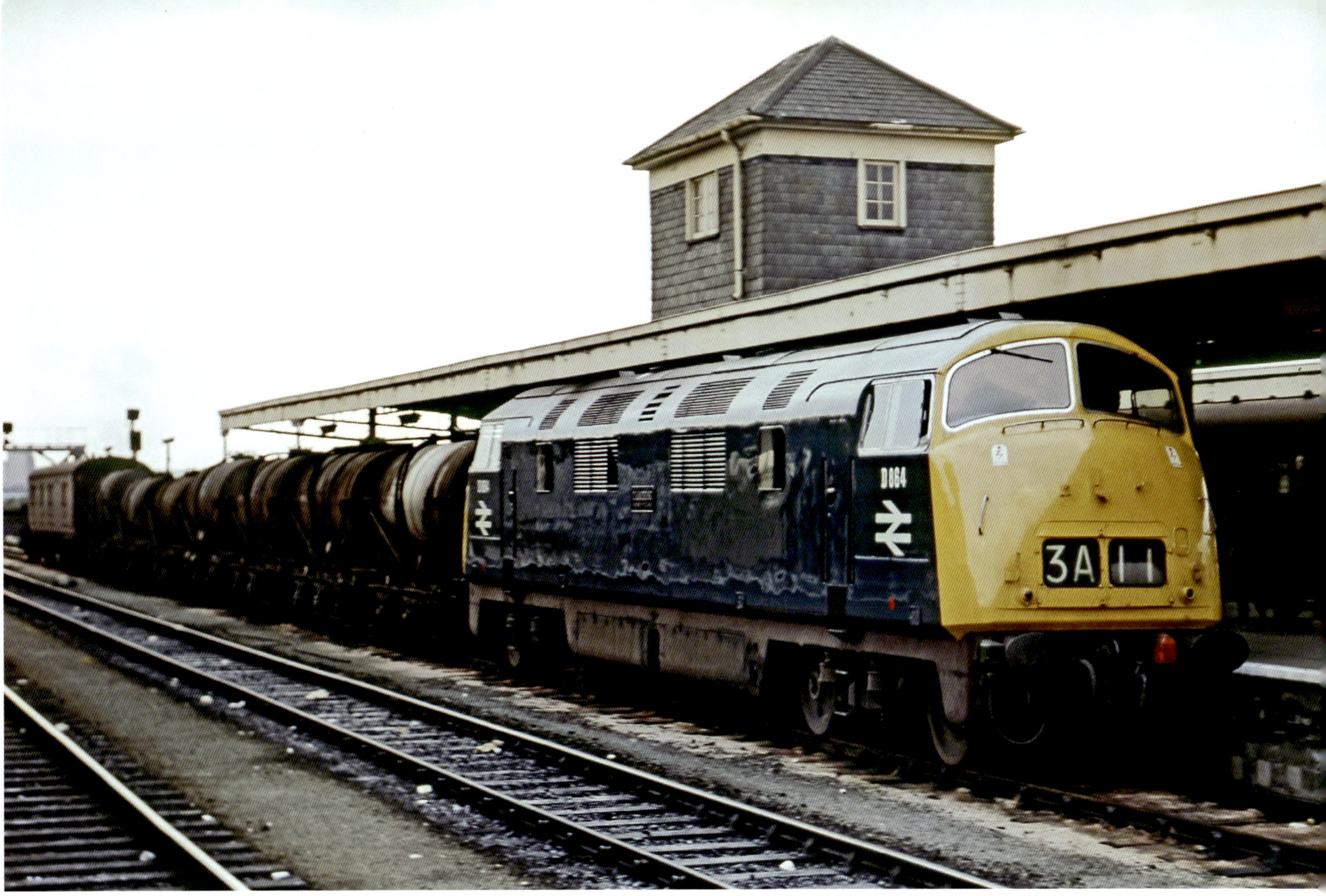

Even though the lower skirt area of D864 Zambesi was unique in a burnt umber brown paint, it too is beyond the range of effective mechanical cleaning seen at Reading in 1968 whilst on an up milk train. ***David Cobbe/Rail Photoprints***

Standing alongside a Swindon built Warship at Exeter St. Davids we find the last built North British Warship 865 Zealous at the head of an inter-regional train for the north. Obviously running out of 'Z' names it was originally envisaged that D864 should have been named Zealous and D865 should have become Zenith. ***Transport Topics***

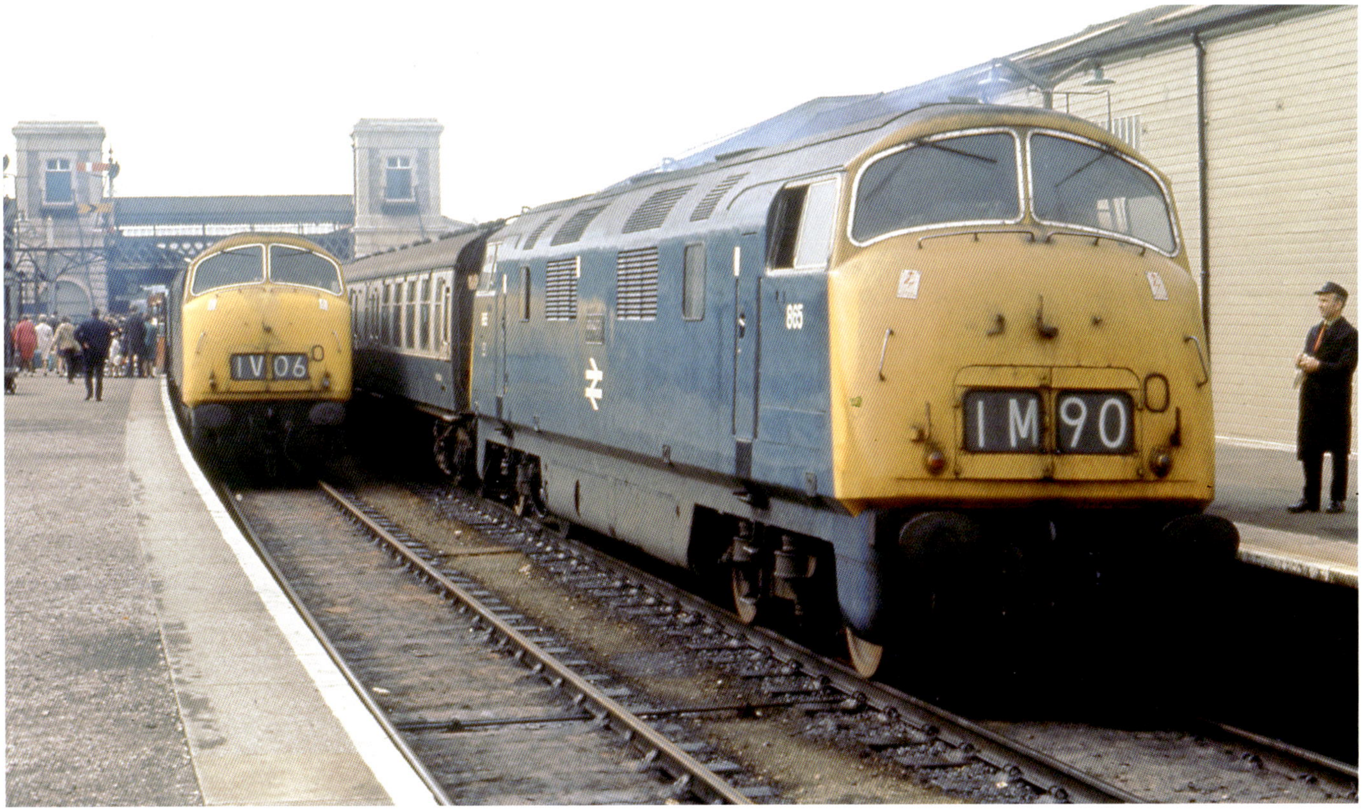

Page left: Most definately one of the rarer Warships for cameramen and no doubt many spotters alike was D863 Warrior with the distinction of being the shortest lived of its type. This view was taken in December 1963 twenty months into its very short career at Old Oak Common. ***Richard Sinclair Collection***

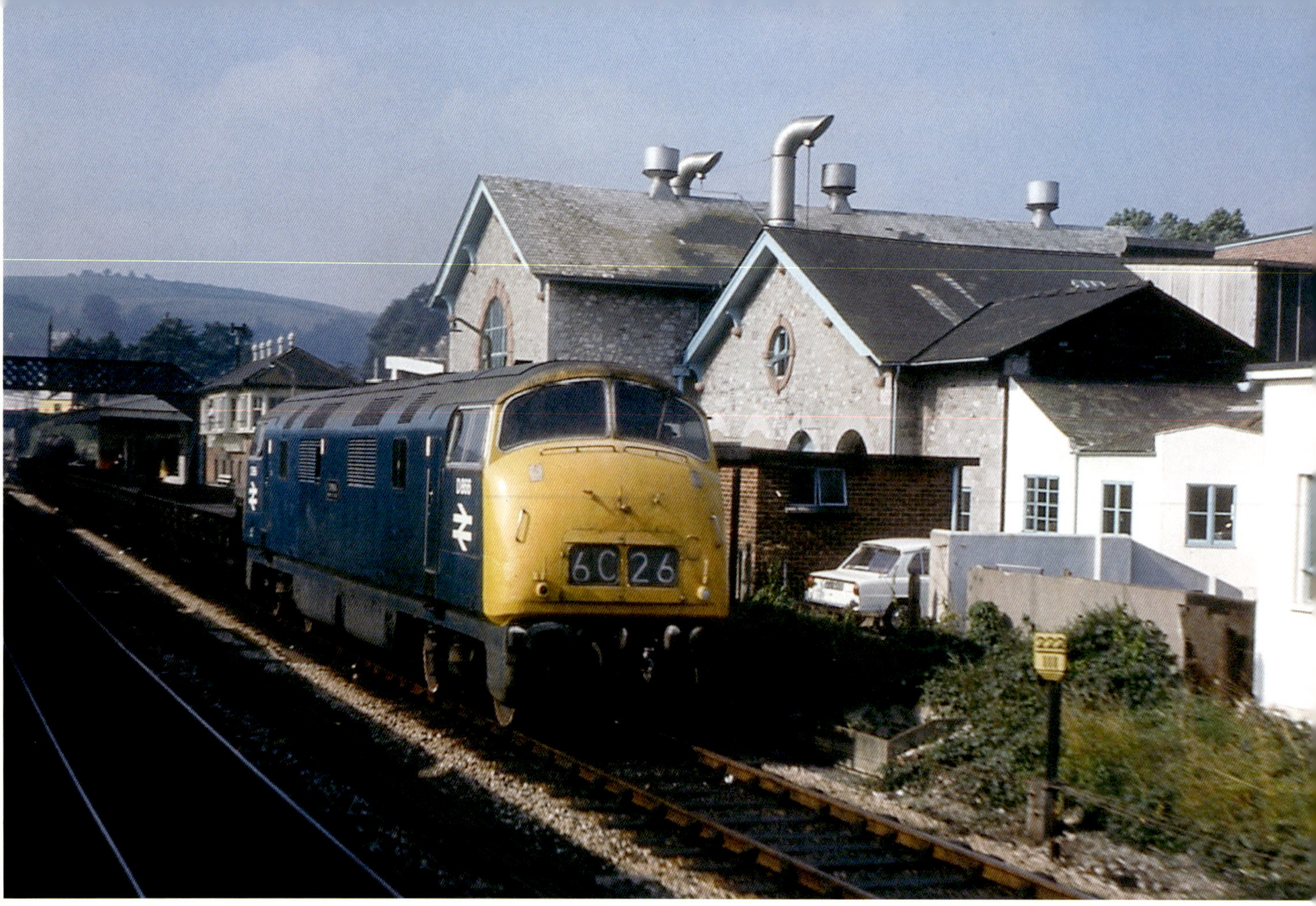

Waiting in the loop at Totnes on 7 September 1971 was D866 Zebra at the head of the 08.45 Plymouth Friary to Severn Tunnel Junction goods. Warships were much rarer into Wales with the occasional trips only as far as Cardiff by this time. ***Peter Crawley***

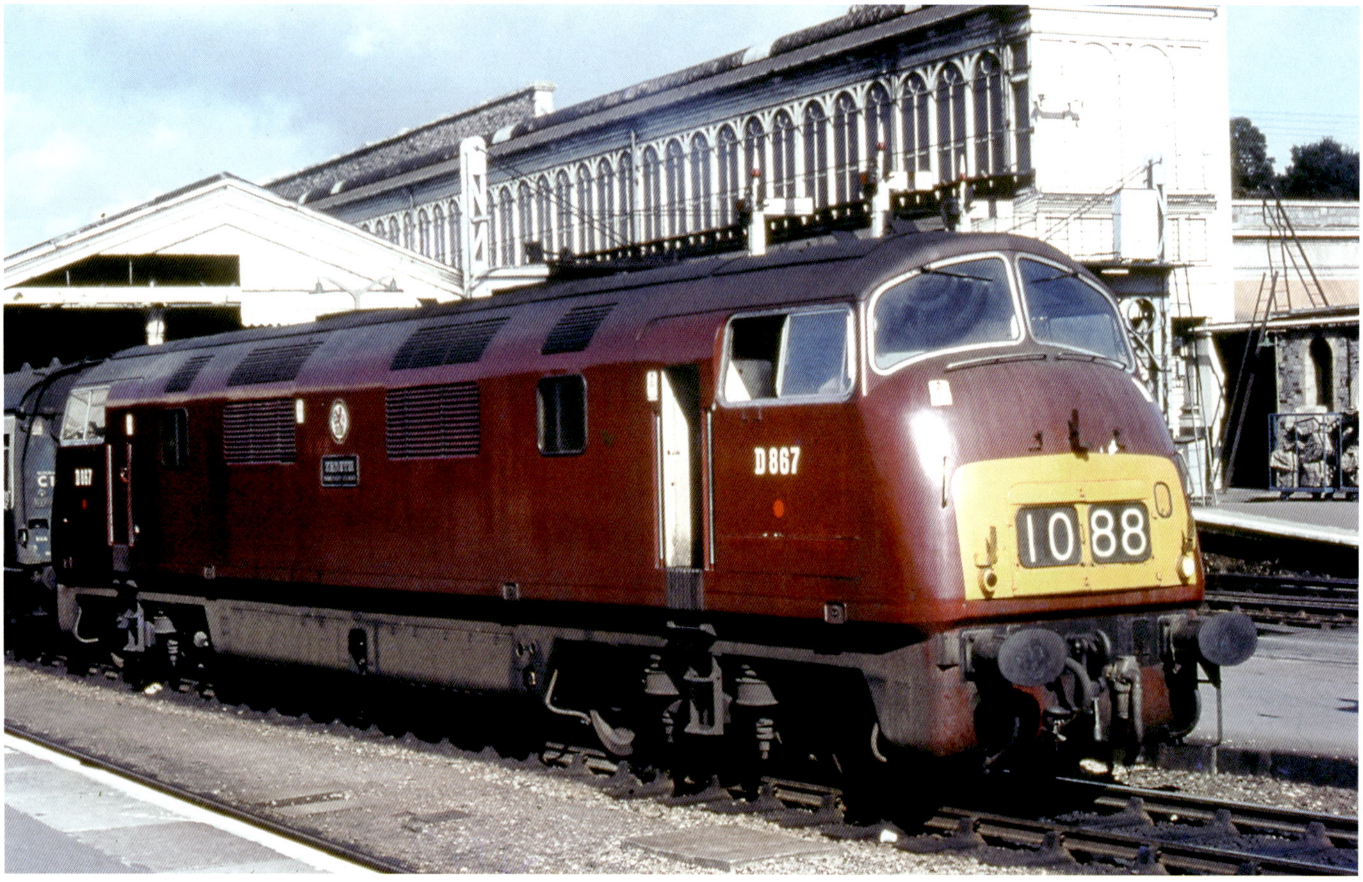

As can be seen the bufferbeam colour for the maroon paint scheme was black as modelled by D867 Zenith whilst waiting at Exeter St. Davids on 23 September 1967. In 1973 after Swindon Works had cut up both Zebra and Zenith identifiable pieces from both locomotives turned up at Kilnhurst near Rotherham in a scrapyard causing some excitement at the time. ***Exe Rail***

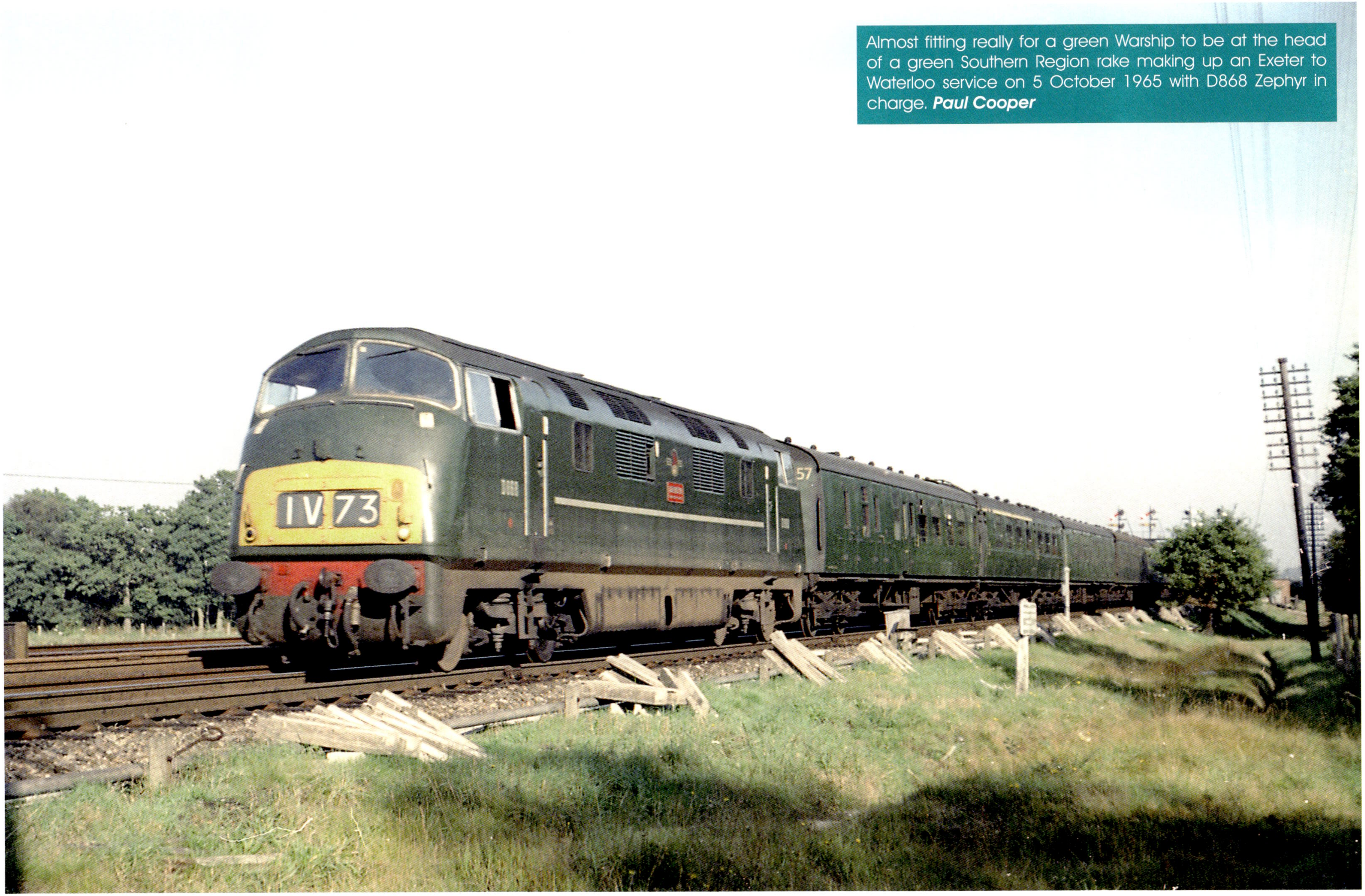

Almost fitting really for a green Warship to be at the head of a green Southern Region rake making up an Exeter to Waterloo service on 5 October 1965 with D868 Zephyr in charge. ***Paul Cooper***

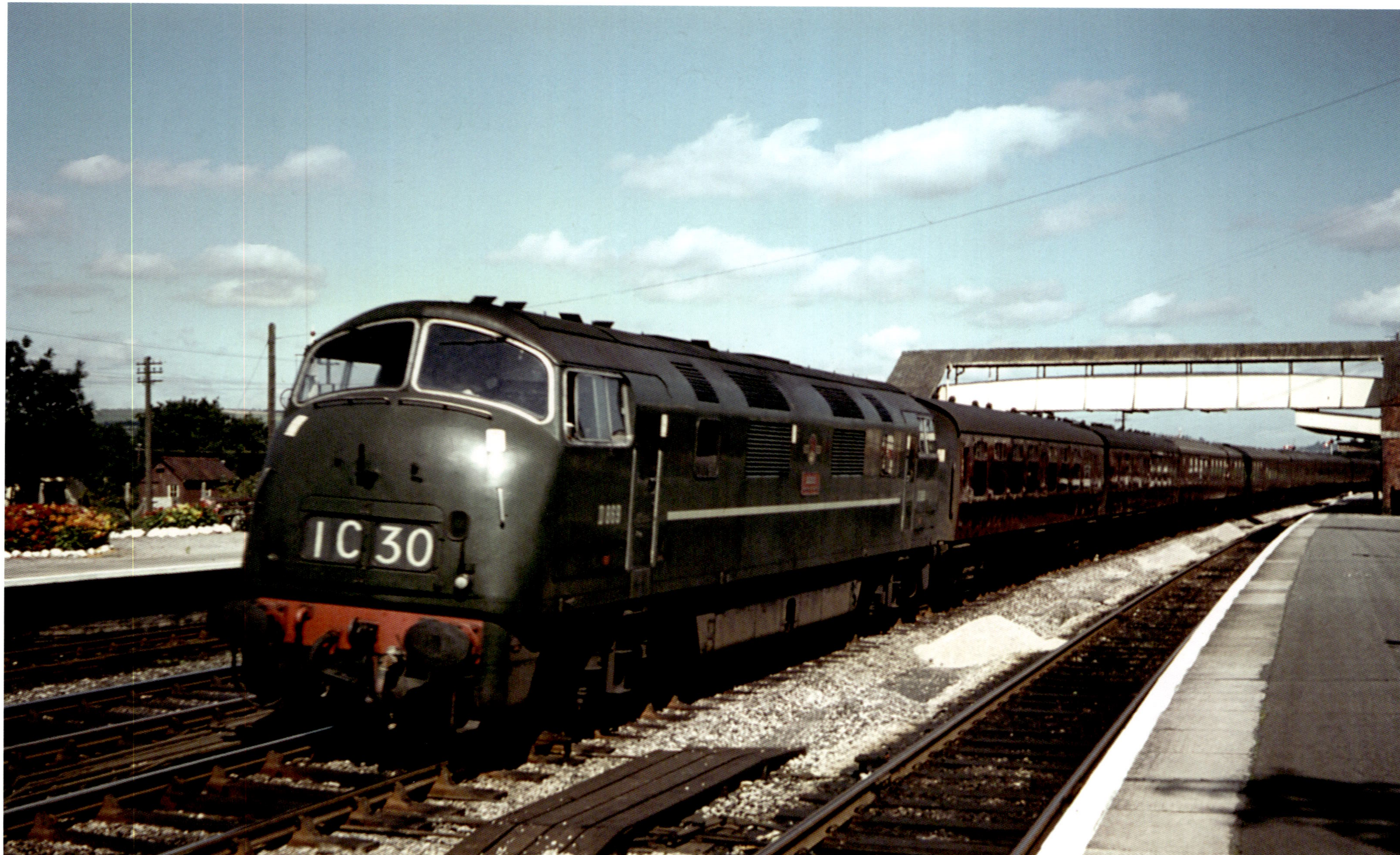

Though when one see's an all green Warship such as D869 Zest at the head of a maroon rake as here at Tiverton Junction with a down express on 7 September 1962, it is easy to see the Western Region's desire to paint its' express diesel fleet into maroon to match the stock. ***Transport Treasury***

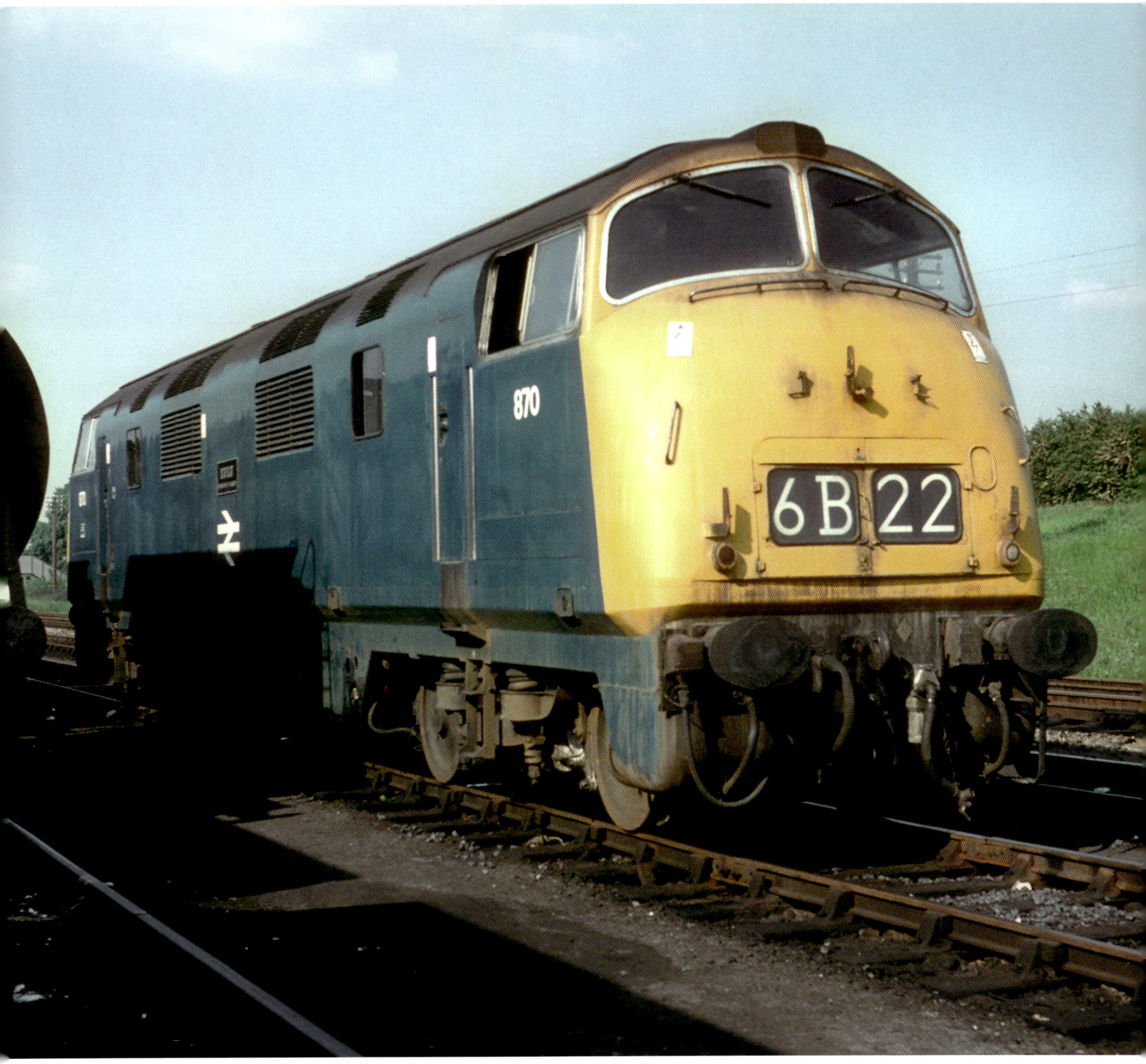

Always easy to spot from afar was 870 Zulu with its distinctive cowling above the roof to house the horns. This modification from new came about as this example was selected for an experiment to fit electric train supply equipment, and the extra space was needed where the warning horns were normally housed behind the bufferbeams in order to host the jumper boxes that would be required. In the event this trial never took place and so it was that Zulu remained visually different throughout its life. The white diamond markings can be just made out amongst the grime on the bufferbeam to denote which locomotives could be paired with each other for dual working. Although all the Warships were originally fitted for dual working most lost this equipment as time went on. However to try and speed up the Paddington to Penzance services for the 1968 summer timetable twenty of the Swindon built Warships had their jumper cables refitted and were marked with these white diamonds. It would appear that D814 Dragon, D816 Eclipse and D857 Undaunted retained their jumper cables and were also coded with white diamonds as well. Whilst from the outset the three prototypes D800-D802 were only ever equiped to work with each other. On 4 June 1970, 870 Zulu rested on Gloucester Horton Road depot. ***Jim Binnie***

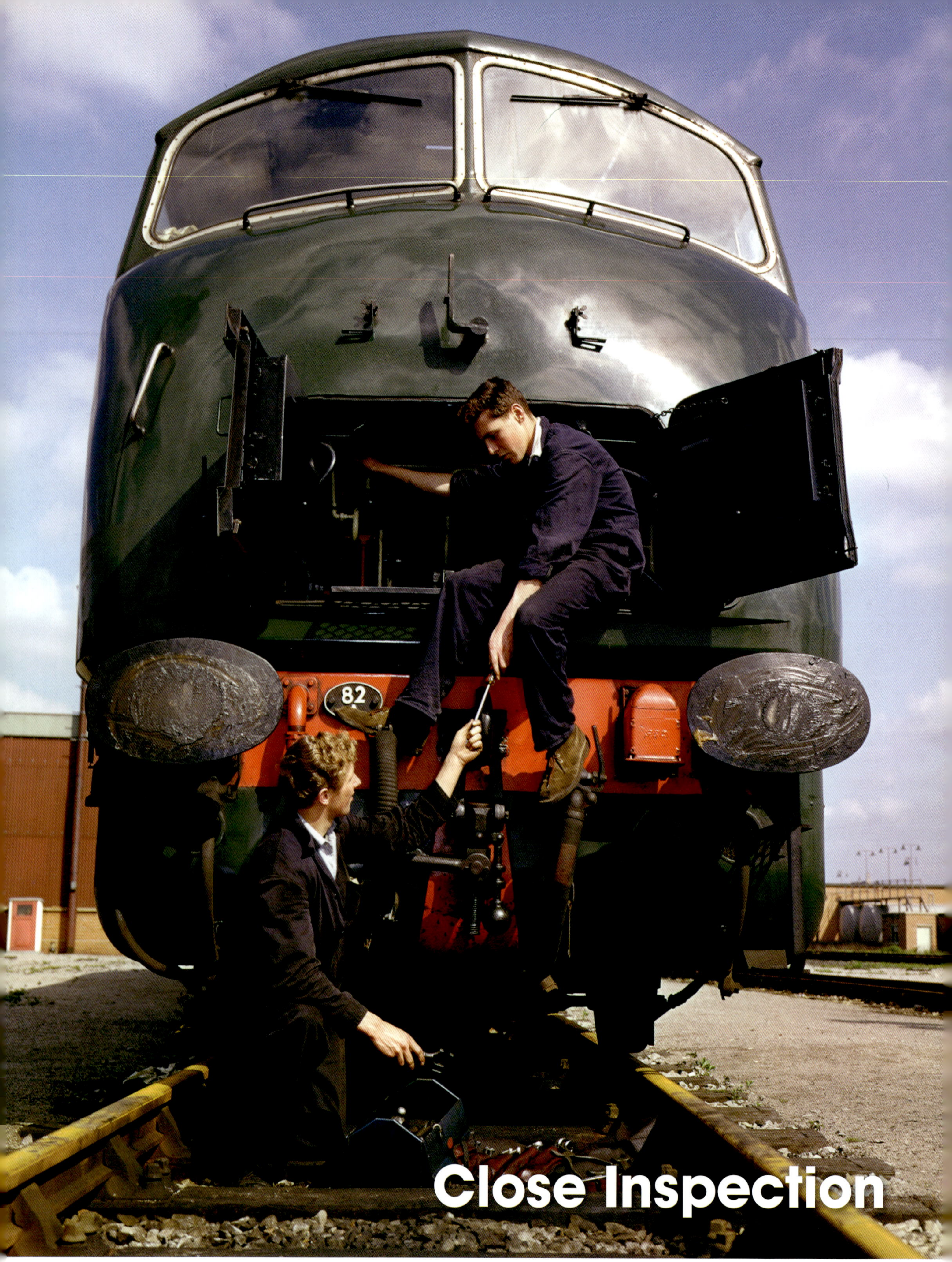

Close Inspection

A delightfully posed official portrait view of an unknown North British Warship at Old Oak Common most likely in the summer of 1961. The red dropdown by the coupling shows up well here and what is also of note is the Bristol Bath Road 82A shedplate as none were based there then. ***Transport Treasury***

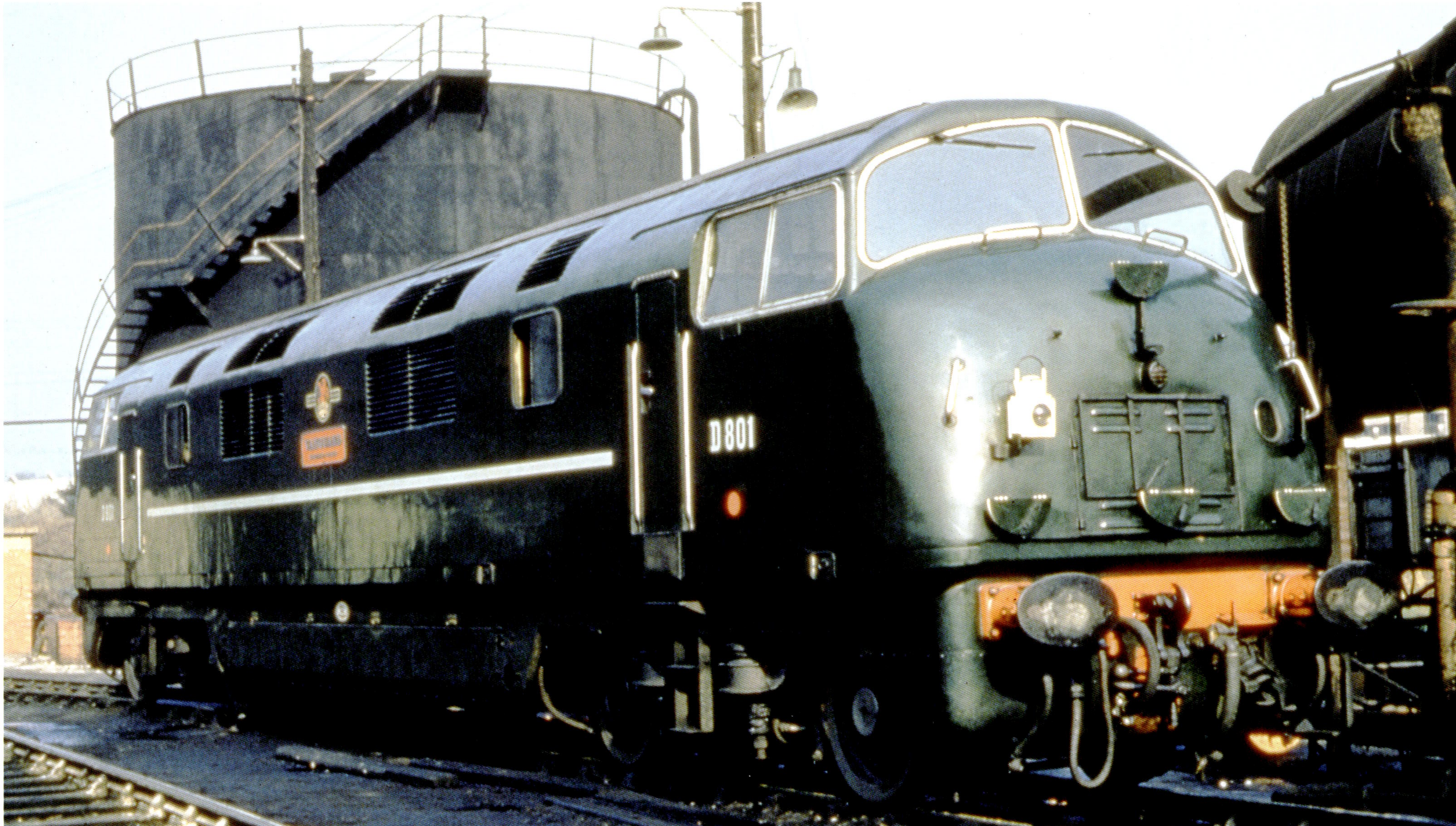

A comparison between the shorter front handrails and the differing styles of headcode arrangements is apparent in this view for the first three prototypes, as modelled by D801 Vanguard in original condition at Old Oak Common in October 1959. The jumper cable boxes are different as well as are the cab door handrails on these first three locomotives, which were bent inwards at the top and bottom whilst the production locomotives were straight. As time went on those shorter front handrails were modified to comply with the rest of the class, as were the headcode boxes too. Another later modification was to the rubber kick strips below the driver's doors which would later be beefed up with alluminium strips. ***Grahame Wareham Collection***

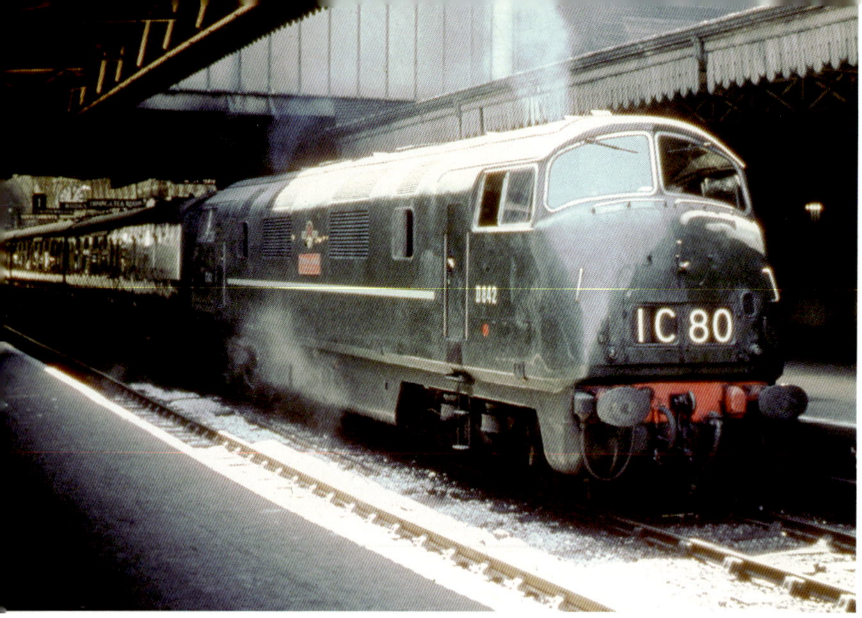

Deliveries from D813 onwards were with the four character headcode boxes as here with D842 Royal Oak at Paddington in this livery until D859 Vanquisher arrived in January 1962. This meant that the last seven locomotives delivered from North British entered service with half yellow fronts. The last Swindon builds from D866 to D870 had all entered service in 1961. ***Strathwood Library Collection***

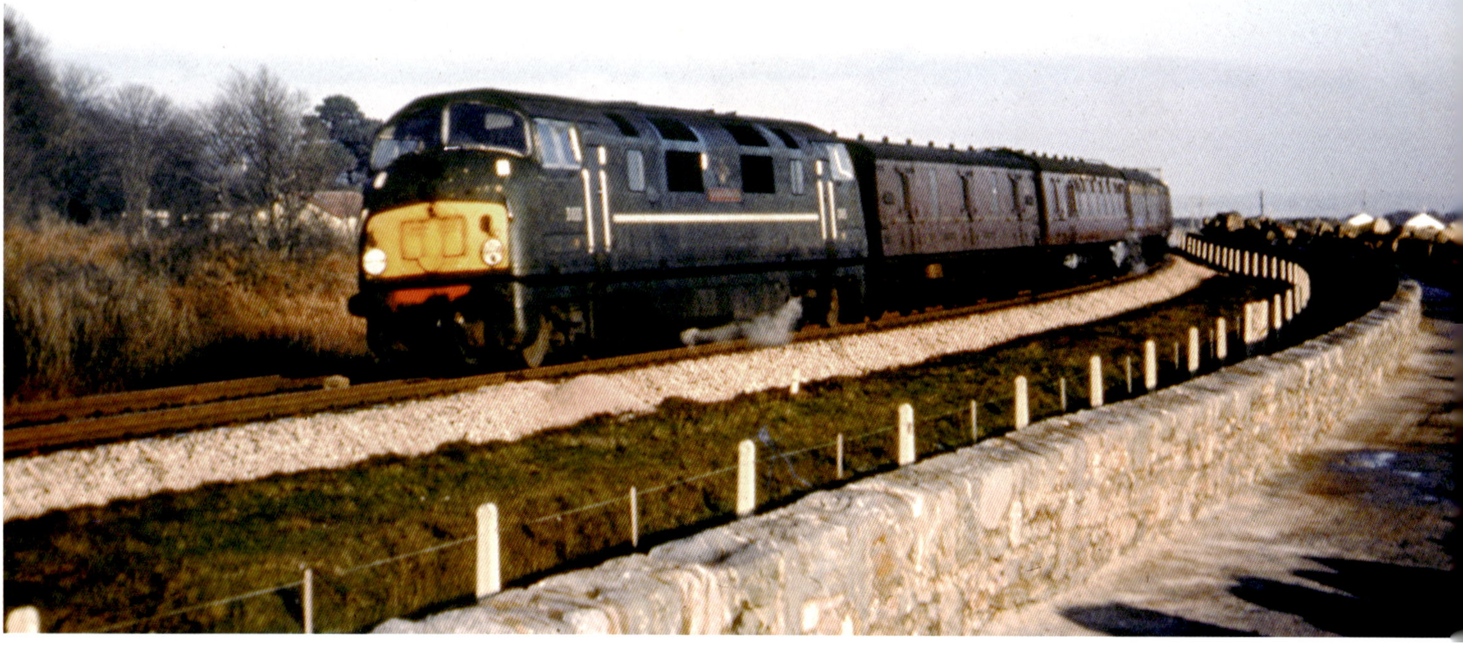

From the first thirteen Warships built with headcode discs it was only D803 Albion that managed to avoid a half yellow panel before it was modifed with four character headcode boxes by early 1965. This is D800 Sir Brian Robertson passing Dawlish Warren on 15 December 1963. ***Strathwood Library collection***

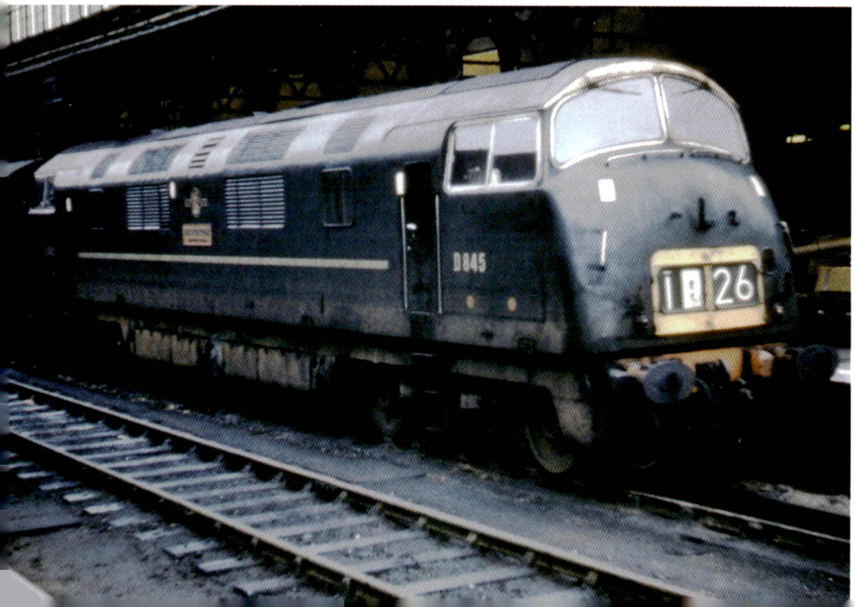

When D845 Sprightly was outshopped from repairs at Swindon in August 1961 it had yellow headcode doors and a white cab stripe affixed as here at Exeter St. Davids on 15 December 1962. The locomotive lost this variation in February 1964 when it gained the normal style of half yellow front. It should be noted that D858 Valorous also carried yellow headcode doors but not the white cab surround for a short while as well until the summer of 1963. ***Strathwood Library Collection***

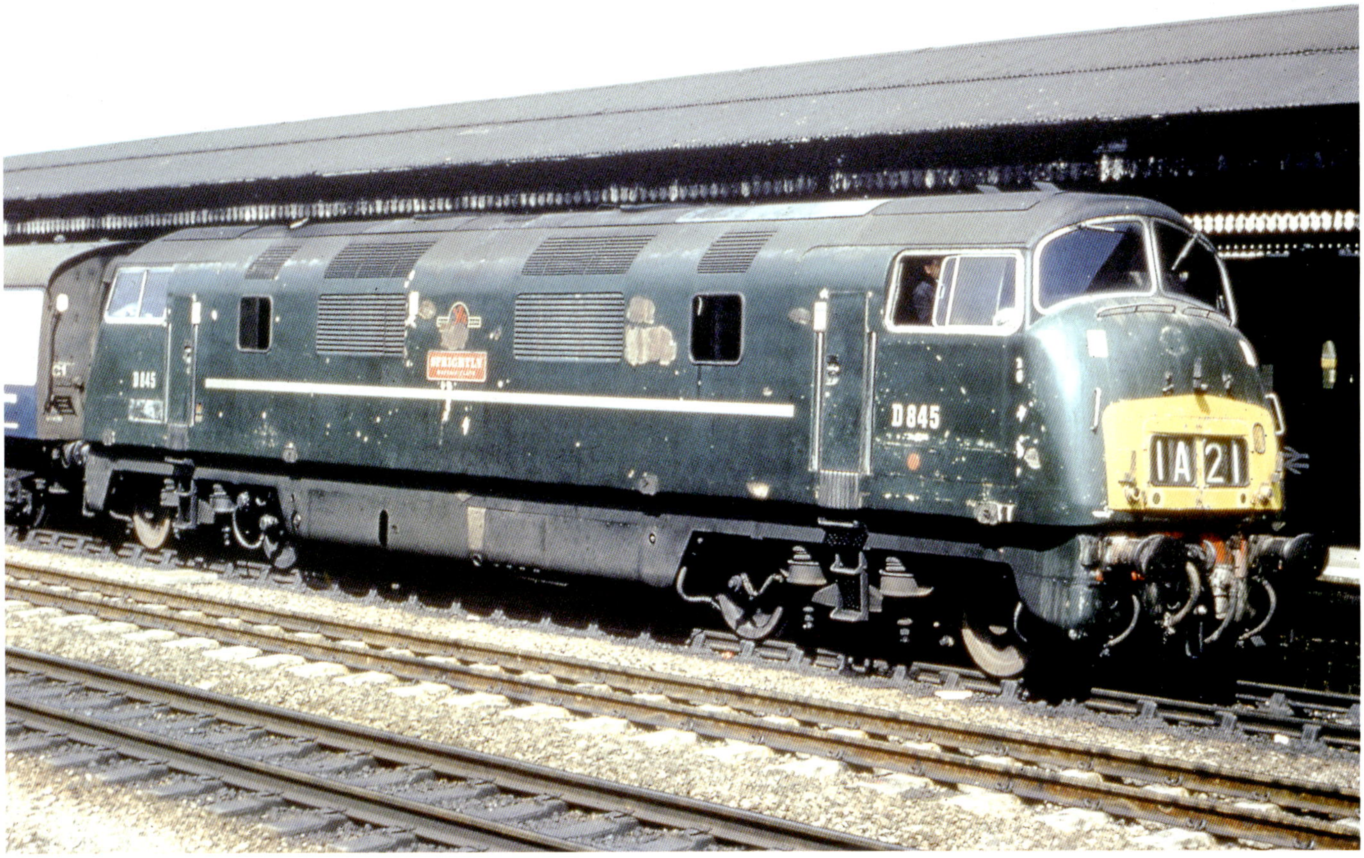

The problems with maintaining a good paint finish on the Warships can be seen on D845 Sprightly at Reading in the summer of 1968. This was no different with the maroon locomotives and many could be seen running with darker and fresher paint patches in an attempt to cover up this problem in the late 1960s. Most notable in the scruffy stakes would be D867 Zenith and with D869 Zest for patching up. ***Colour Rail***

As already mentioned D808 Centaur gained full yellow fronts whilst still in green in December 1967, whilst the only other class member to share this scheme was D810 Cockade from January 1968 until the spring of 1970, we see her here at Exeter St. Davids during 1969. ***Exe Rail***

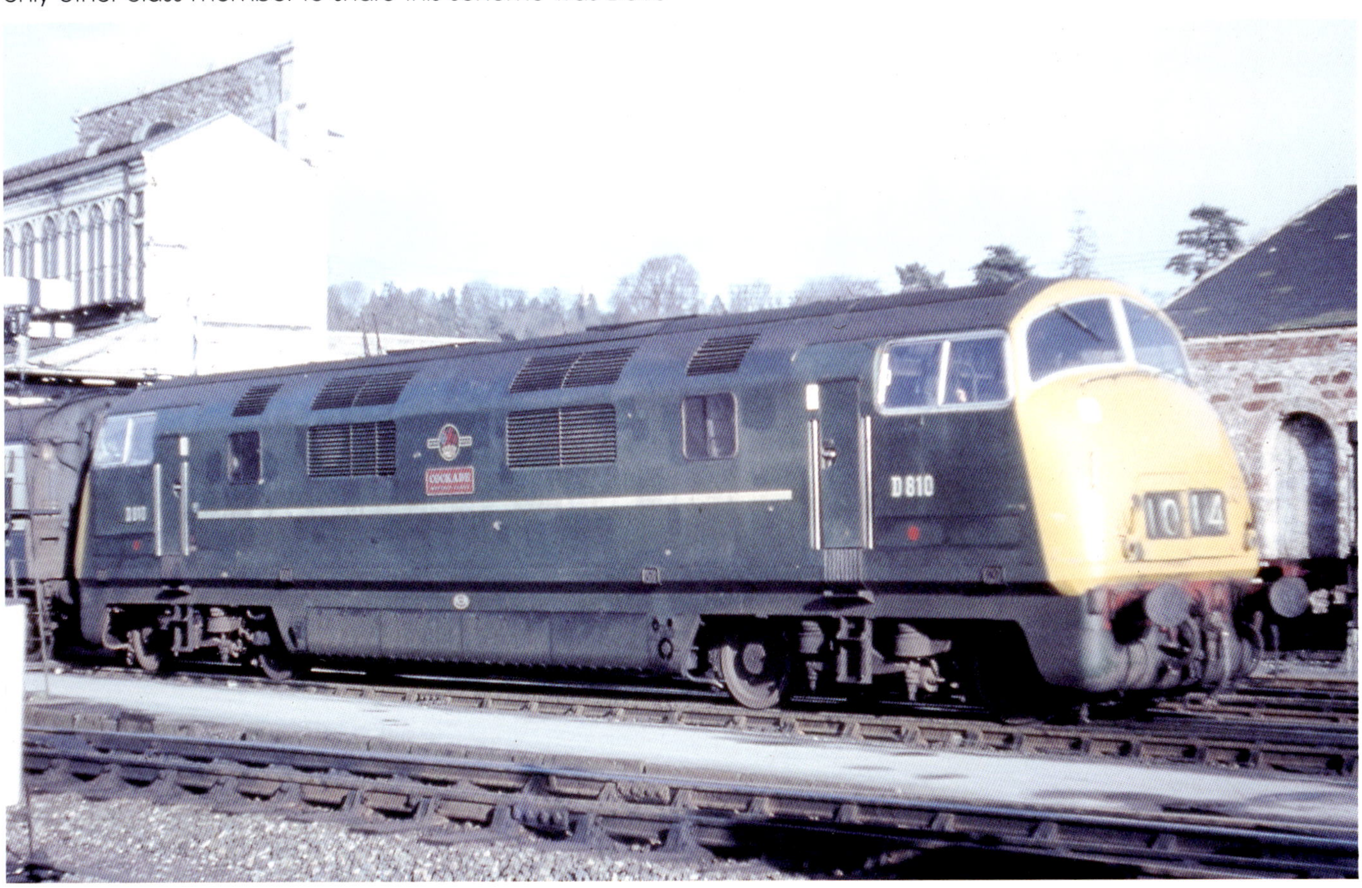

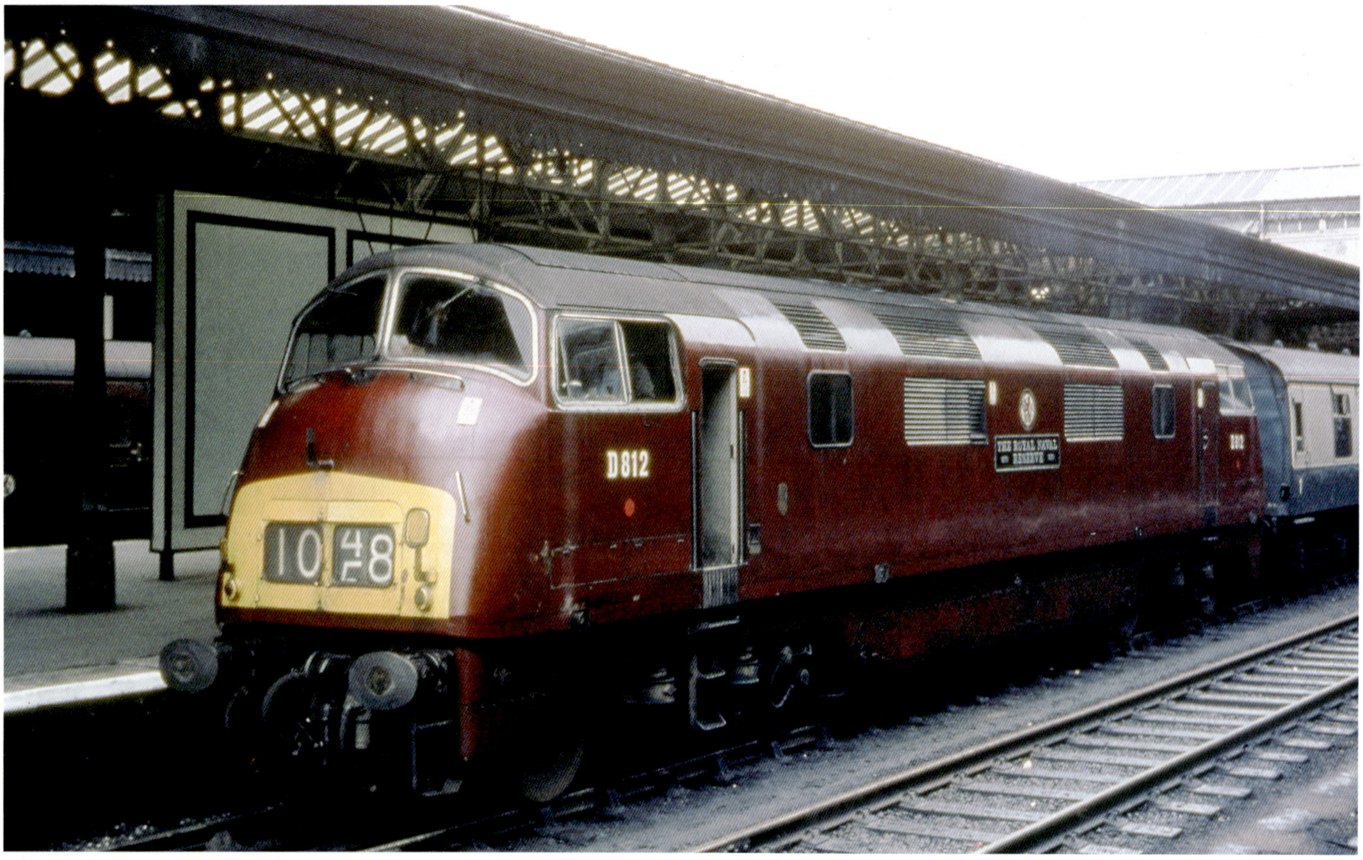

Almost half of both classes of Warships would eventually be turned out by Swindon Works from November 1965 until October 1966 in maroon with half yellow fronts including D812 The Royal Naval Reserve 1859-1959 seen here at Exeter St. Davids. ***Strathwood Library Collection***

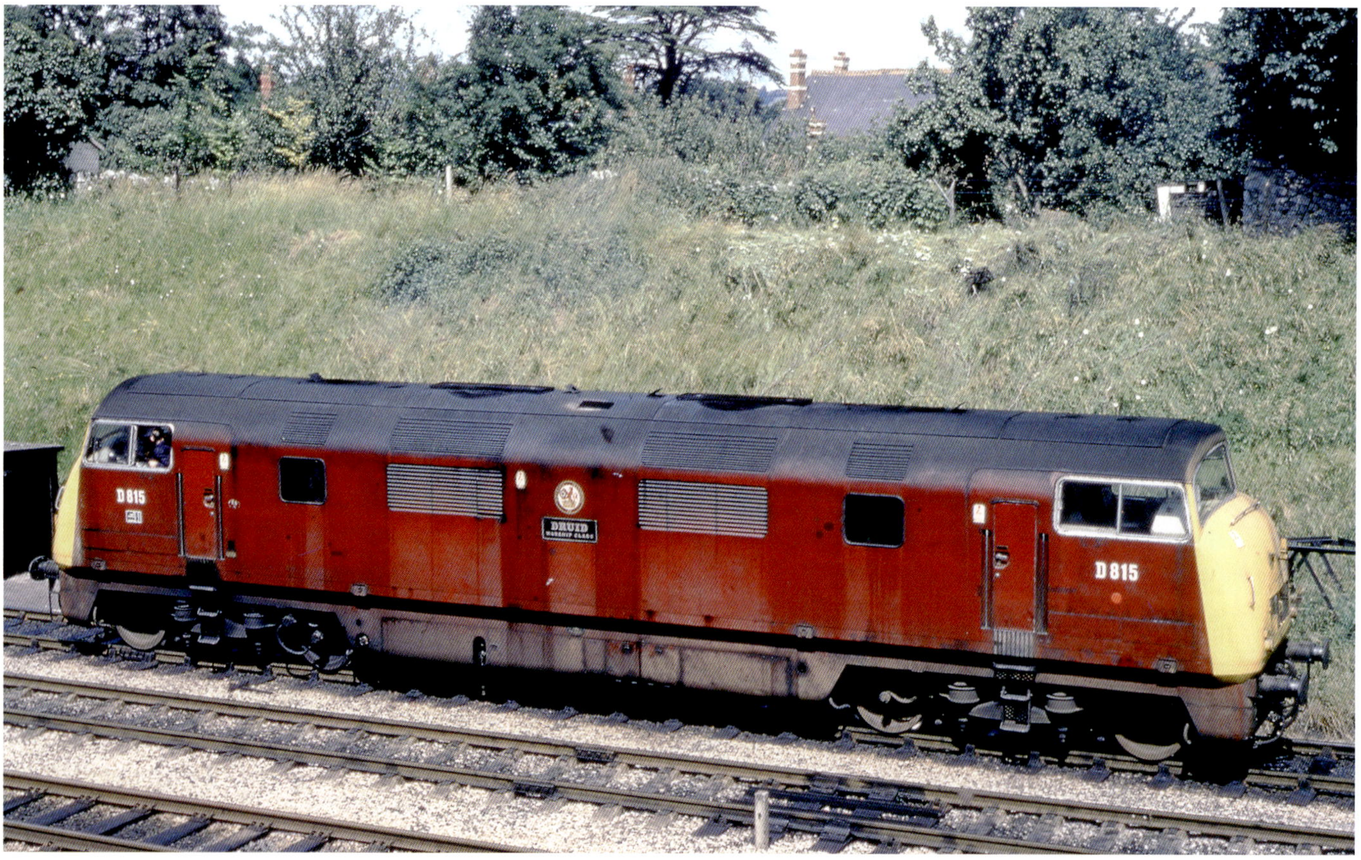

There are a number of differences within the Warships on their roof details. The Swindon built locomotives with Maybach engines required pre-heating and had this small rectangular exhaust port on the drivers side as seen here on D815 Druid at Newton Abbot on 8 July 1969. These Maybach locomotives had their main engine exhaust in the centre of the roof, whilst D830 with it's Paxman engine and the North British built MAN engined Warships could be started from cold and the main exhaust was on the drivers side of the roof, they also carried a pronounced guard around the ventilation fans as well. ***Strathwood Library Collection***

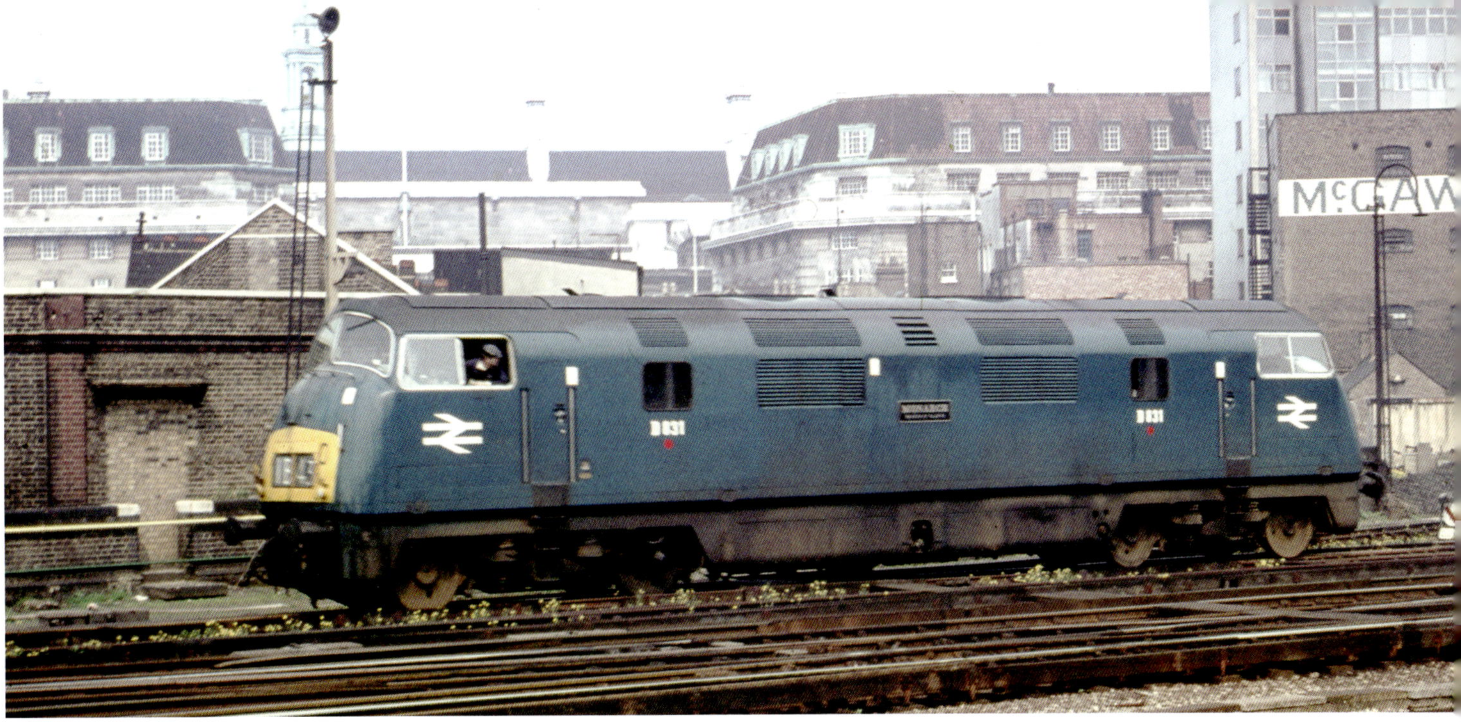

As the last of the maroon Warships left the works at Swindon the painters began interpreting the new orders to finish locomotives into blue. This led to D831 Monarch being turned out like this in November 1966 with two large arrows each side and numbers amidships as seen at Waterloo on 3 June 1967. ***Strathwood Library collection***

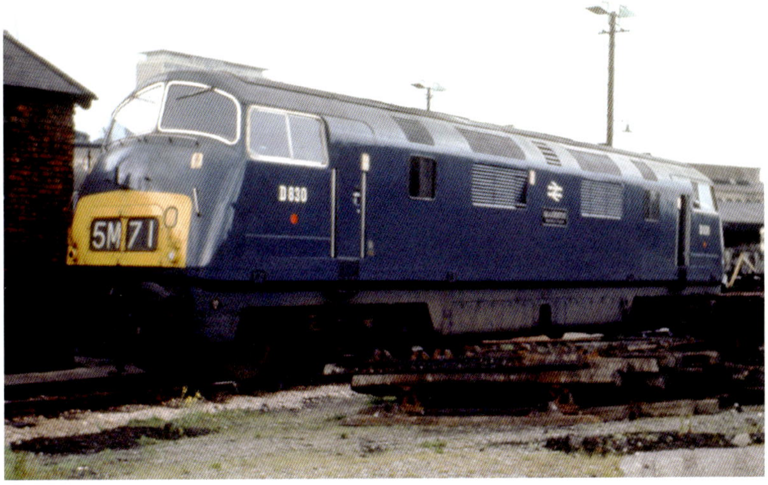

Next out was the Paxman engined D830 also with half yellow fronts but one smaller set of arrows above the nameplates and numbers as they were on the maroon scheme seen here at Exeter in May 1967. ***Grahame Wareham***

Swindon also tried on D864 Zambesi seen recently ex-works in May 1967 two larger arrows under the Serif style of numbering, in addition to the full yellow front a maroon/brown umber skirt was applied. This unique variation was retained right through to scrapping as seen on page 95. ***Grahame Wareham***

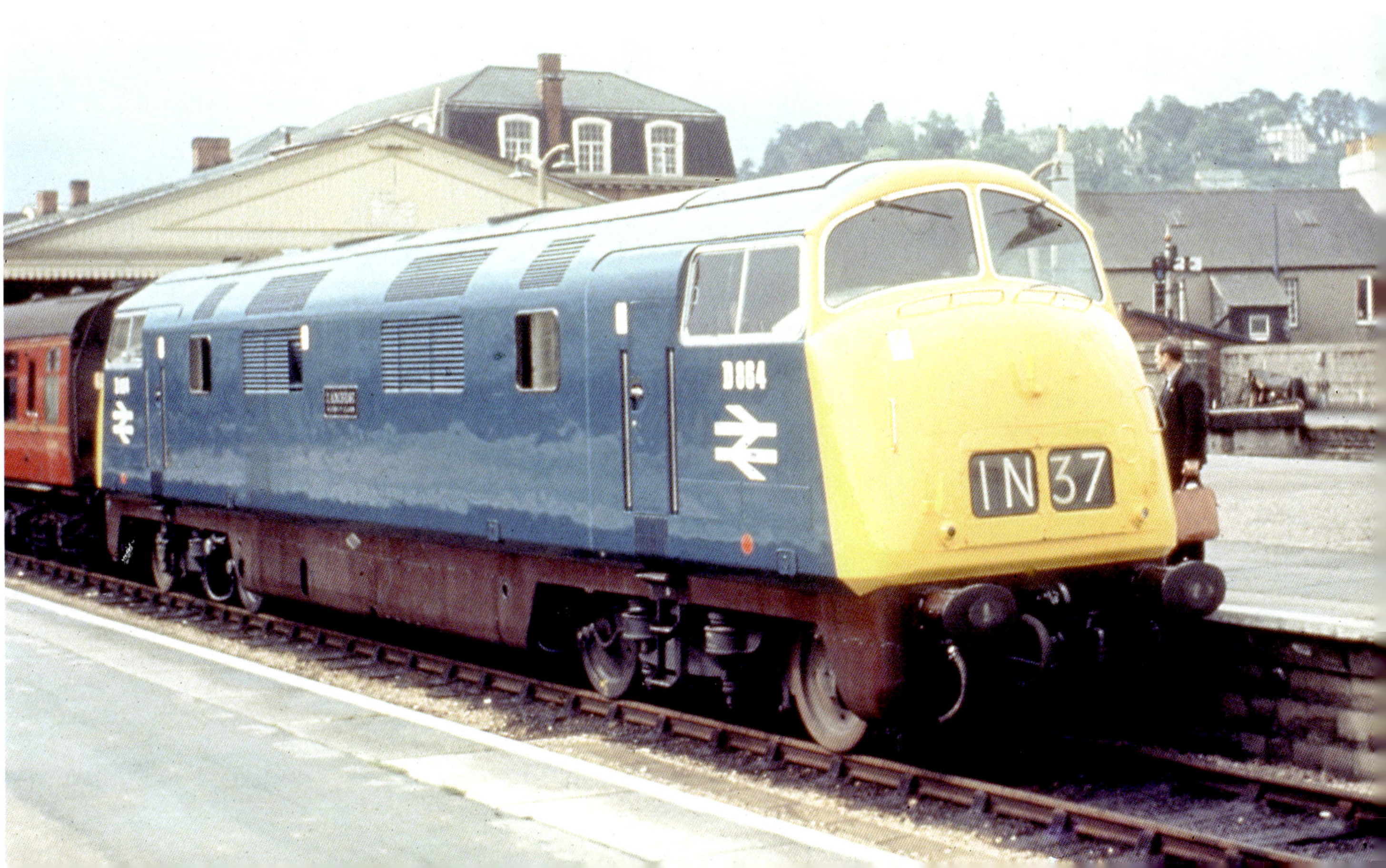

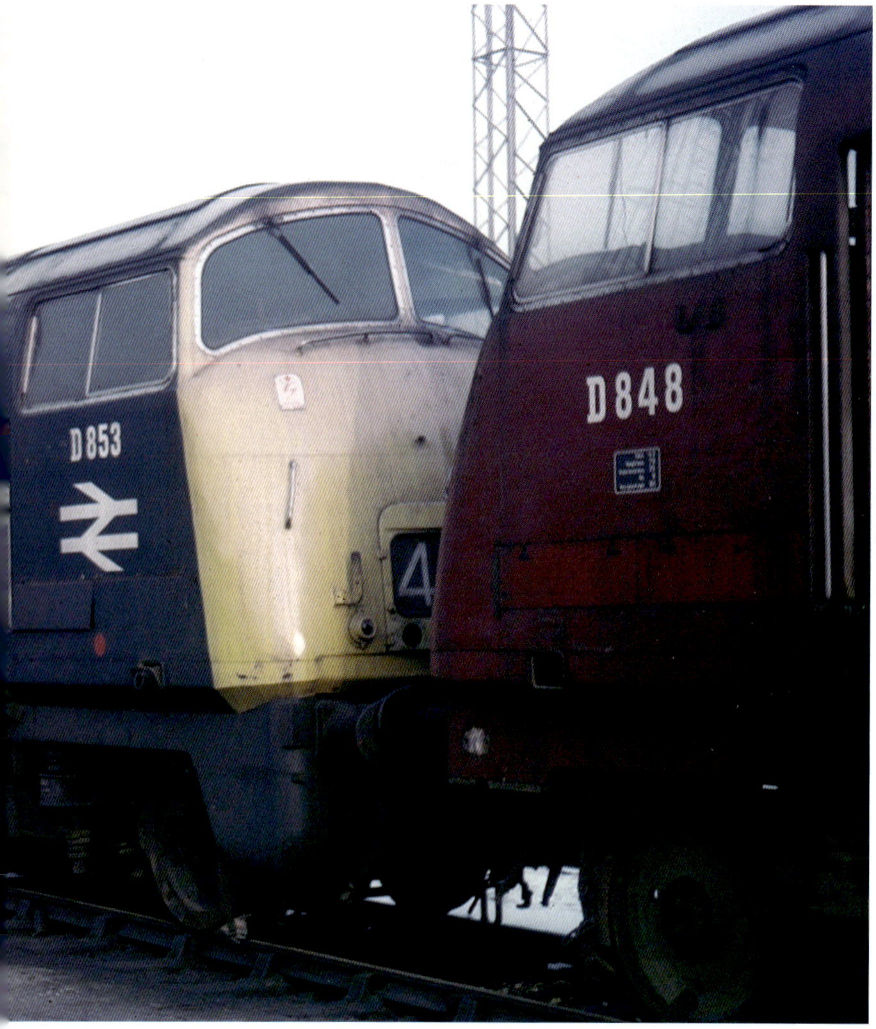

This issue of the style of numbering and the exact positioning varies tremendously, here we have the stored D853 Thruster which went into blue livery in October 1967 here buffered up to the withdrawn D848 Sultan in late 1969 at Old Oak Common, the latter has also gained a data description sticker with a blue background. ***Strathwood Library Collection***

Coupled to D850 is D835 Pegasus wearing the later Gill Sans style of numbering complete with D prefix above two larger arrows affixed to each cab again at Old Oak Common this time in June 1968. Both examples have the red spot route indicator placed low down below those troublesome access hatches. ***Derek Everson***

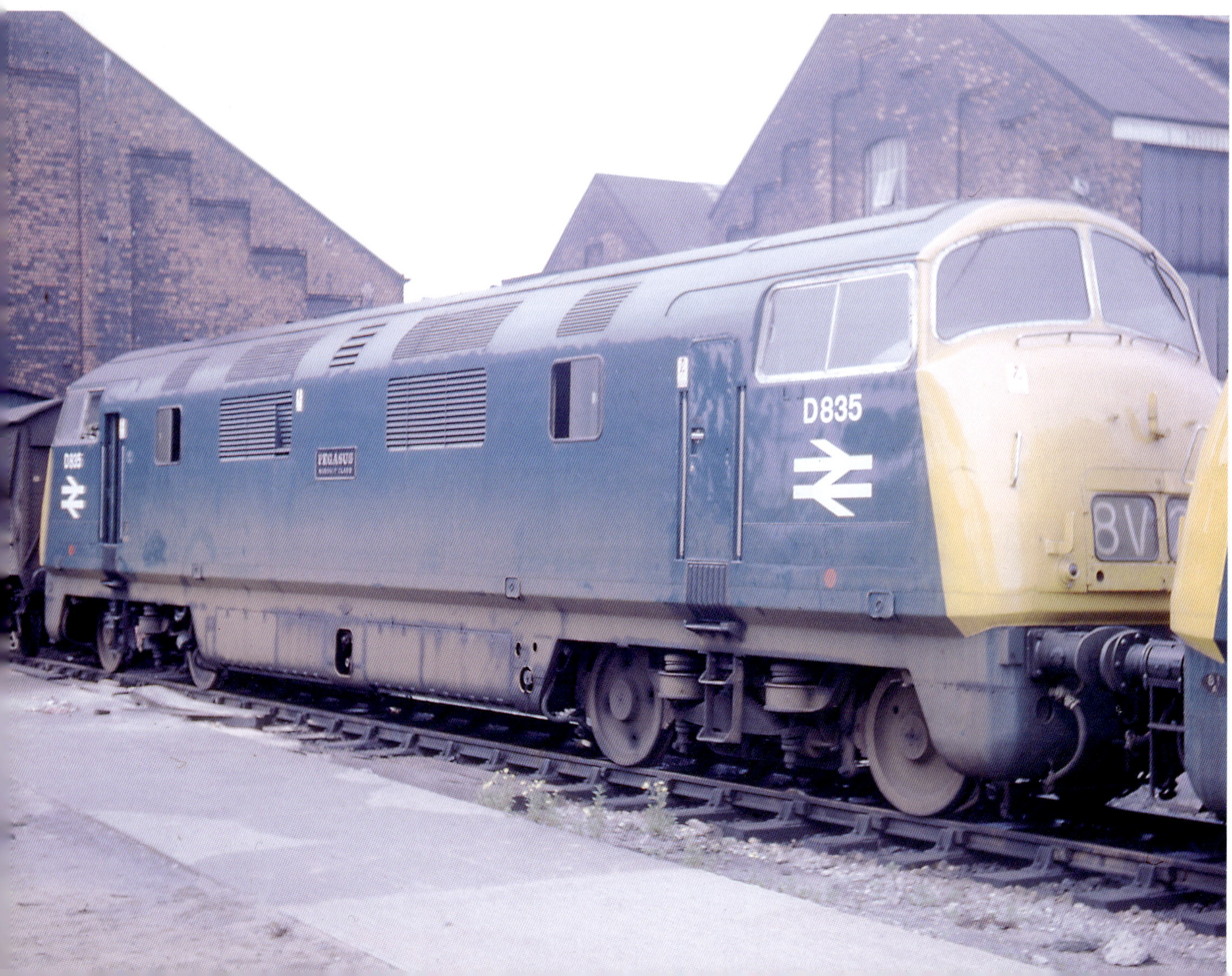

Another variation this time on D847 Strongbow at Old Oak Common in June 1968 shows the locomotive with Serif style D numbers affixed slightly lower down and a single small arrow above the nameplate. ***Derek Everson***

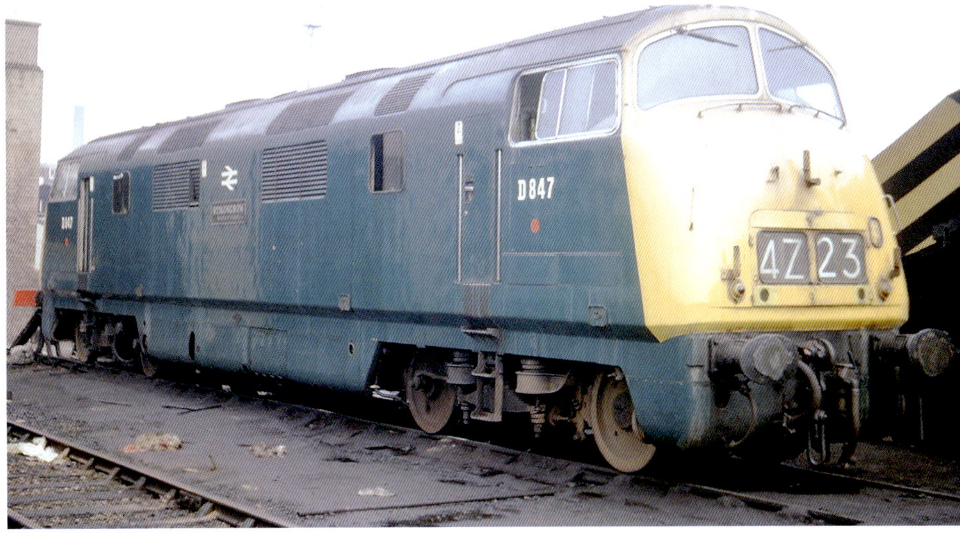

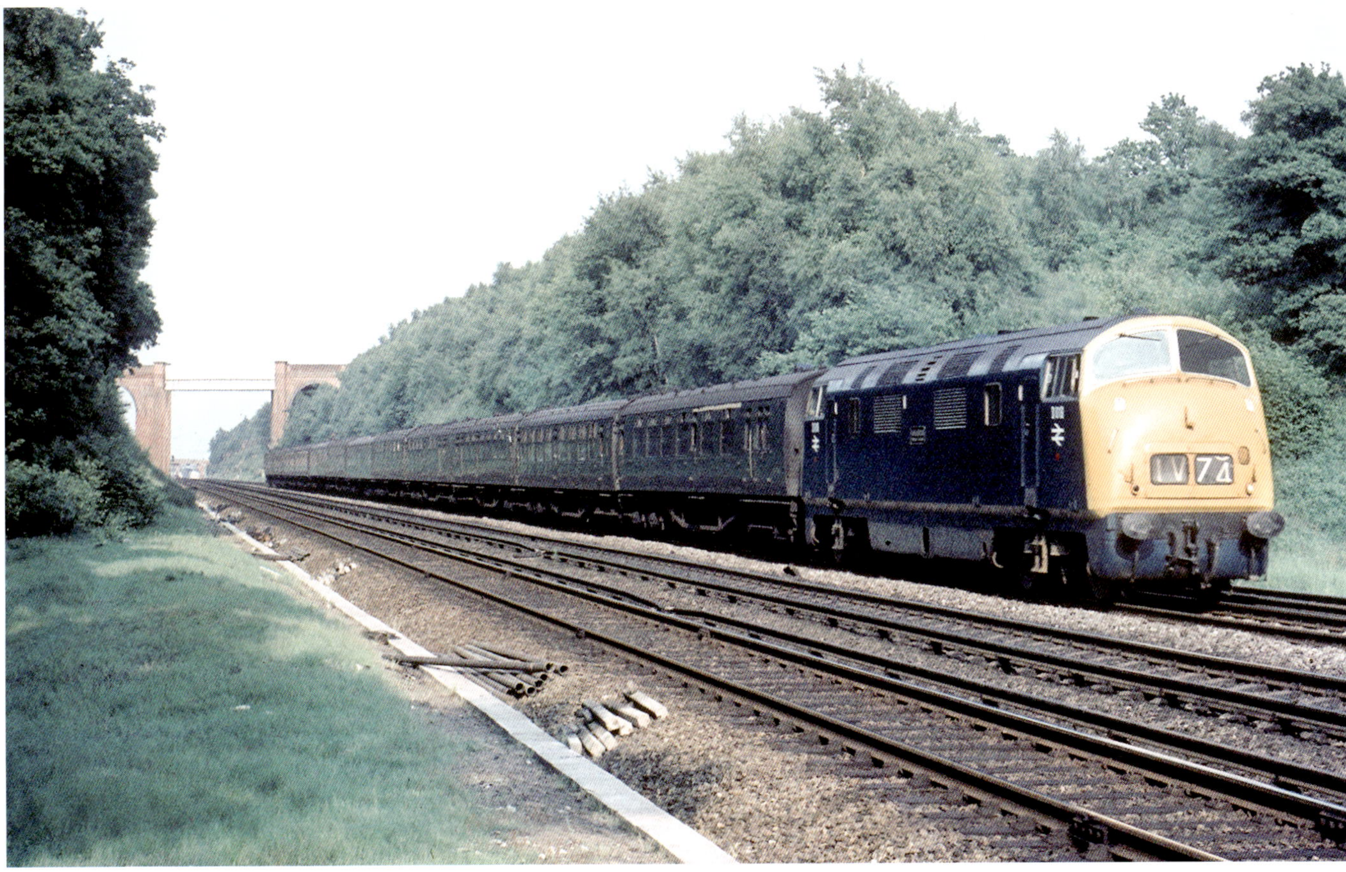

Whilst D816 Eclipse also has Serif style D numbers closer to the cabside windows and with a set of small arrows and a red route dot below each one, as it passes Fleet in October 1967. ***Paul Cooper***

It is Gill Sans numbers only and a single large arrow below the nameplate for 831 Monarch now in August 1969 after a repaint earlier in March of that year. ***Strathwood Library Collection***

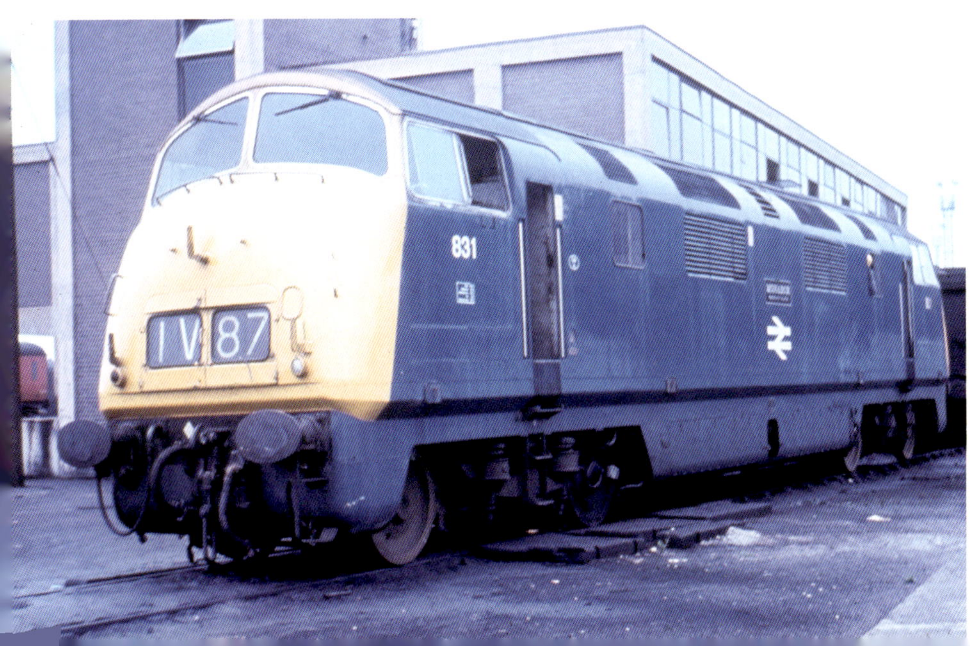

Warship Signals

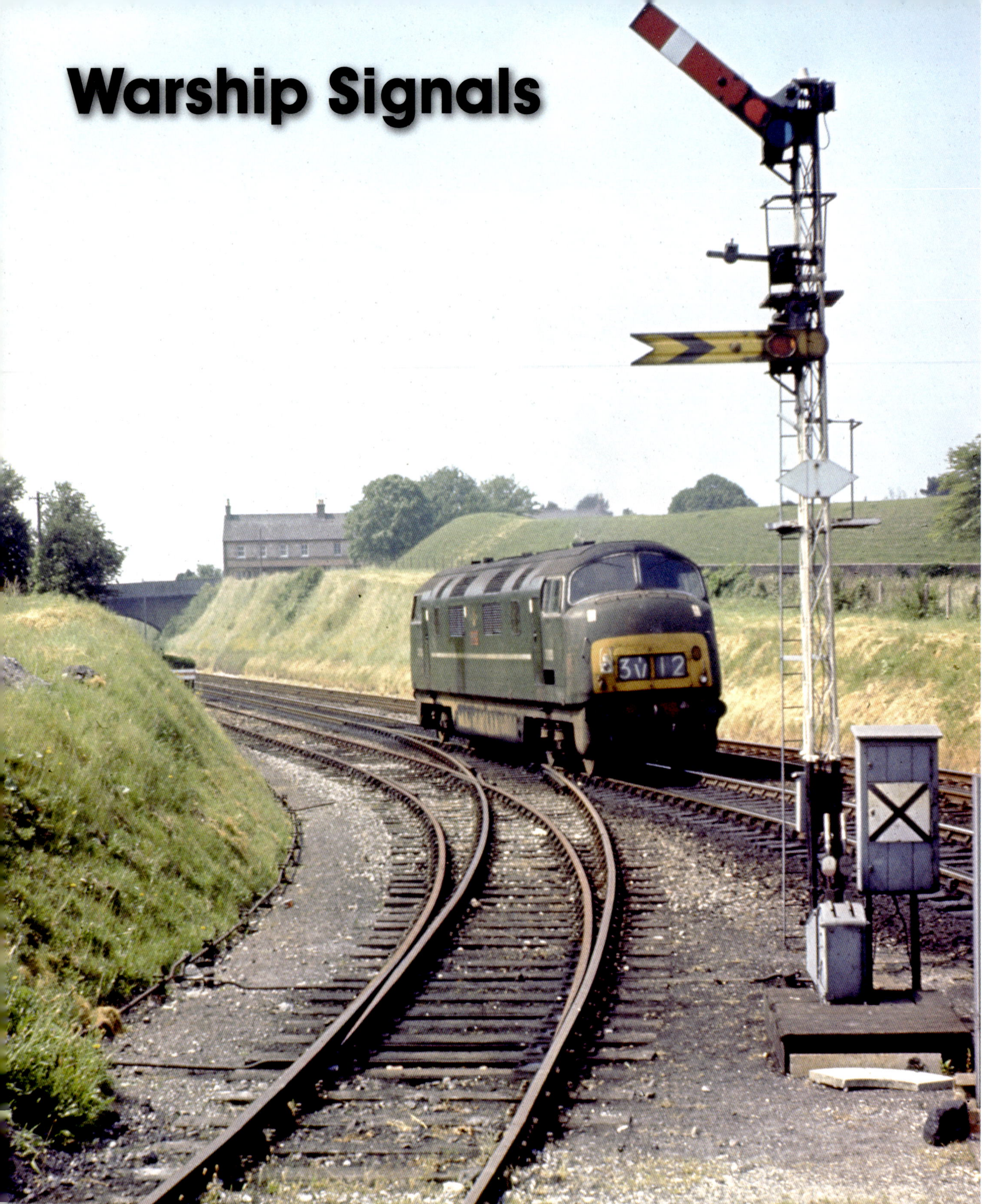

A little light engine movement for D803 Albion alongside an ex London & South Western Railway semaphore at Barnstaple in June 1966. This Laira based locomotive has lost one of the side access flaps below the leading cab for the time being. ***Bernard Mills***

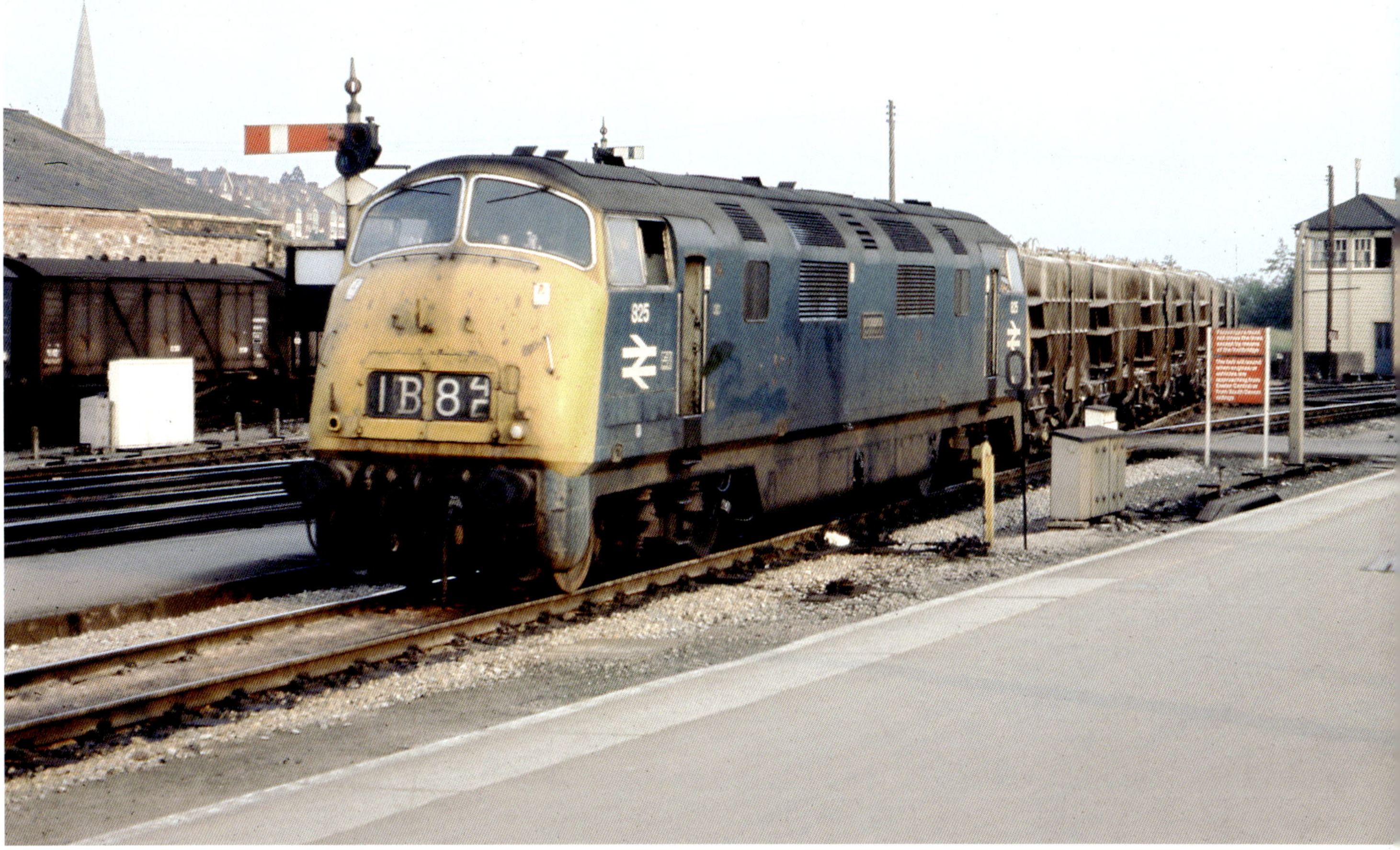

Doing its best with a fitted rake of empty pressflos in order to hold back their decent from Exeter Central into Exeter St. Davids in June 1971 was 825 Intrepid, this working would be bound for Westbury and the Associated Portland Cement works which was shunted by fellow hydraulic D9526 in industrial service there at the time. ***Bernard Mills***

On 22 October 1967 D857 Undaunted was to be found on permanent way duties at Tavistock North, the sights of these North British Class 43 Warships on the former London & South Western Railway's metals was more commonplace the further west one went. ***Bernard Mills***

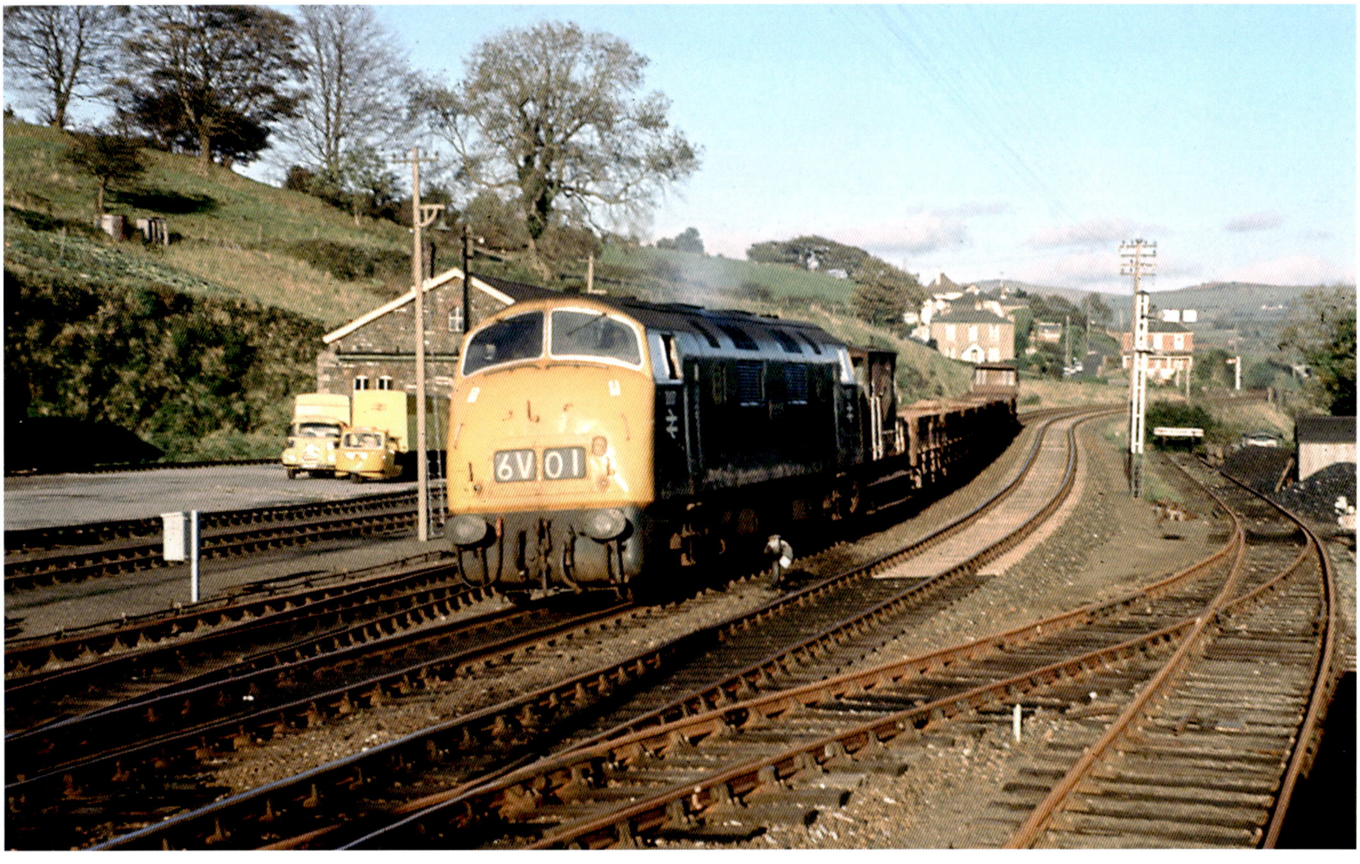

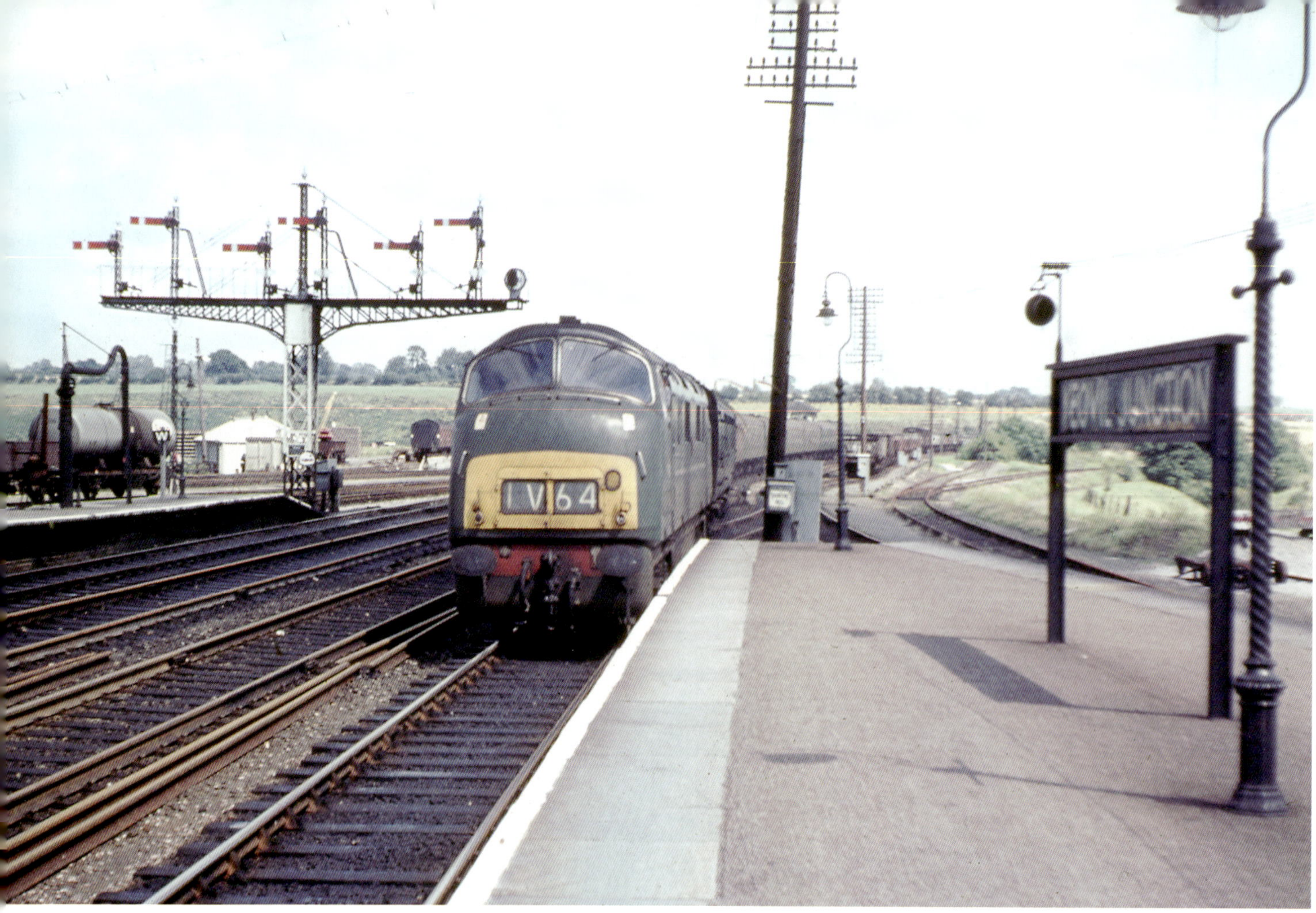

It is the imprssive latice post gantry in the background that catches our eyes, along with the overhead telegraph wiring and posts, barley twist lampost, water column and the long Yeovil Junction nameboard that greet D808 Centaur's arrival at this once busy location in June 1966. ***Bernard Mills***

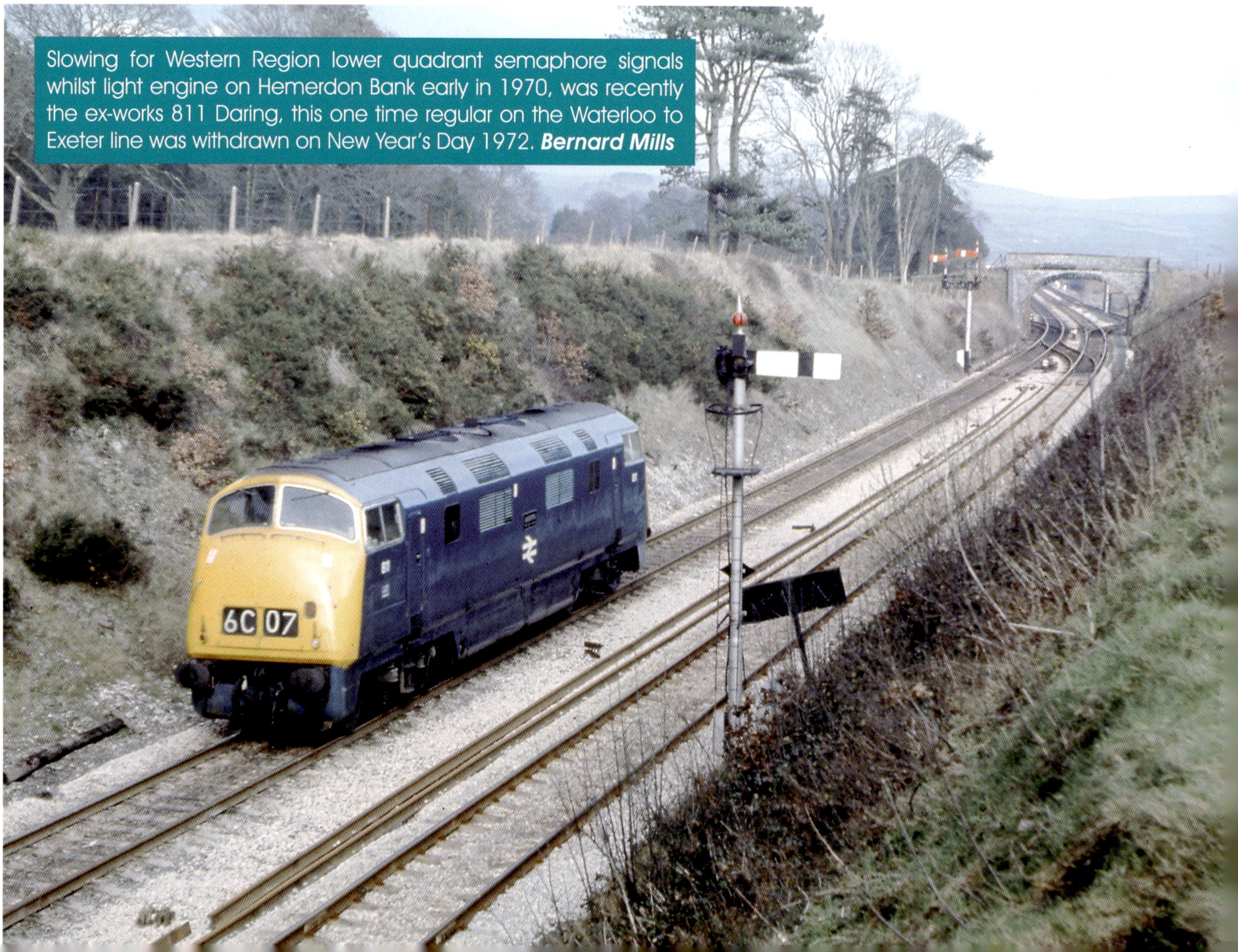

Slowing for Western Region lower quadrant semaphore signals whilst light engine on Hemerdon Bank early in 1970, was recently the ex-works 811 Daring, this one time regular on the Waterloo to Exeter line was withdrawn on New Year's Day 1972. ***Bernard Mills***

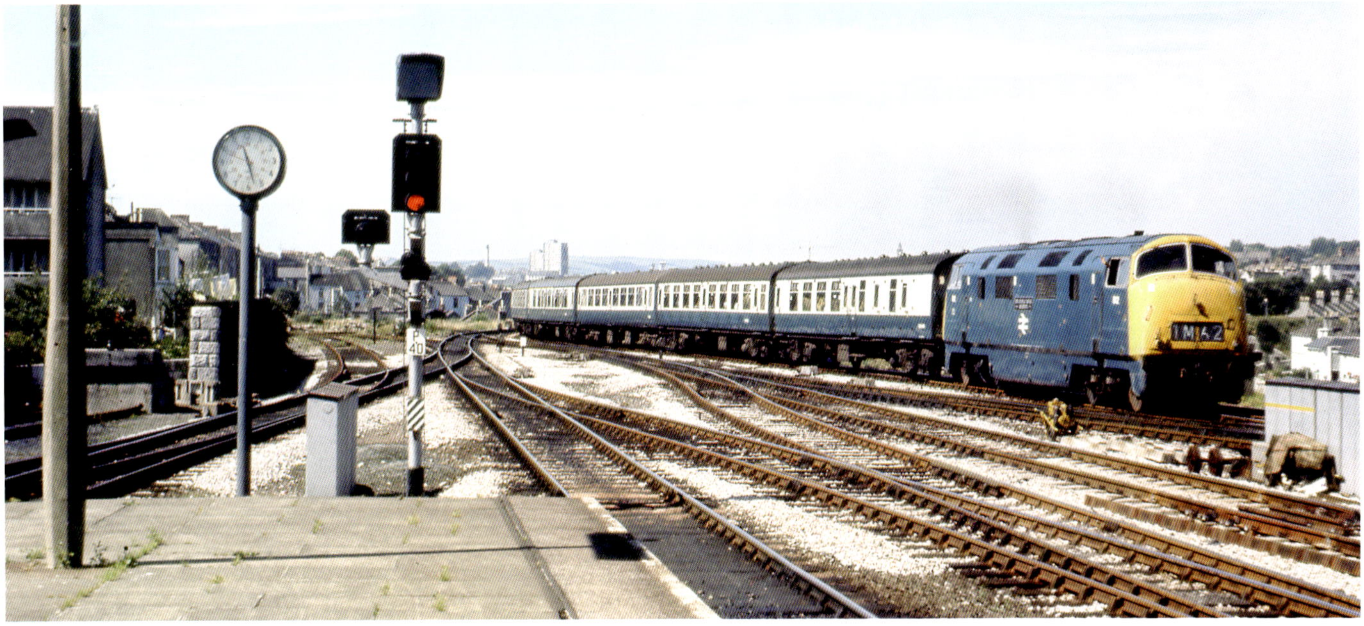

The large nameplates of 812 The Royal Naval Reserve 1859-1959 betray this Warship's identity before it arrives at Plymouth North Road station on 12 August 1972. ***Bernard Mills***

Waiting at Barnstaple Town in May 1966 in charge of the 11.05 Paddington to Ilfracombe today is D803 Albion. The line through to Ilfracombe and stations like Barnstaple Town would close completely in 1970. ***Bernard Mills***

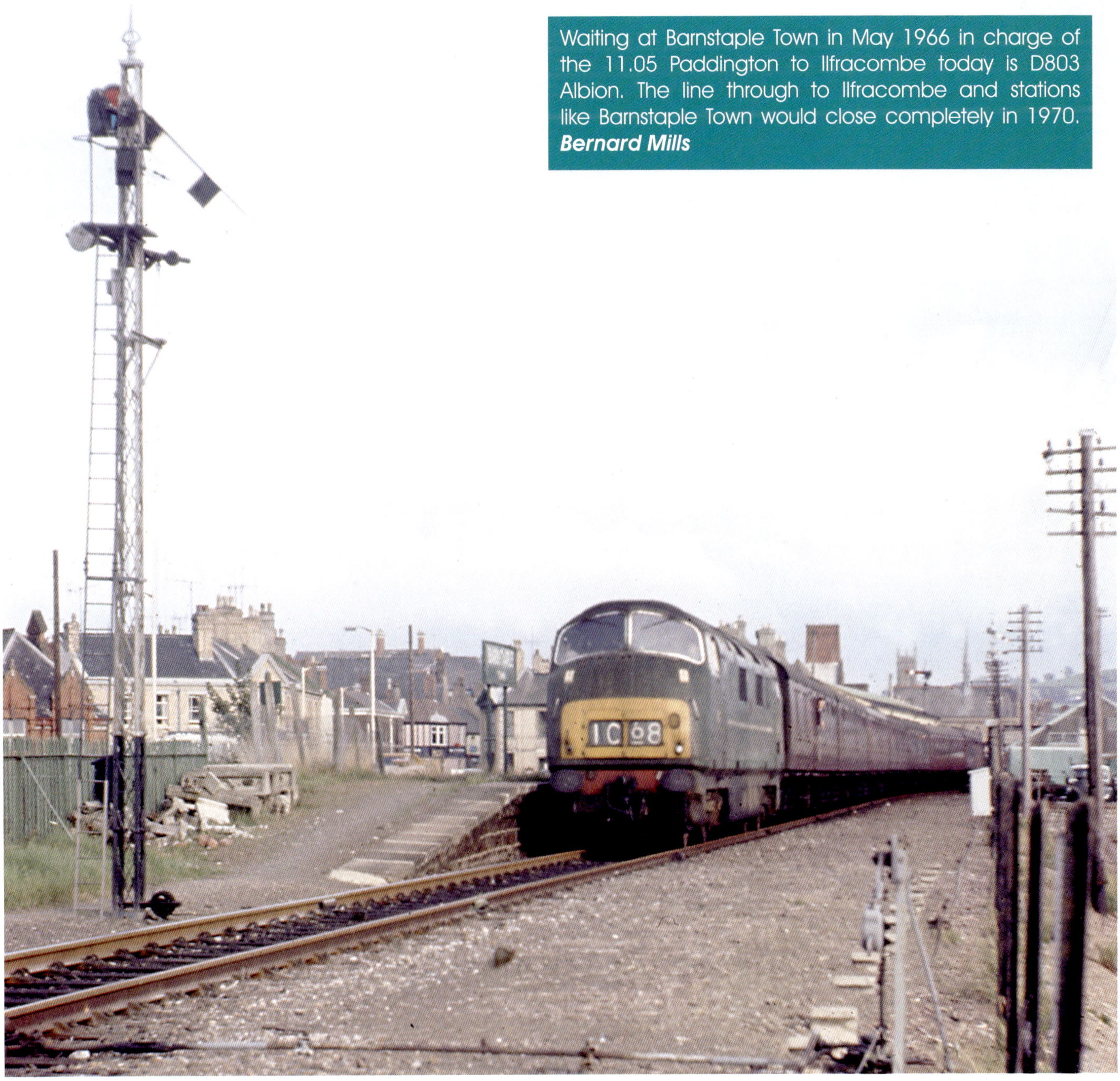

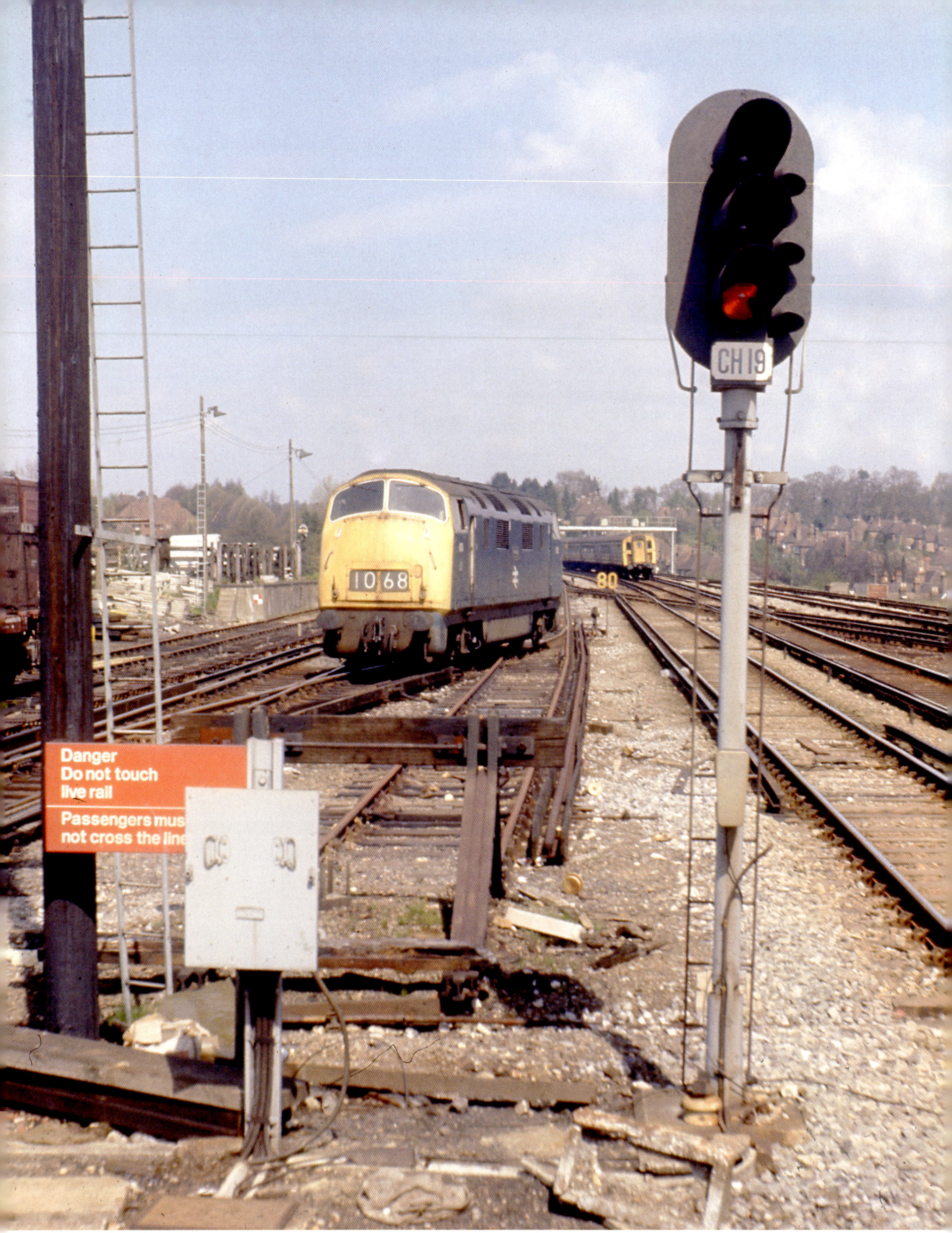

An unusual visitor to Chichester on 16 April 1972 was 810 Cockade which was running round having arrived as part of a trip around the Southern Region arranged by the Plymouth Railway Circle and the Great Western Society as their Bluebell Railtour. The day's duties were shared with 821 Greyhound which handled the legs back and forth from Plymouth to Salisbury. ***Bernard Mills***

By the Water

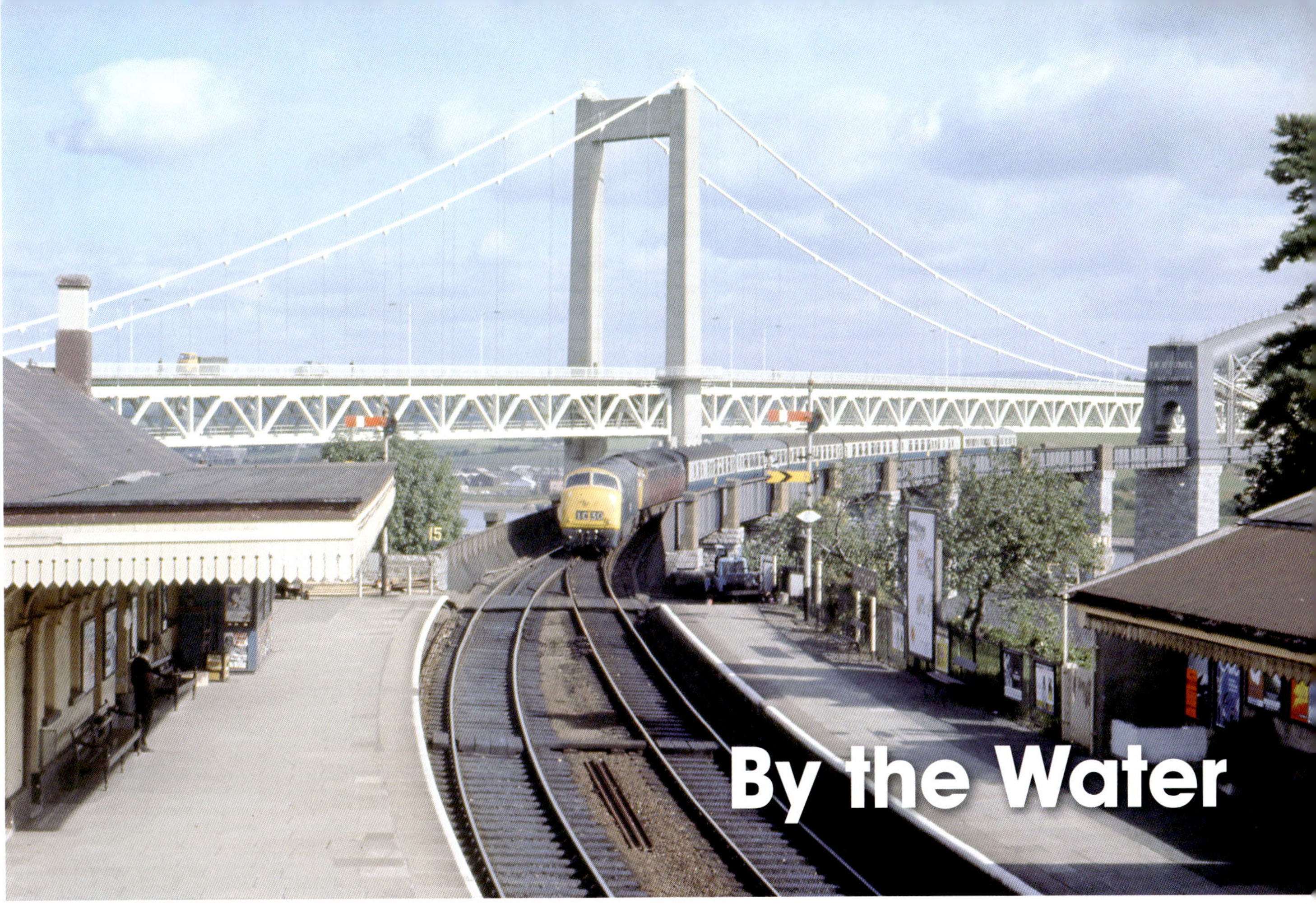

This unknown Warship pairing brings a very lightly loaded 08.30 Paddington to Penzance into Saltash station over the River Tamar in the spring of 1968 ***Bernard Mills***

Its an even lighter loading for D870 Zulu with a local stopping service at Dawlish a few weeks on into the summer months during the same year. ***Bernard Mills***

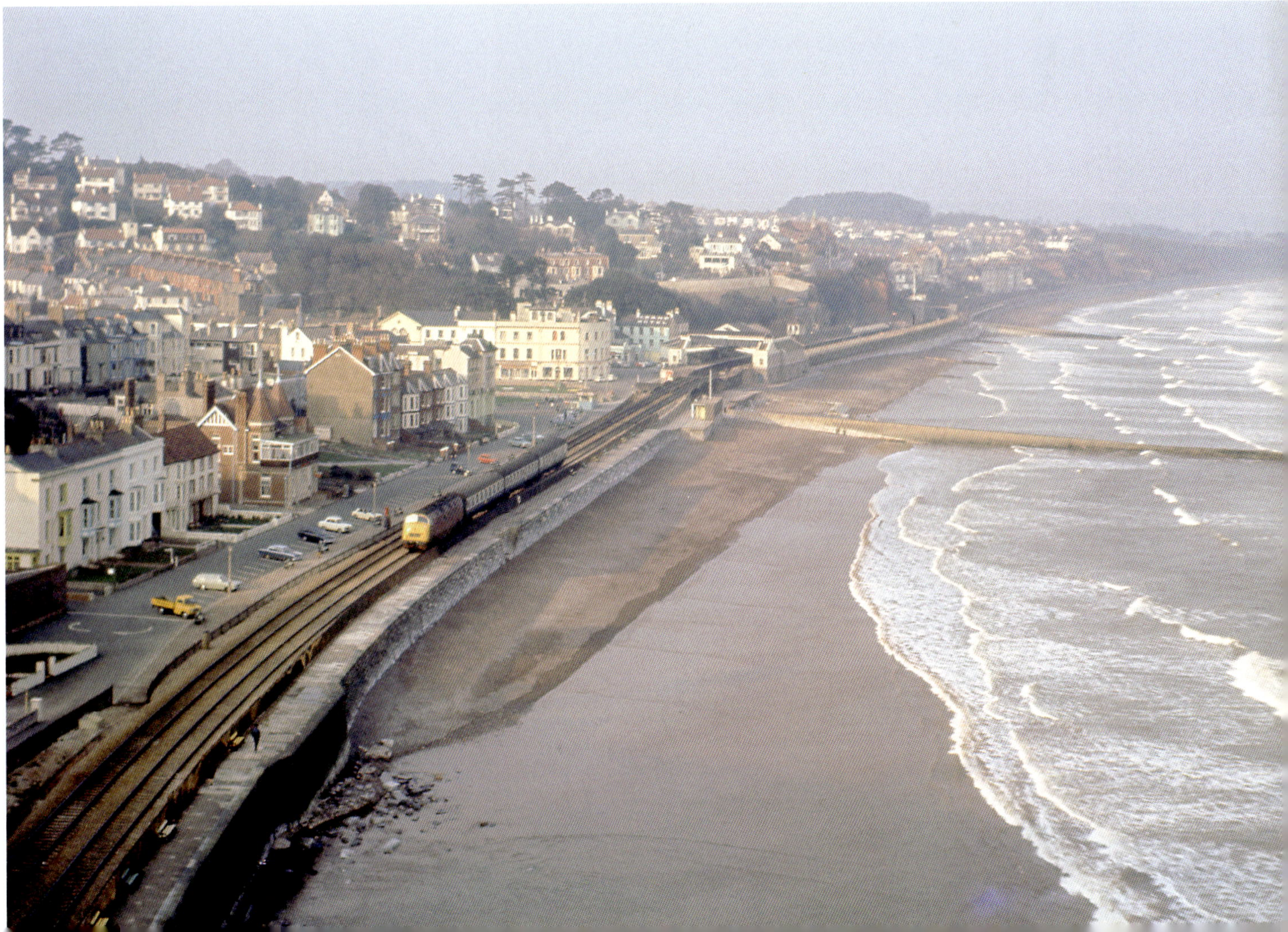

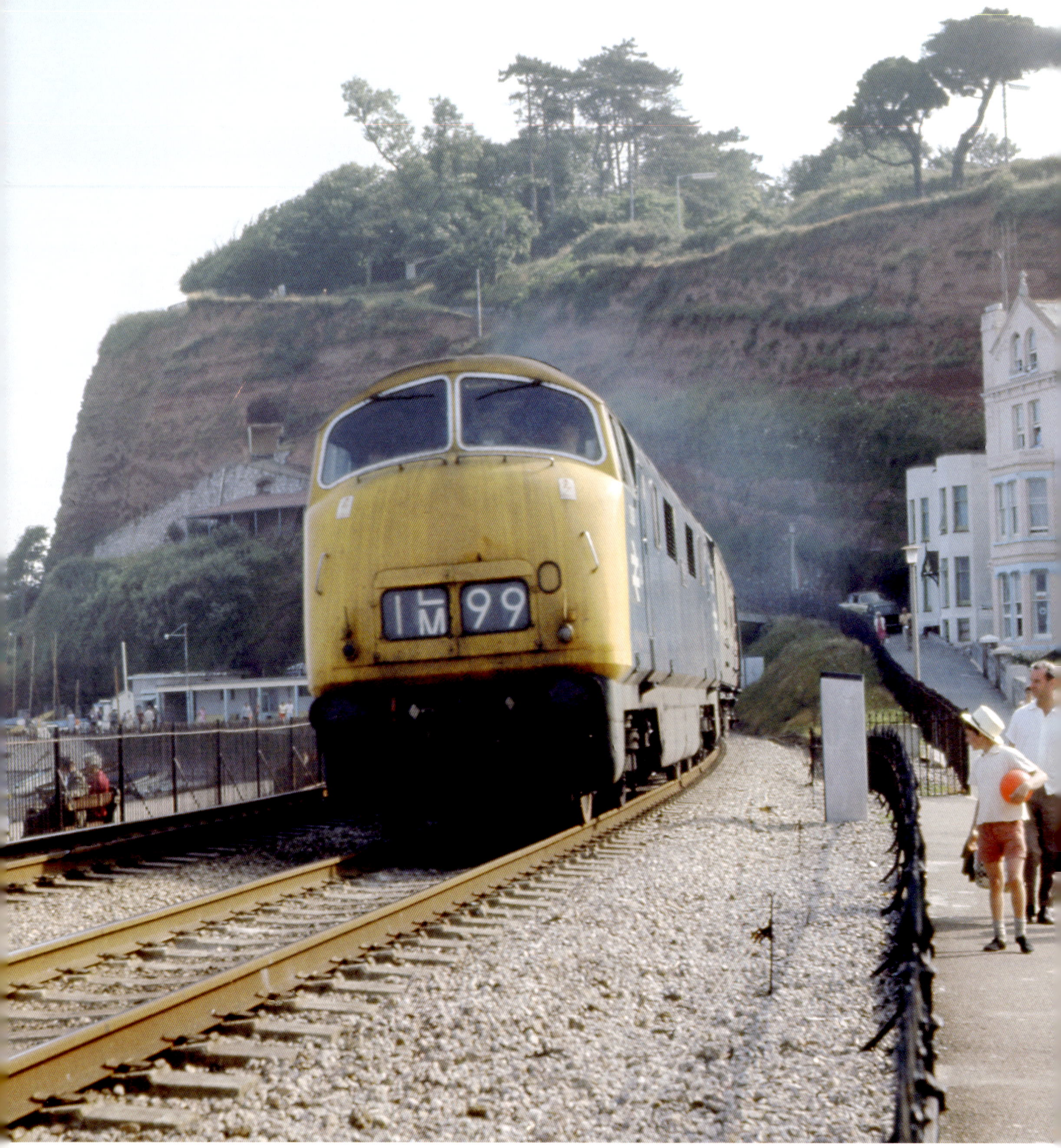

When the headcode discs were changed to four character headcode boxes on the first thirteen Warships all except D801 and D804 lost their headboard clips, whilst all but D801/4/6/9/12 lost their upper lamp backets as well, as shown here on D808 Centaur running into Dawlish on 23 July 1969, this gave a much cleaner appearance to the nose end of these Warships. ***Bernard Mills***

Page opposite: D855 Triumph casts an almost perfect reflection as it runs light near Laira in June 1967. ***Bernard Mills***

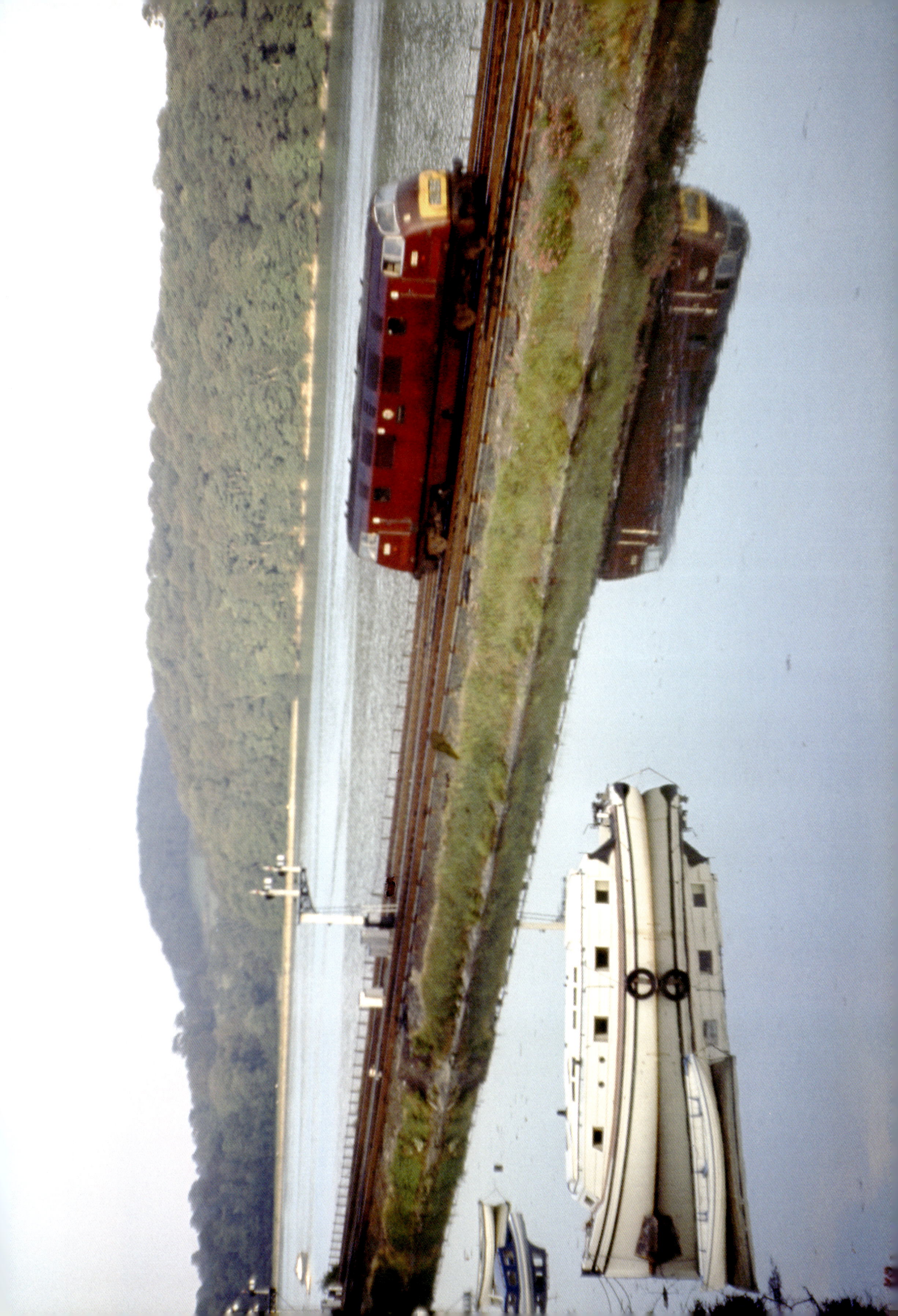

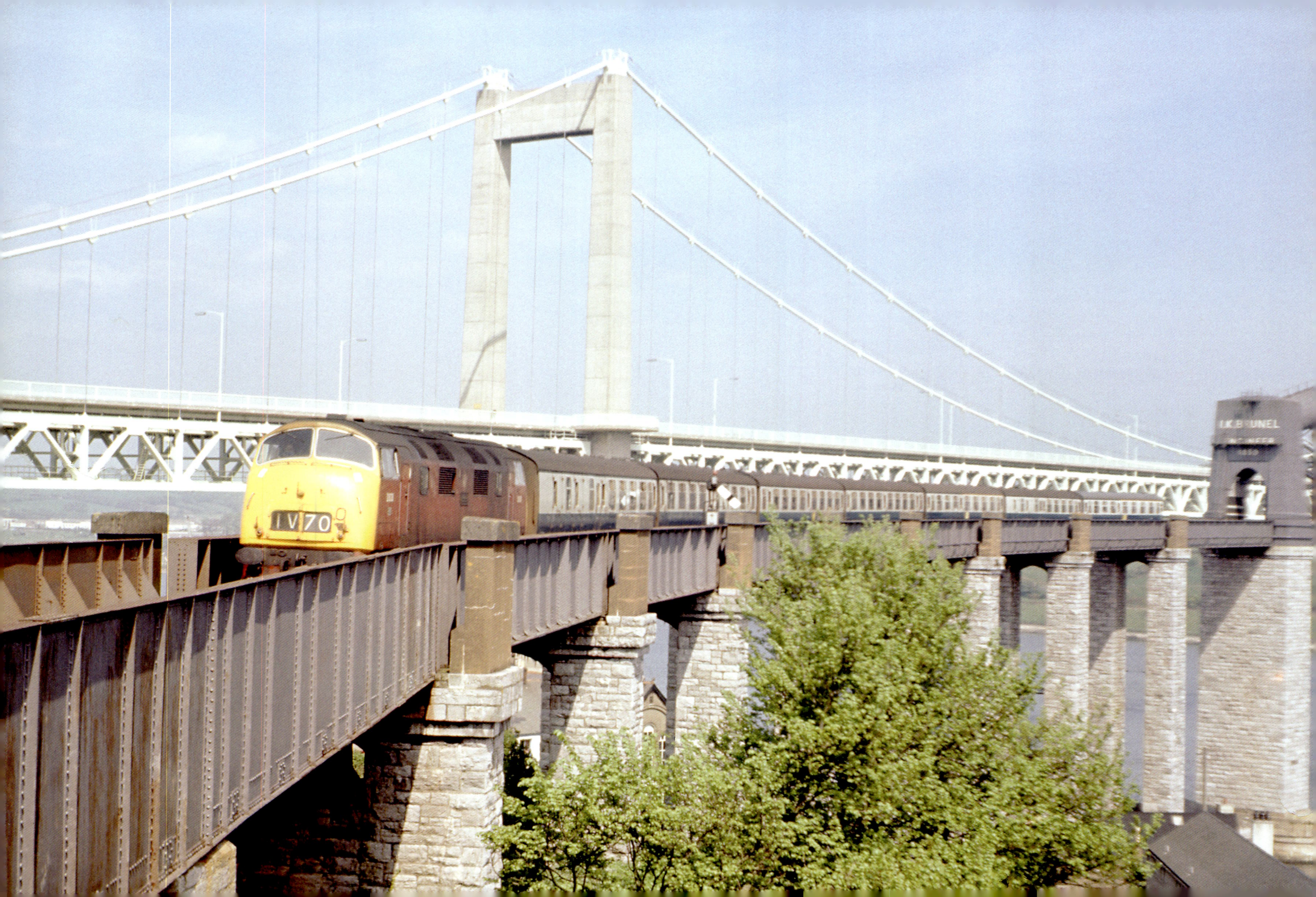

1V70
I.K.BRUNEL

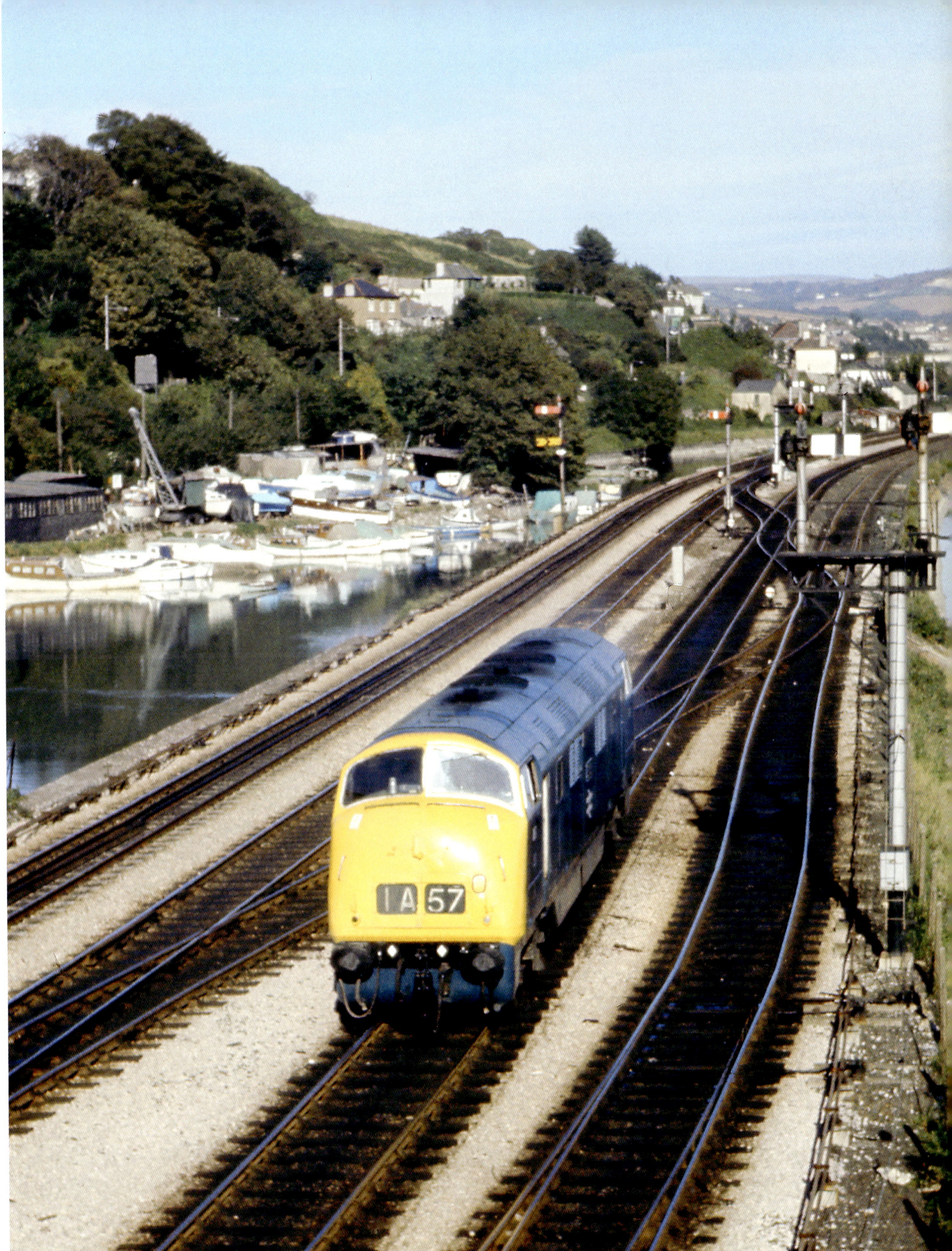

Page left: Observing the speed restriction on Brunel's wonderful bridge and into the platforms at Saltash in 1969 our enthusiastic cameraman caught D838 Rapid with seven Mark I coaches in tow. ***Bernard Mills***

Two large distinctive white diamond coupling codes stand out on an ex-works 867 Zenith running briskly as a light engine near Laira in September 1970. Up until this point D867 Zenith had been one of the scruffiest Warships in the fleet in its final days as a maroon locomotive. ***Bernard Mills***

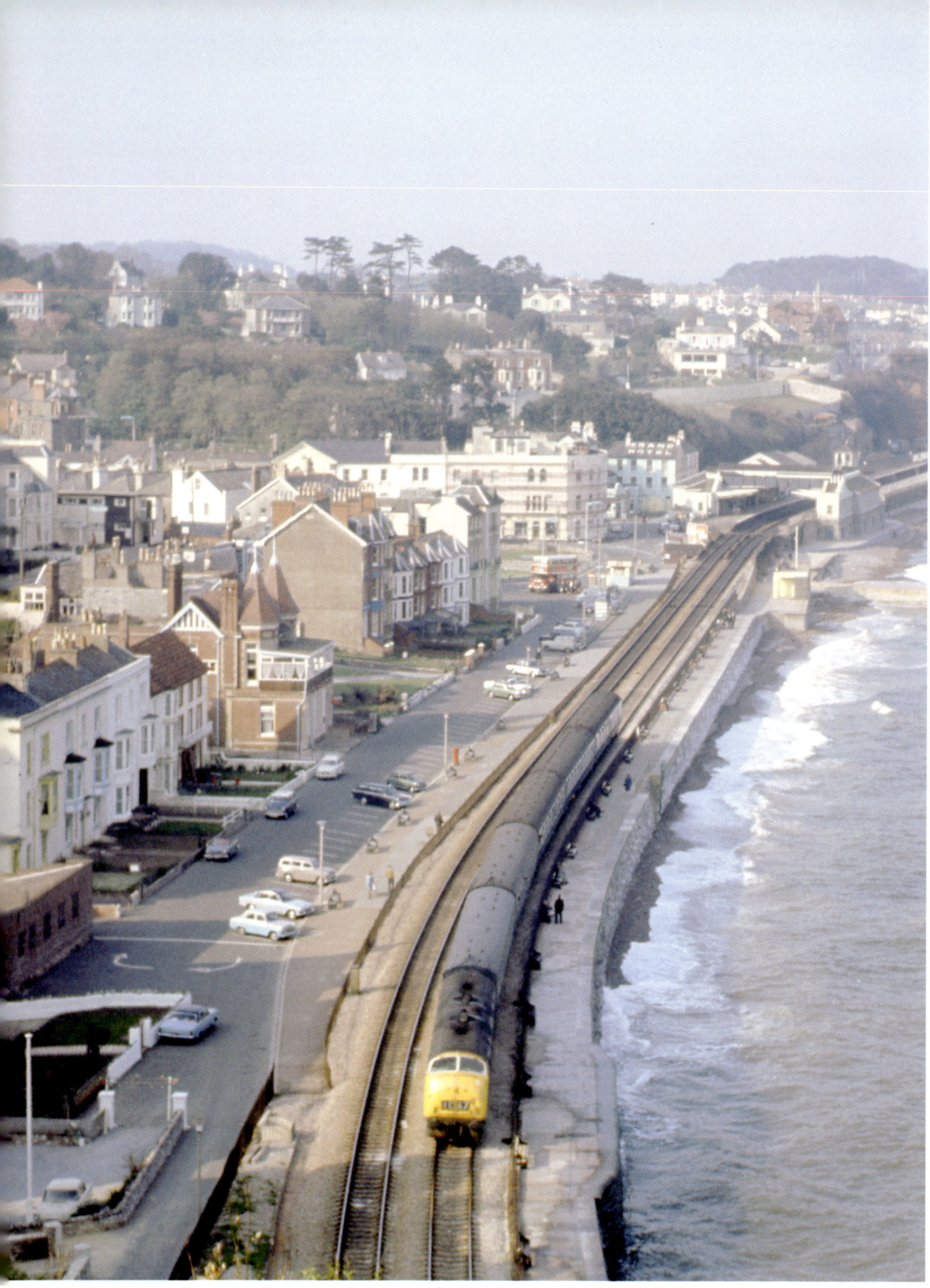

The classic location overlooking the shore and Dawlish station has been a popular spot for many photographers over the years, these two fine views were taken on 23 July 1969, firstly with D820 Grenville with a service from Paignton, and then with D804 Avenger on another local service with just four coaches being required. ***Both: Bernard Mills***

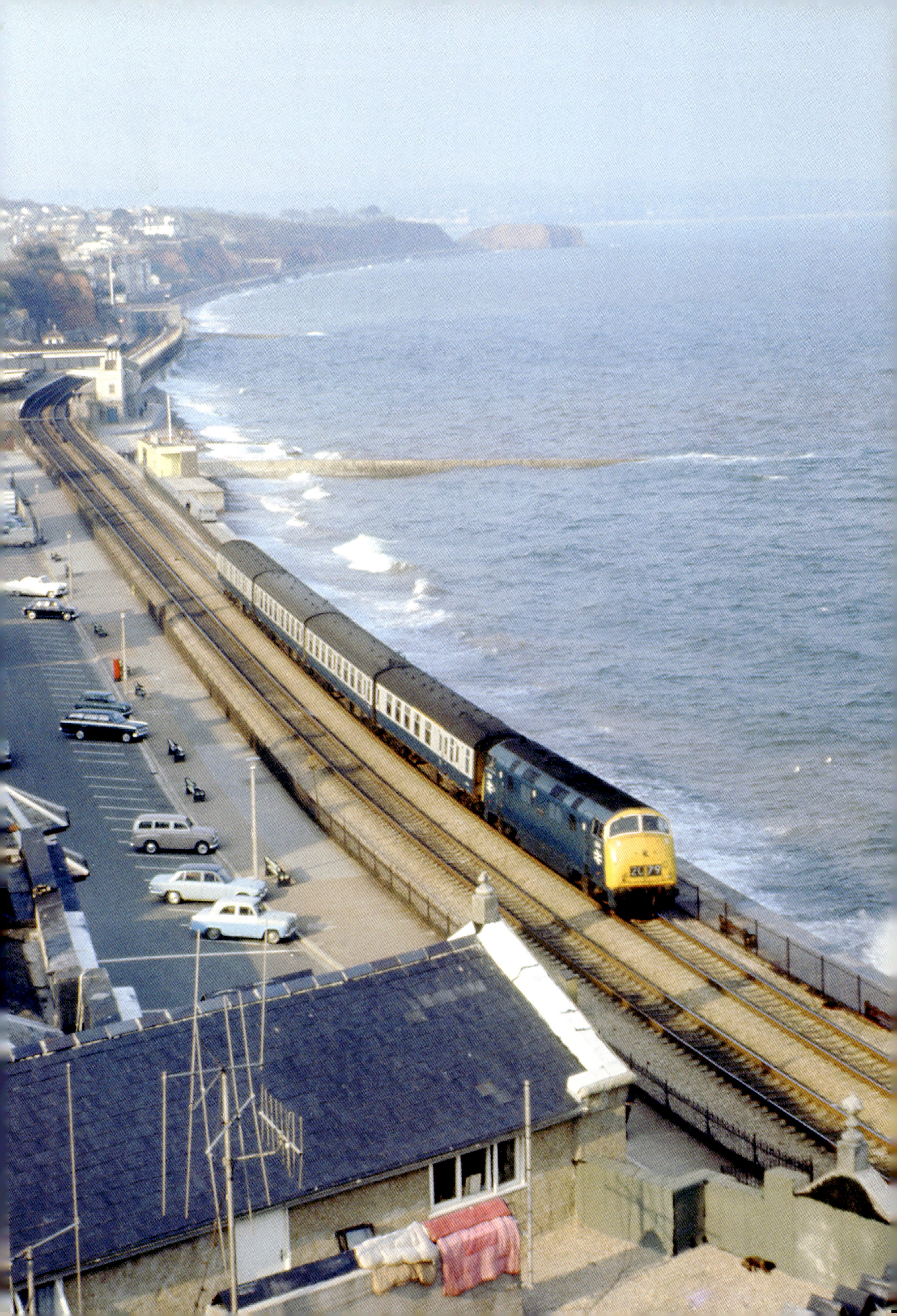

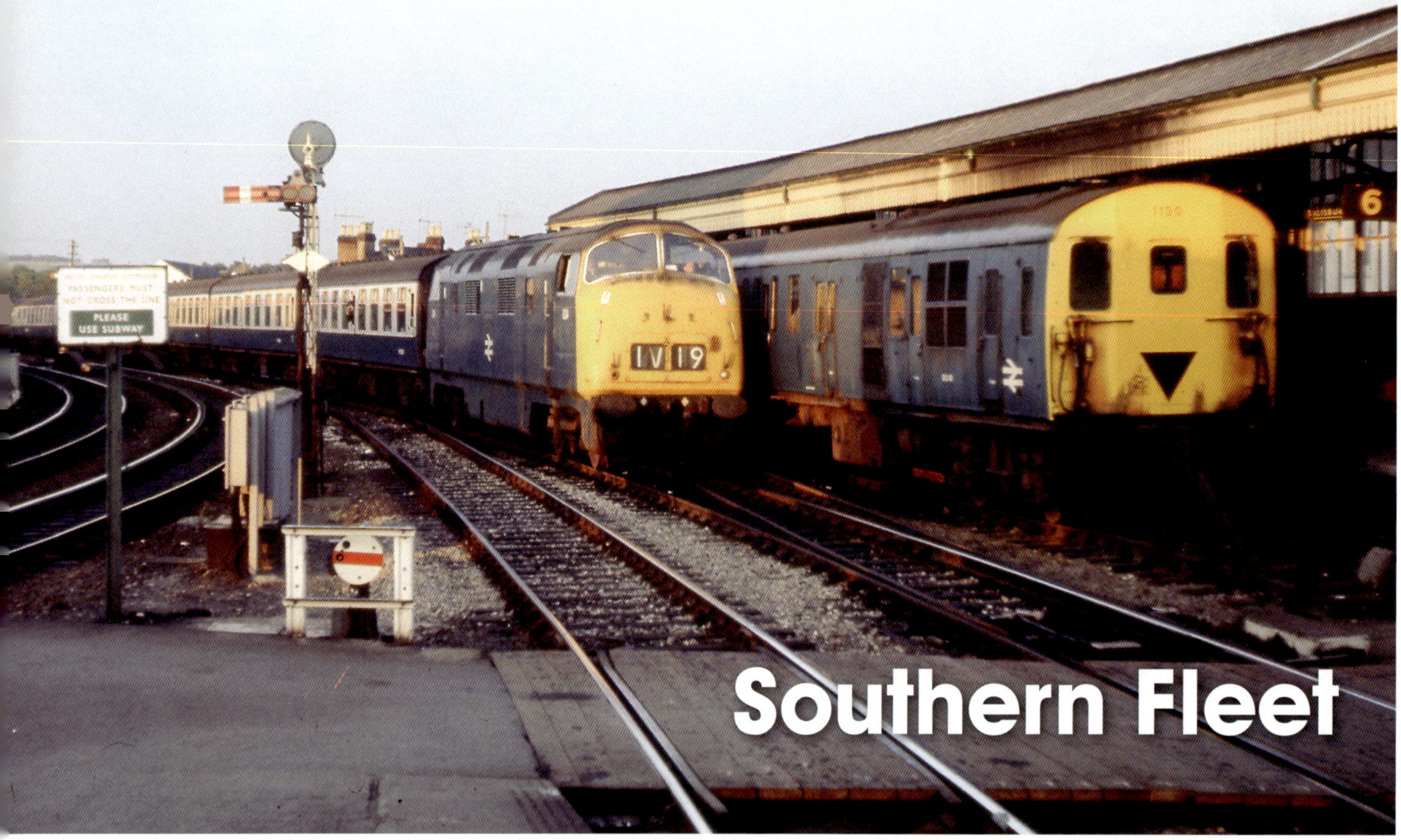

Southern Fleet

From 1964 the Swindon built Warships took over the Exeter to Waterloo express services ousting the Bulleid Pacifics. Although no Warships were shedded on the Southern Region it was Newton Abbot's allocation that did the bulk of the work. Here 824 Highflyer arrives with a down service at Salisbury on 29 May 1969. ***Bernard Mills***

It was kept to the Swindon machines for Southern Region duties to reduce the extra driver training that would have been required to include the North British locomotives. This is D814 Dragon being faithfully recorded at Basingstoke in 1966. ***Strathwood Library Collection***

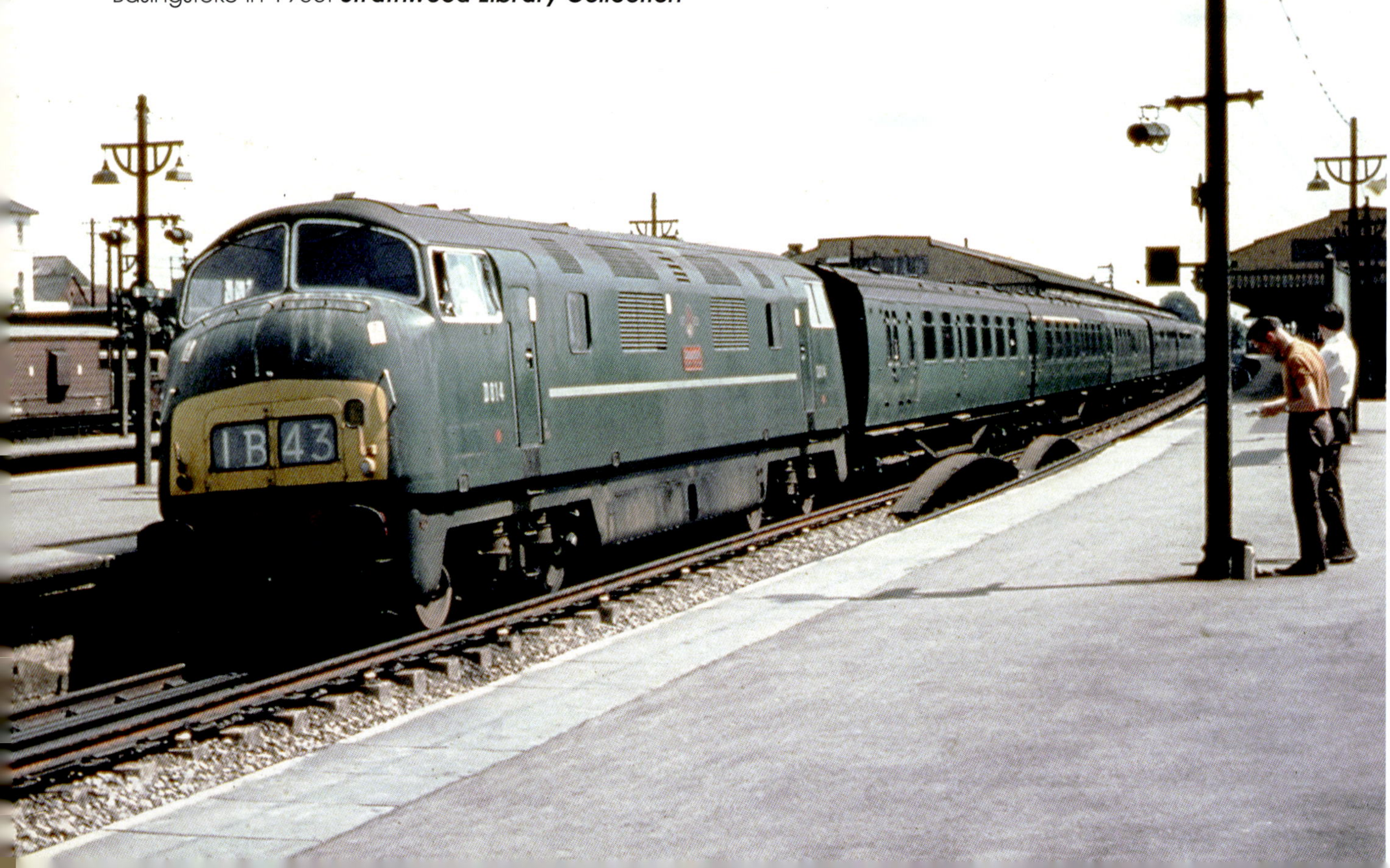

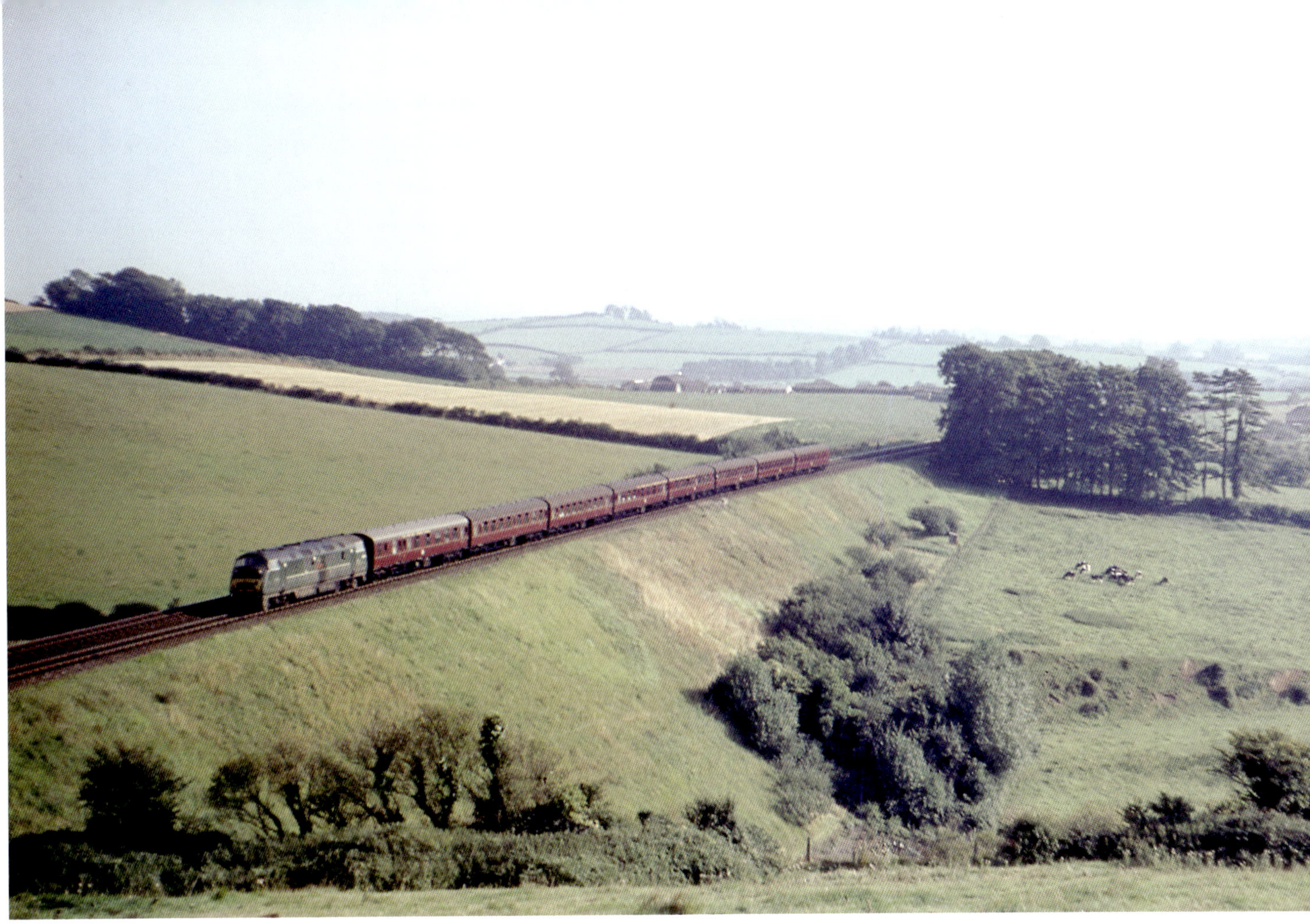

It would be a Western Region crew working the 16.30 Weymouth to Wolverhampton in July 1966 as North British built D840 Resistance growls up Upwey Bank away from the Dorset port. ***Bernard Mills***

Judging from the exhaust the driver has the power on for 811 Daring as his train sweeps under the flying junction at Battledown with the 10.10 Exeter St. Davids to Waterloo on 25 August 1971. ***Bernard Mills***

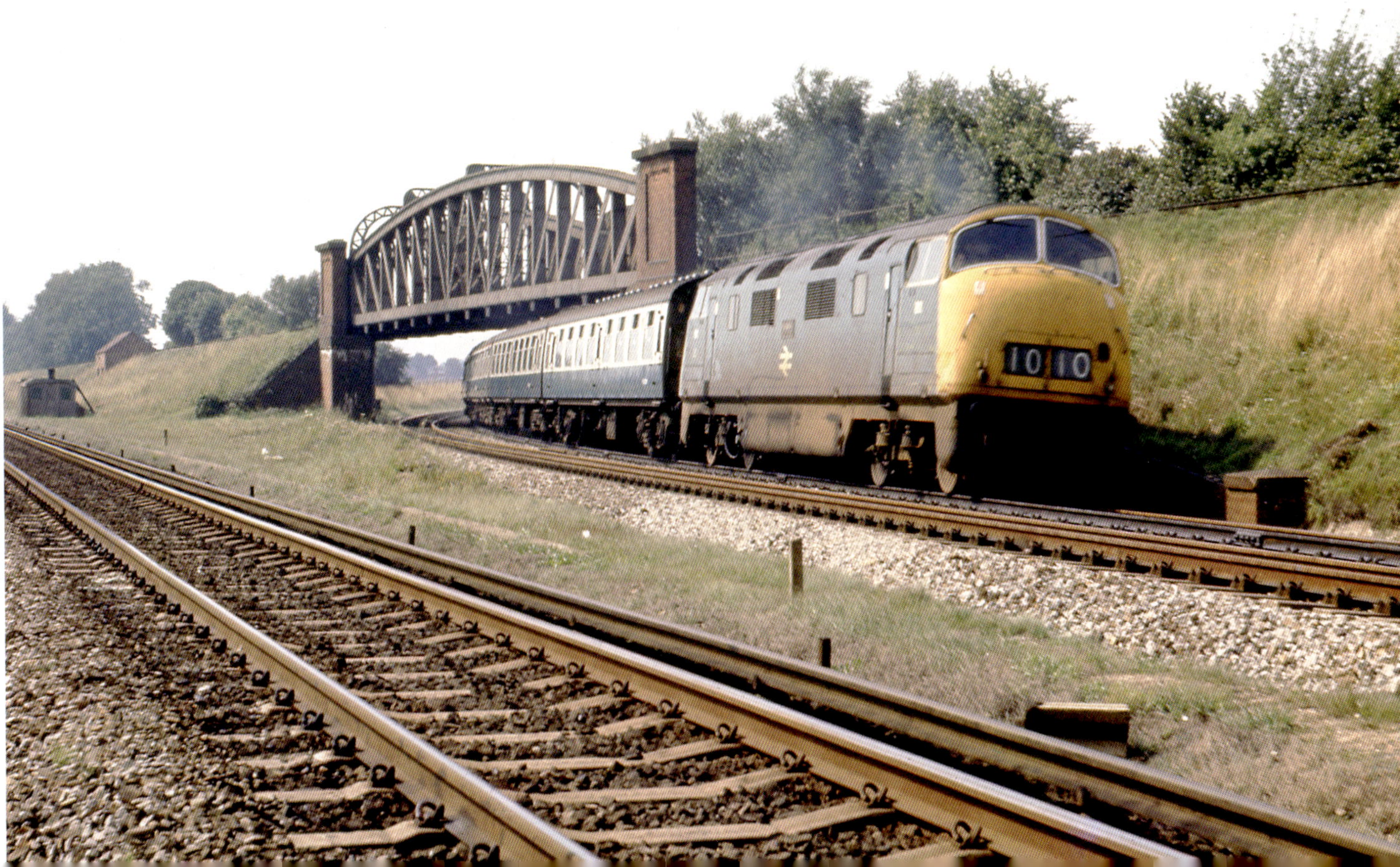

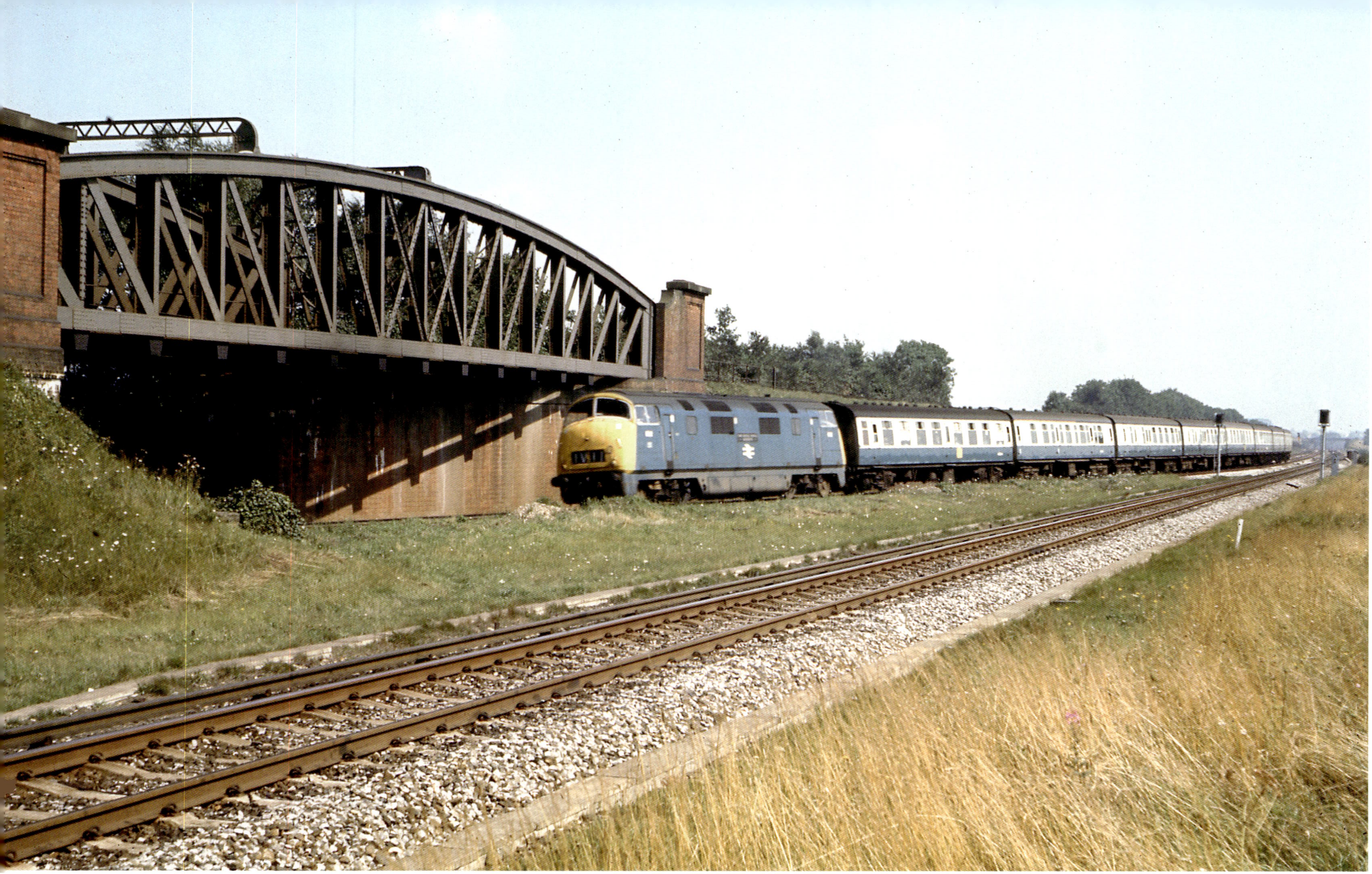

A short walk along the fence in the farmer's field the same day to record another blue Warship 812 the Royal Naval Reserve 1859-1959 with a reverse working also at speed. At this late date Class 33s were appearing more and more on these workings until they finally won through completely late in 1972. ***Bernard Mills***

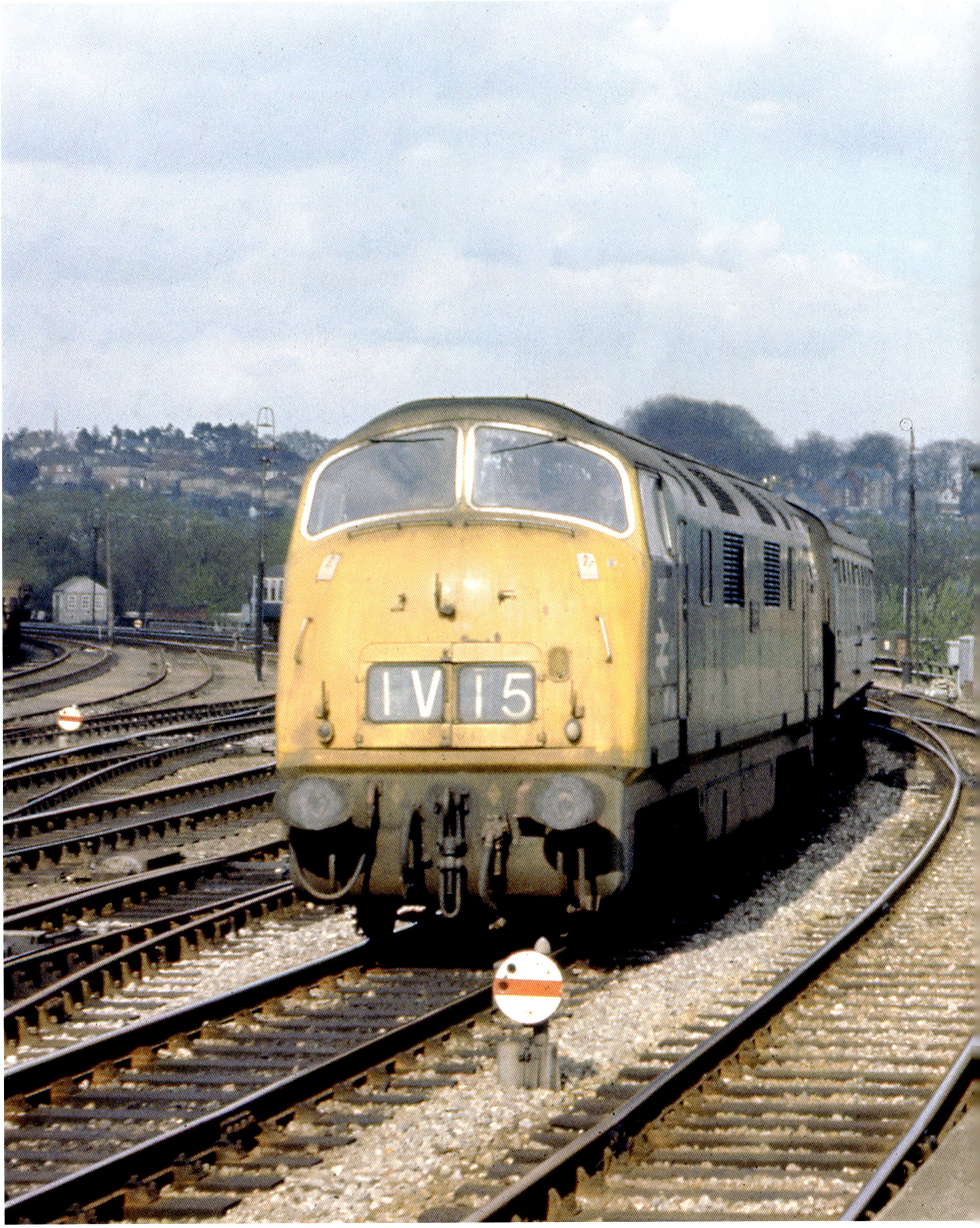

Drawing around the curve to east of Salisbury station and taking heed of the permanent speed restriction was D827 Kelly on 29 April 1970. This was the site of a terrible crash on 1 July 1906, when a London & South Western Railway boat train from Plymouth Friary to London Waterloo failed to navigate the very acute curve at this point. The curve had a speed limit of 30 mph, but the express had been travelling at more than 70 mph. The train was derailed completely, and smashed into a milk train and a light engine, tragically killing 28 people including the locomotive crew. ***Bernard Mills***

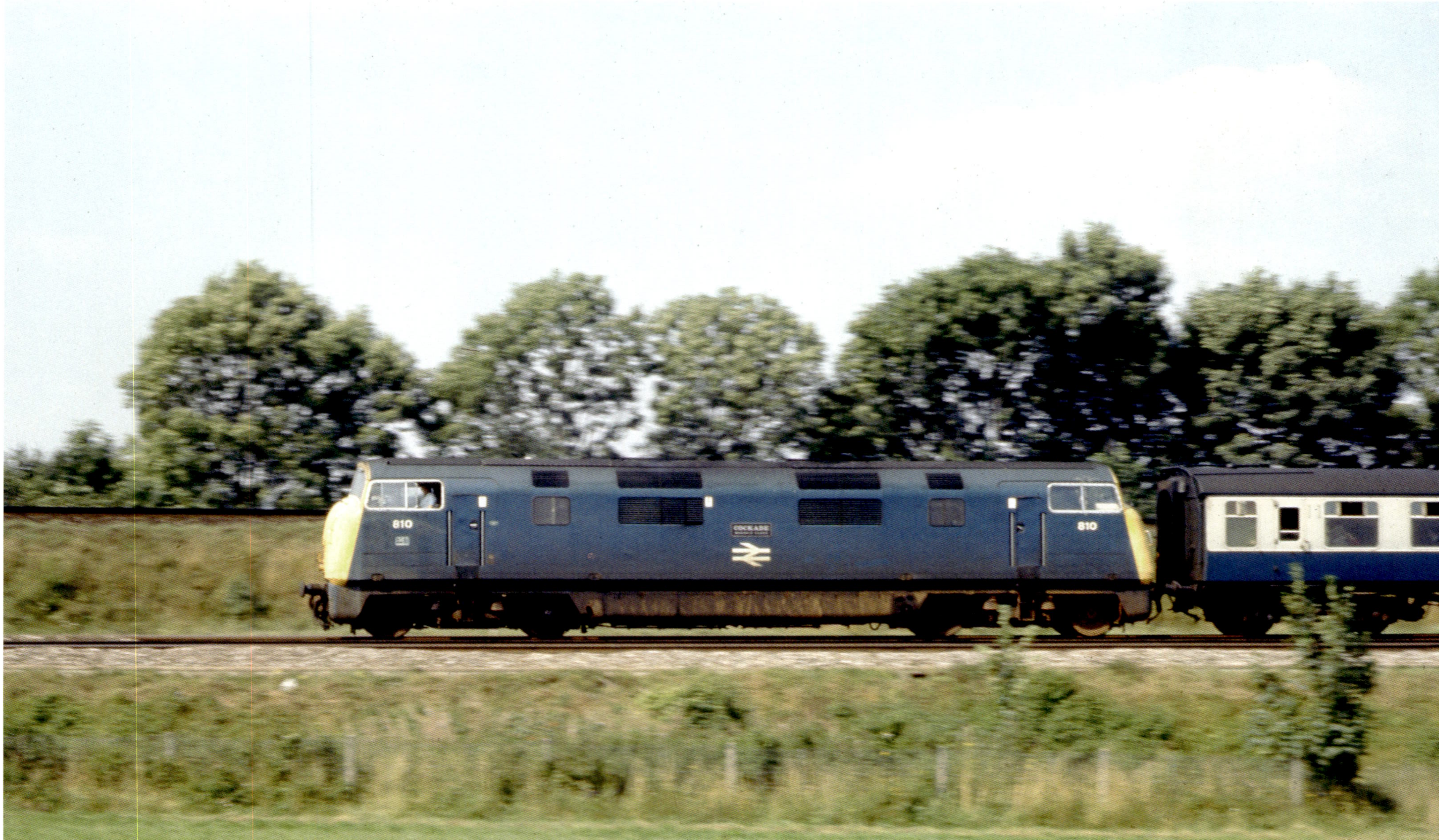

To complete the run of three consecutive numbered Warships on the Waterloo to Exeter route on 25 August 1971 we see 810 Cockade heading westwards and underneath the Bournemouth up line at Worting Junction with the 13.08 Waterloo to Exeter St. Davids. ***Bernard Mills***

Page opposite: Onboard a Waterloo to Salisbury service on 29 May 1970 with 824 Highflyer up front as we head west into the setting sun. ***Bernard Mills***

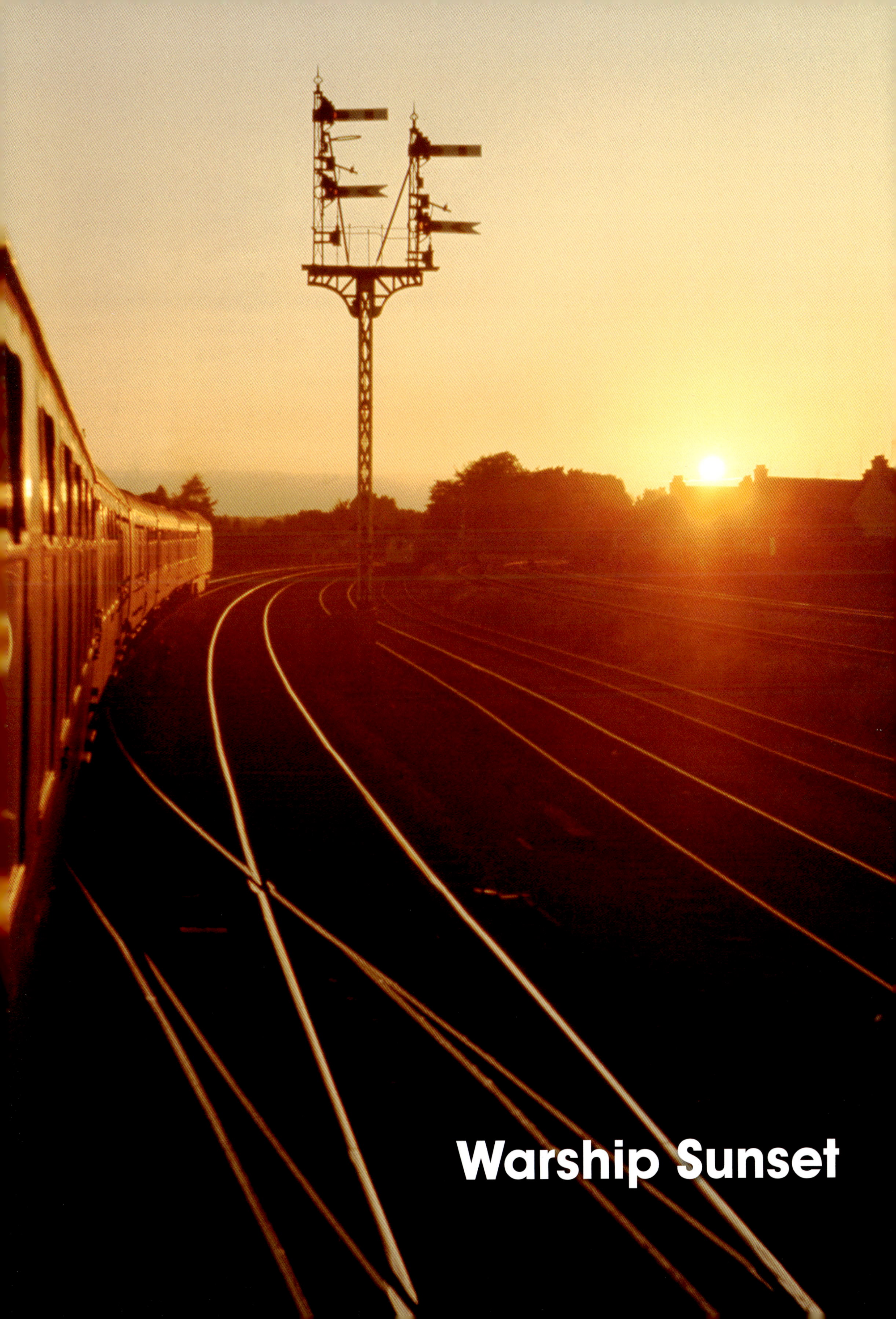

Warship Sunset

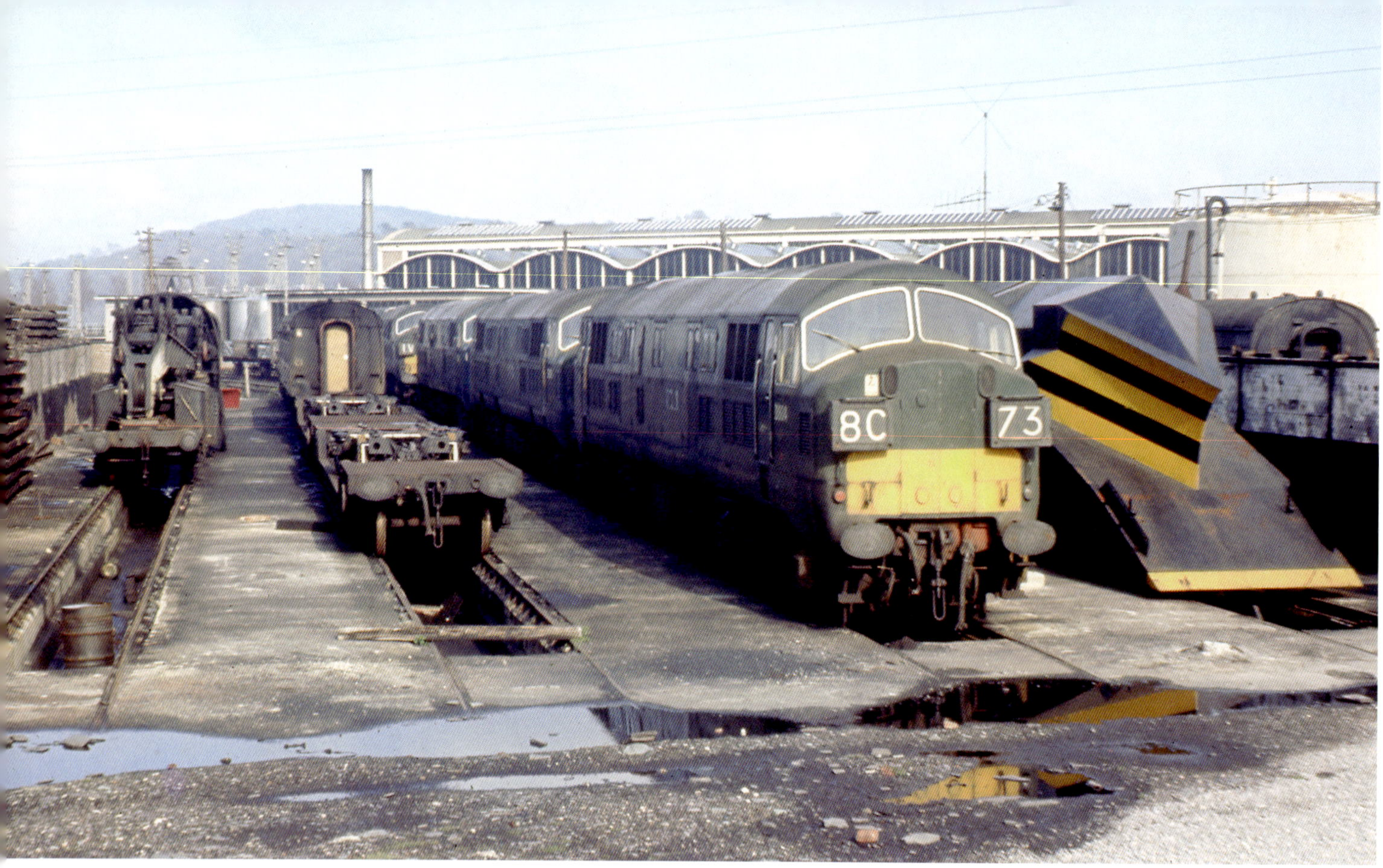

Their nameplates removed and ready for the scrapman's tenders the North British Class 41 fleet are fronted by D604 Cossack early in 1968 at Laira. This example along with D602 Bulldog and D603 Conquest would be purchased for cutting up by John Cashmore's scrapyard at the Western Dry Dock Sidings in Newport, leaving Laira in early August 1968, with D603 to be the last cut up by the year's end. As sadly the planned use for the class at Landore previously came to nothing in the end. ***Bernard Mills***

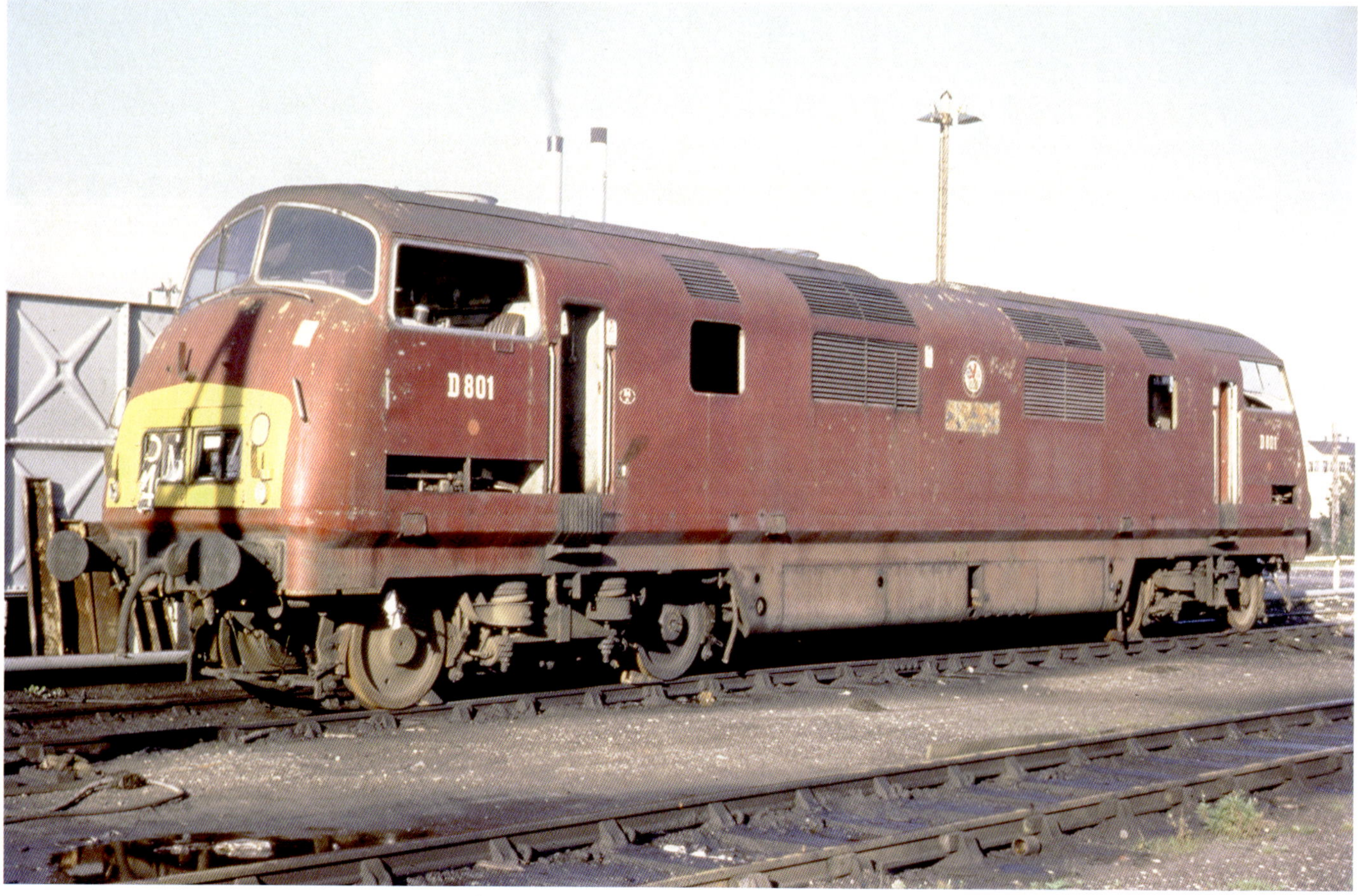

When withdrawn on 3 August 1968, D801 Vanguard had already been in store at Laira since June. It was progressively robbed of spares until it was in this sorry state before the locomotive moved off to Swindon Works in May 1970. By the end of that October the cutters of C Shop had completed their task. ***Strathwood Library Collection***

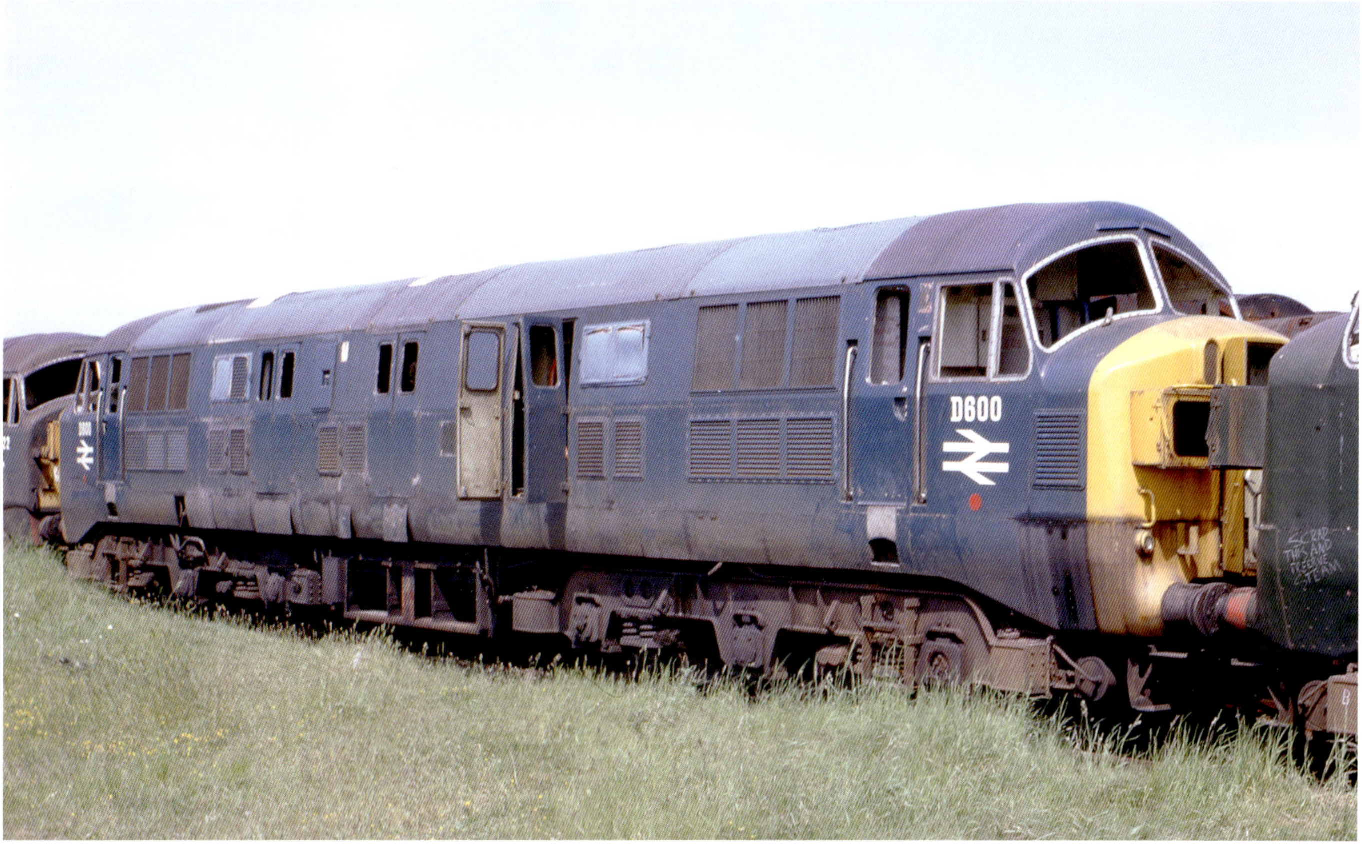

Sandwiched between fellow North British products D6122 and classmate D601 Ark Royal we find D600 Active in the famous Woodham's yard at Barry in July 1969, the Warships arrived here the previous July and Active would be the first of these three to perish in early March 1970. ***Brian Tucker Collection***

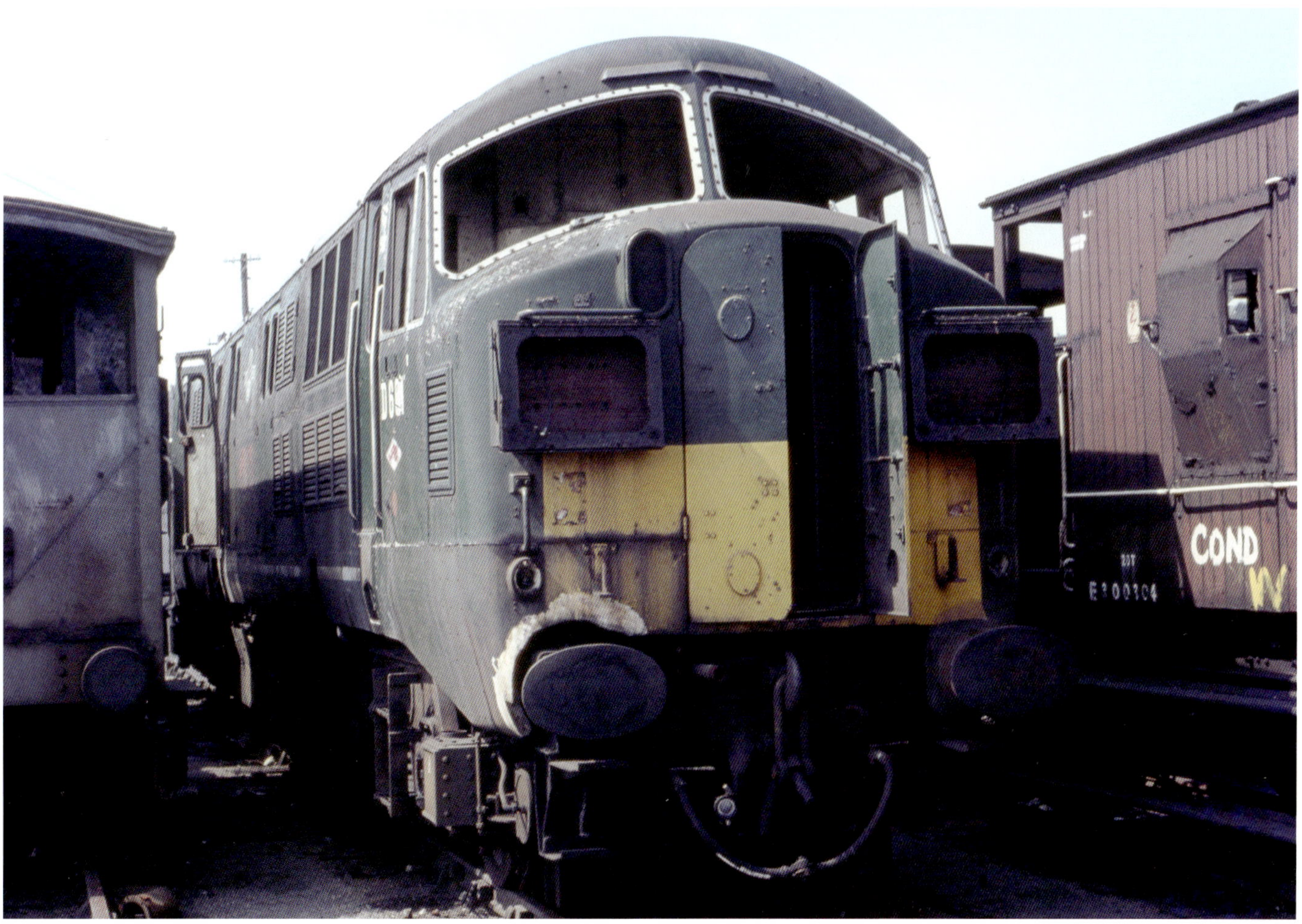

As the various steam locomotives left the yard for preservation this trio was split up in the shunting movements before D600 Active was cut up. This was D601 Ark Royal early in 1970, it would be another ten years before the cutters turned their attentions away from wagons to this last survivor and the Class 21 number D6122. ***Tom Bigley/Strathwood Library Collection***

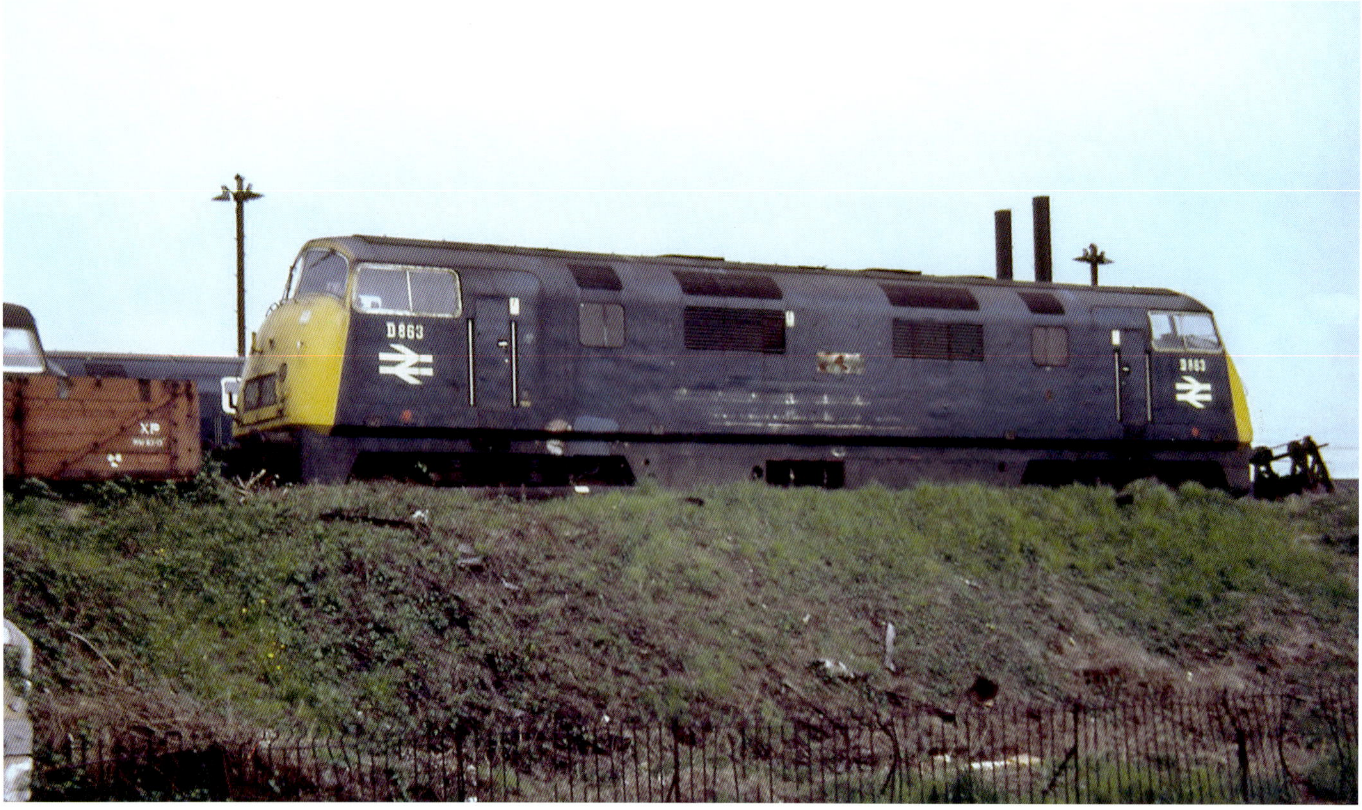

Certainly the rarest Warship to be photographed in blue must be D863 Warrior, aside from being the shortest in mainline service with just two weeks short of eight years use. We must consider it ran in blue for only fourteen months and was in maroon for only two years as well! It was withdrawn on 26 March 1969 and remained here at Newton Abbot in the open until going to John Cashmore's yard at Newport on 21 July 1969 and very quickly cut up within a few weeks of arrival. ***Paul Dalton***

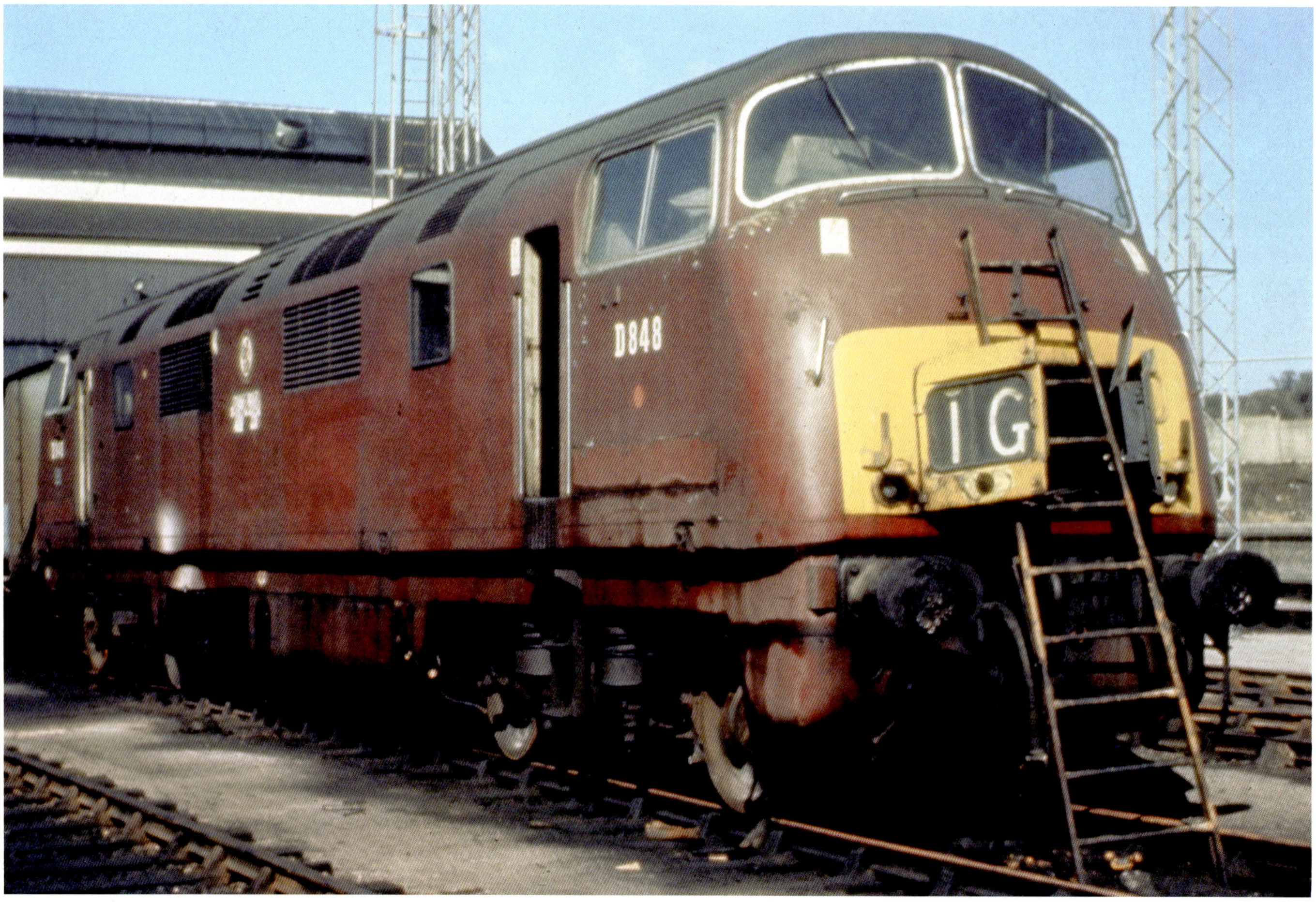

As already stated D848 Sultan was robbed of parts at Old Oak Common by the fitters to keep other Class 43s in service, this was the locomotive being made ready to travel to Swindon Works in April 1970' where it too was soon disposed of. ***Strathwood Library Collection***

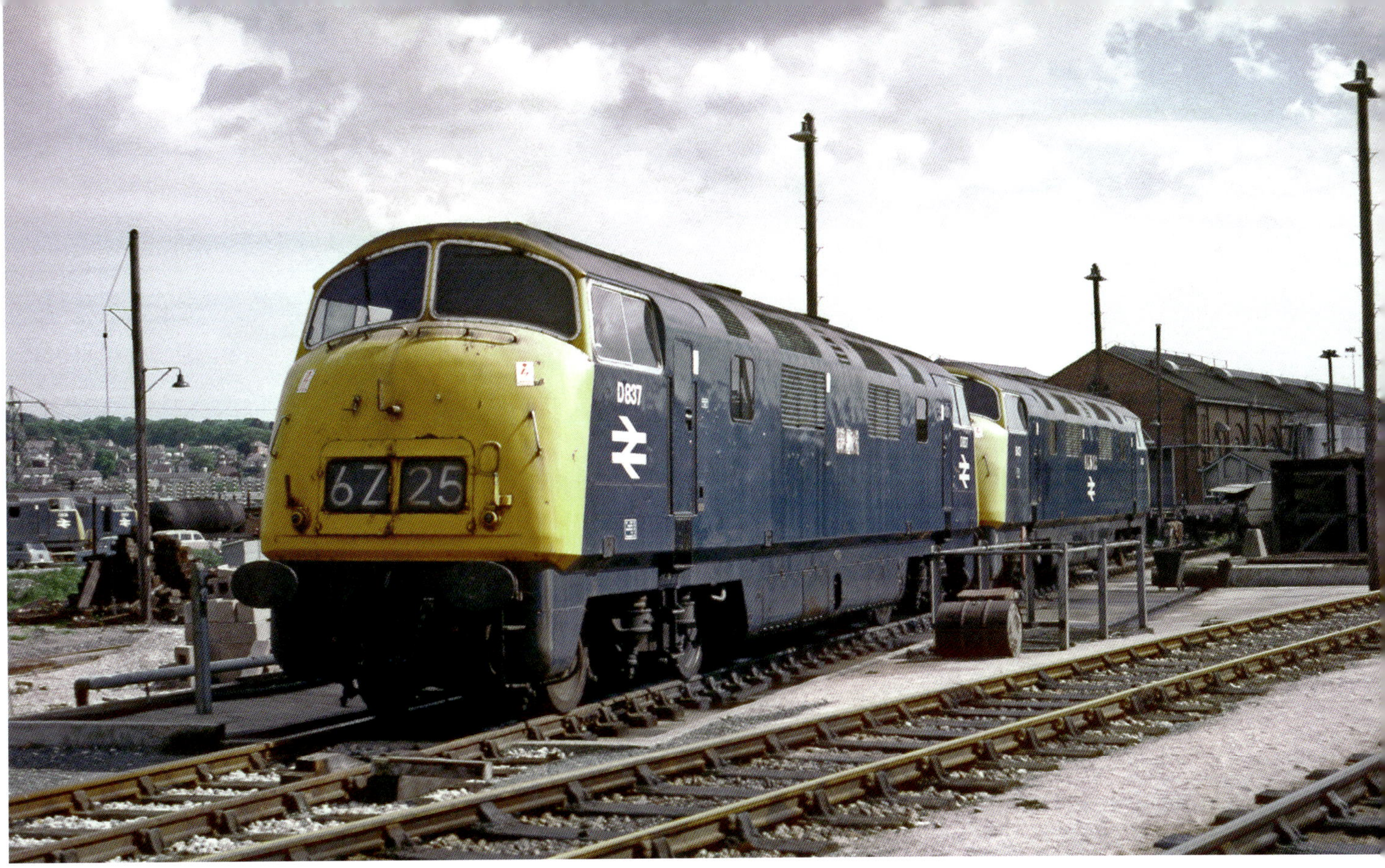

Newton Abbot's collection of withdrawn Warships was bolstered once more with D837 Ramilies and 843 Sharpshooter both minus nameplates on 16 May 1971. The former would go direct to Swindon Works, whilst Sharpshooter would join the waiting ranks at Marsh Junction before making its last trip to Wiltshire. ***Jim Binnie***

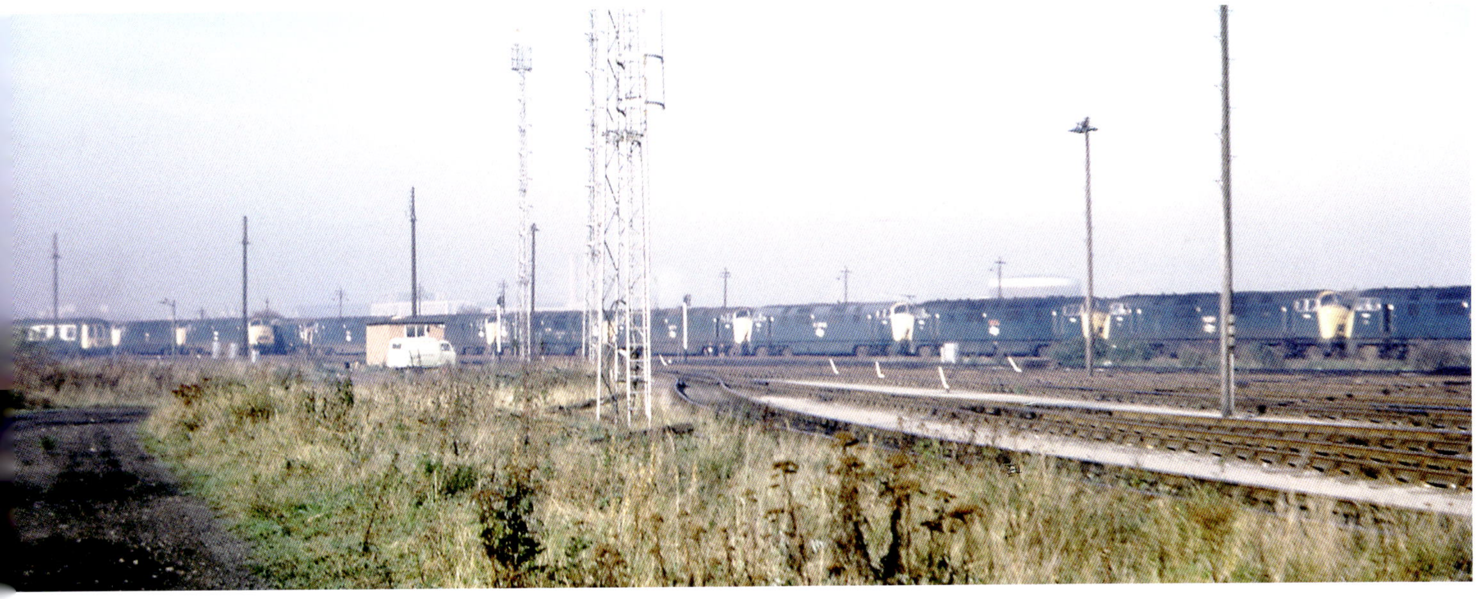

This was the long line up at Marsh Junction in Bristol on 30 October 1971 of once fine machines bound for Swindon's cutters. ***Both: Phil Bidwell***

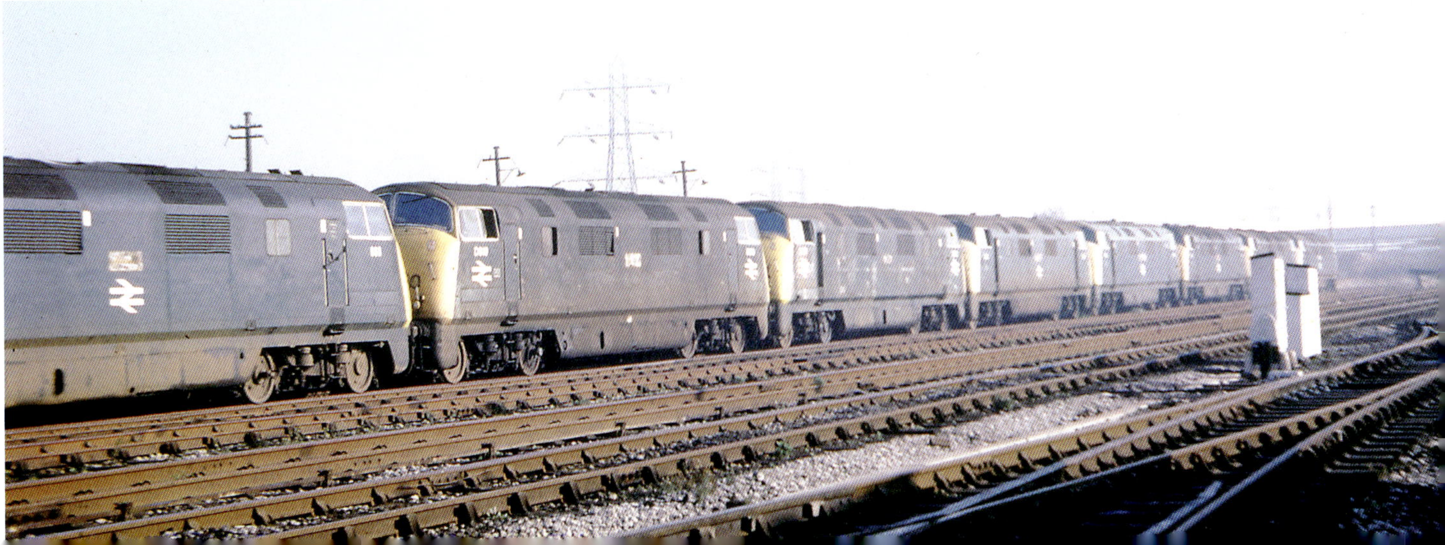

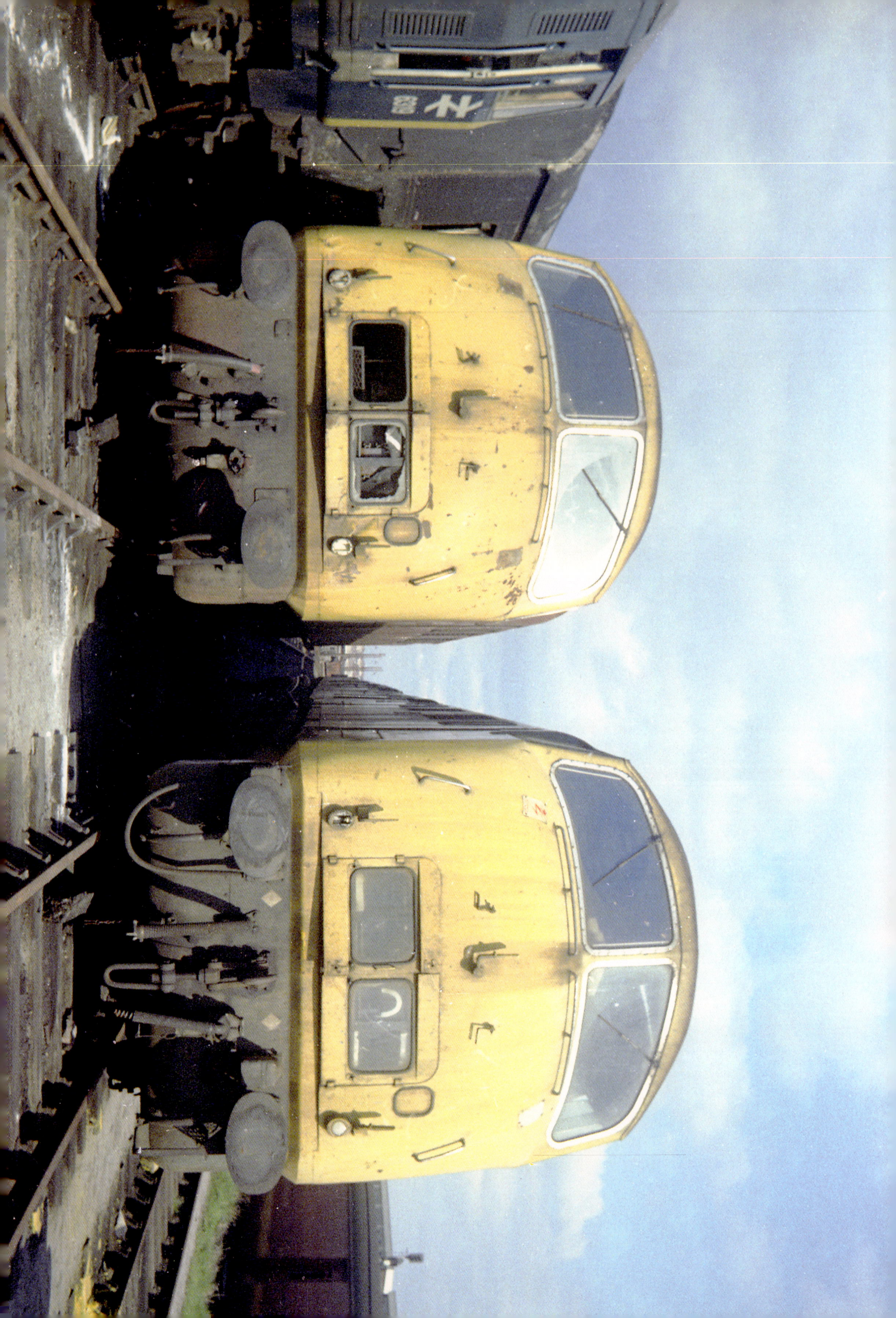

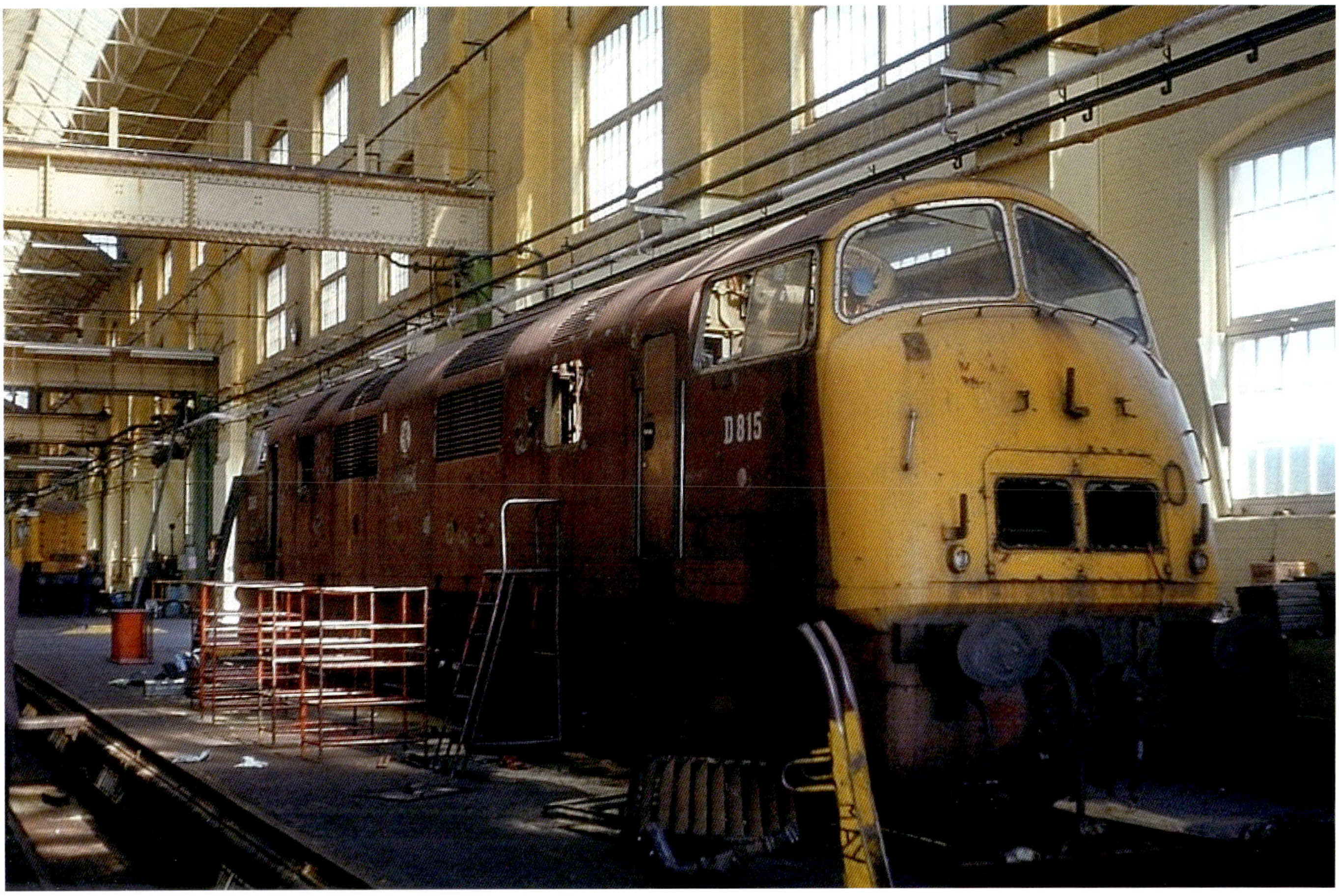

Having arrived at Swindon Works the previous day we find the wreck that was once D815 Druid already inside the workshops being stripped of what might be useful or valuable on 23 August 1972. ***Peter Crawley***

Swinging the camera around to find fellow Class 42 Warship and another once proud product of Swindon Works back here for the last time also being gutted the same day before being shunted out into the yard for cutting up. ***Peter Crawley***

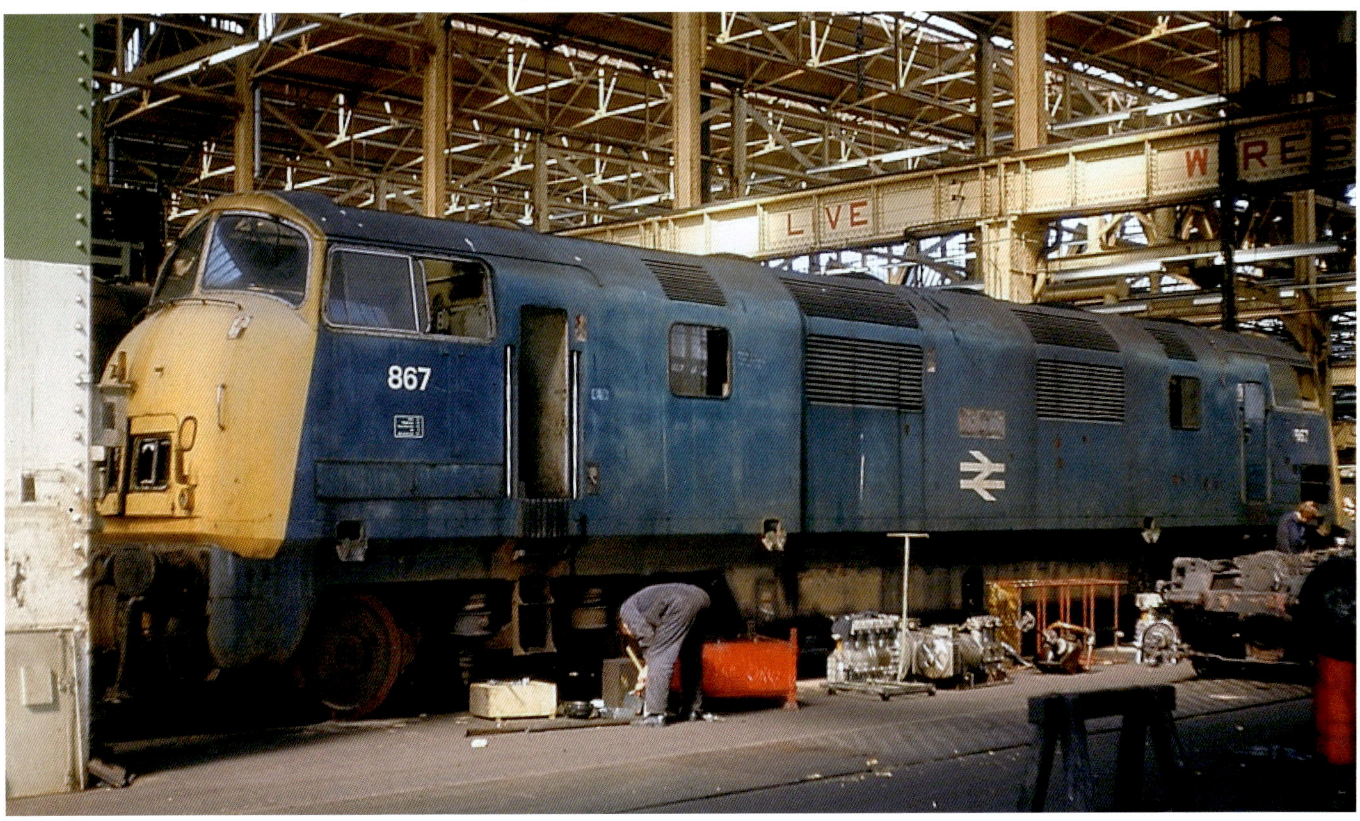

Page left: The same pairing of D815 Druid and 867 Zenith seen above were stored together side by side amongst the withdrawn Class 22s and Hymeks in the sidings at Marsh Junction on 13 December 1971. ***R Ranson/Brian Tucker Collection***

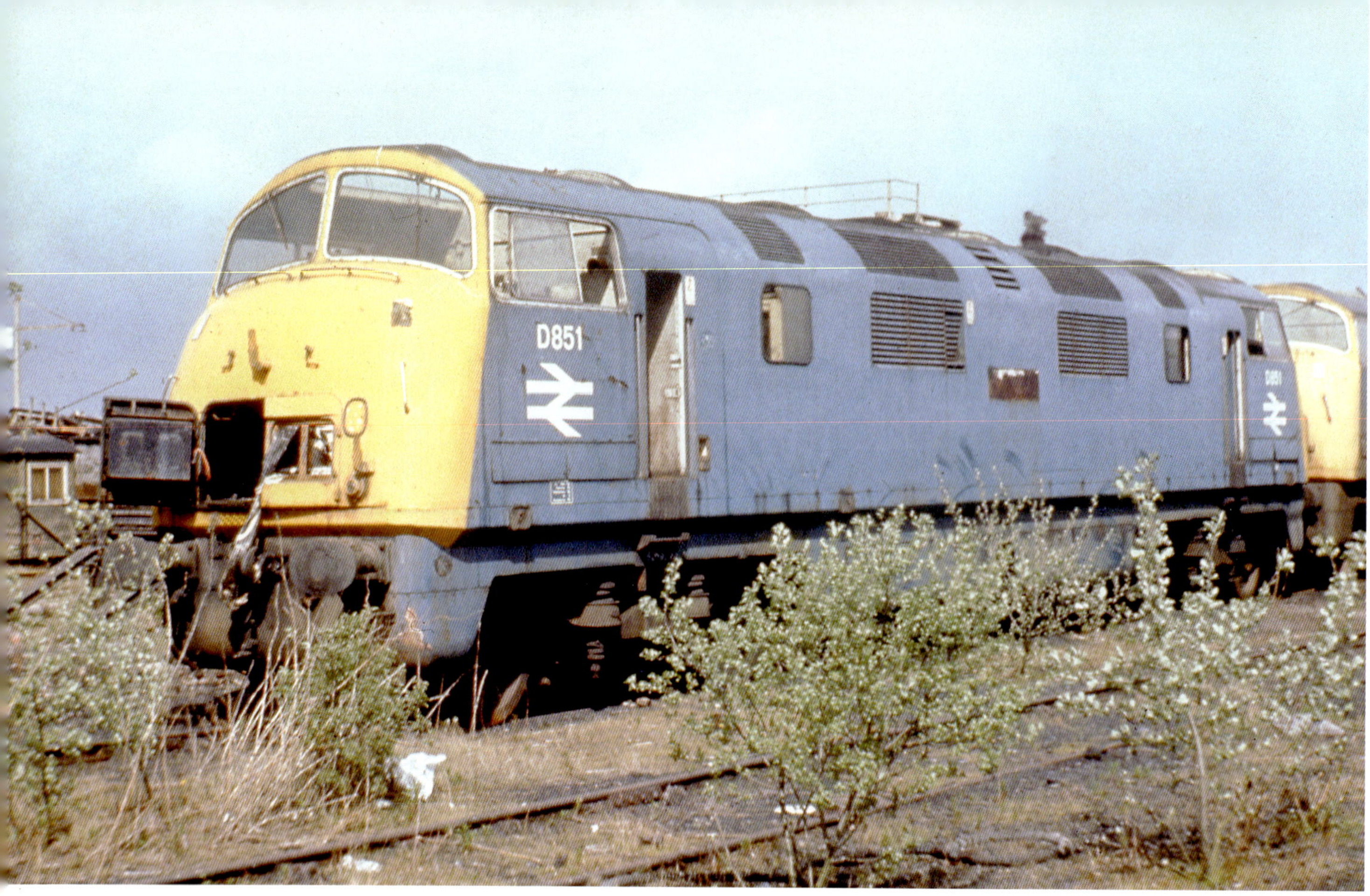

The blue paintwork last applied in May 1968 to D851 Temeraire has faded badly now as she lay awaiting the torches in the lines at Swindon Works in April 1972, the end for this old favourite would come just over a month later. ***Strathwood Libary Collection***

Below & Page opposite: The Swindon Works Open Day in August 1971 allowed many enthusiasts the chance to clamber all over the abandoned hulks such as D864 Zambesi, D860 Victorious, 856 Trojan and 870 Zulu as they awaited their fate in the warm summer sunshine that day. ***Both: Strathwood Library Collection***

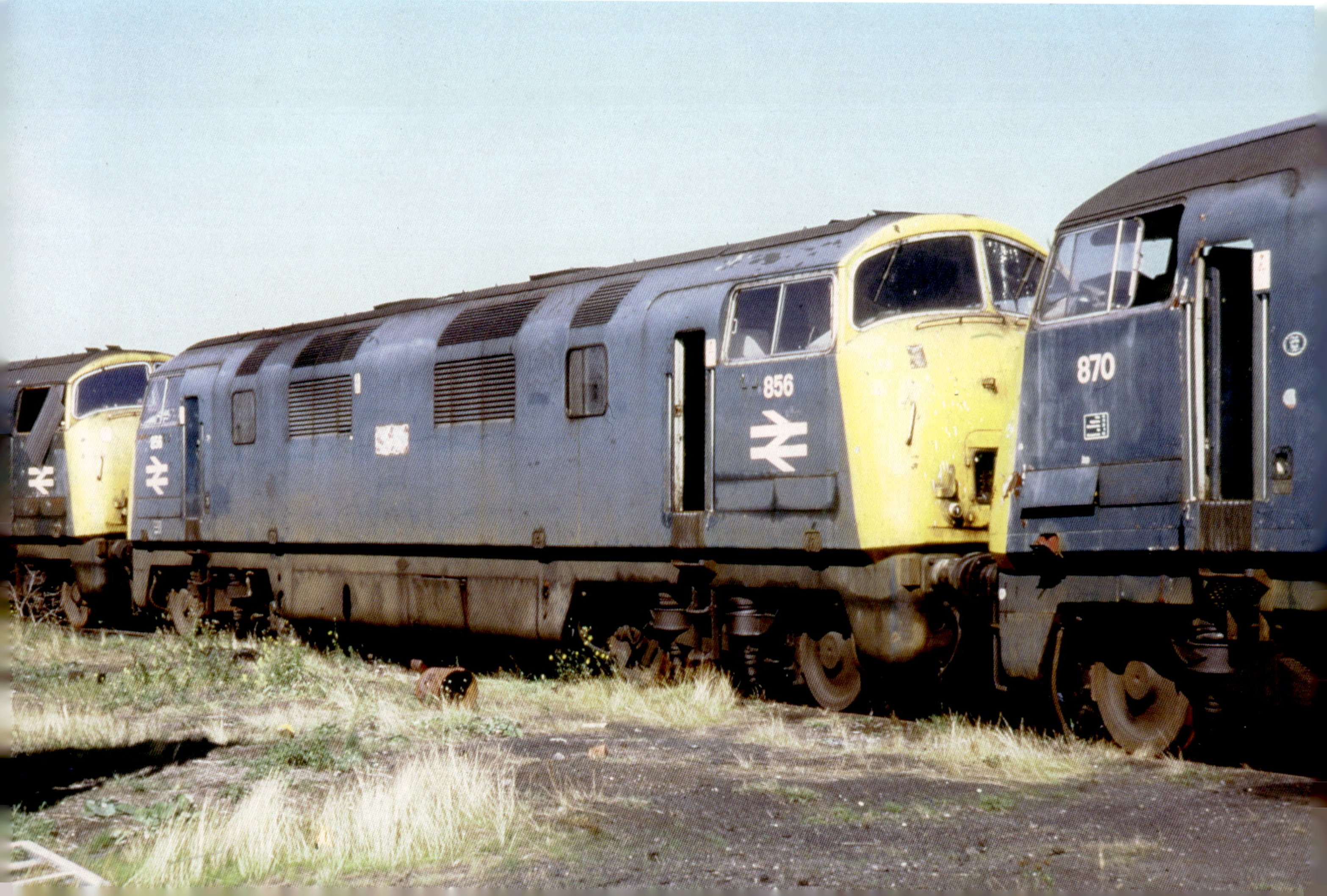

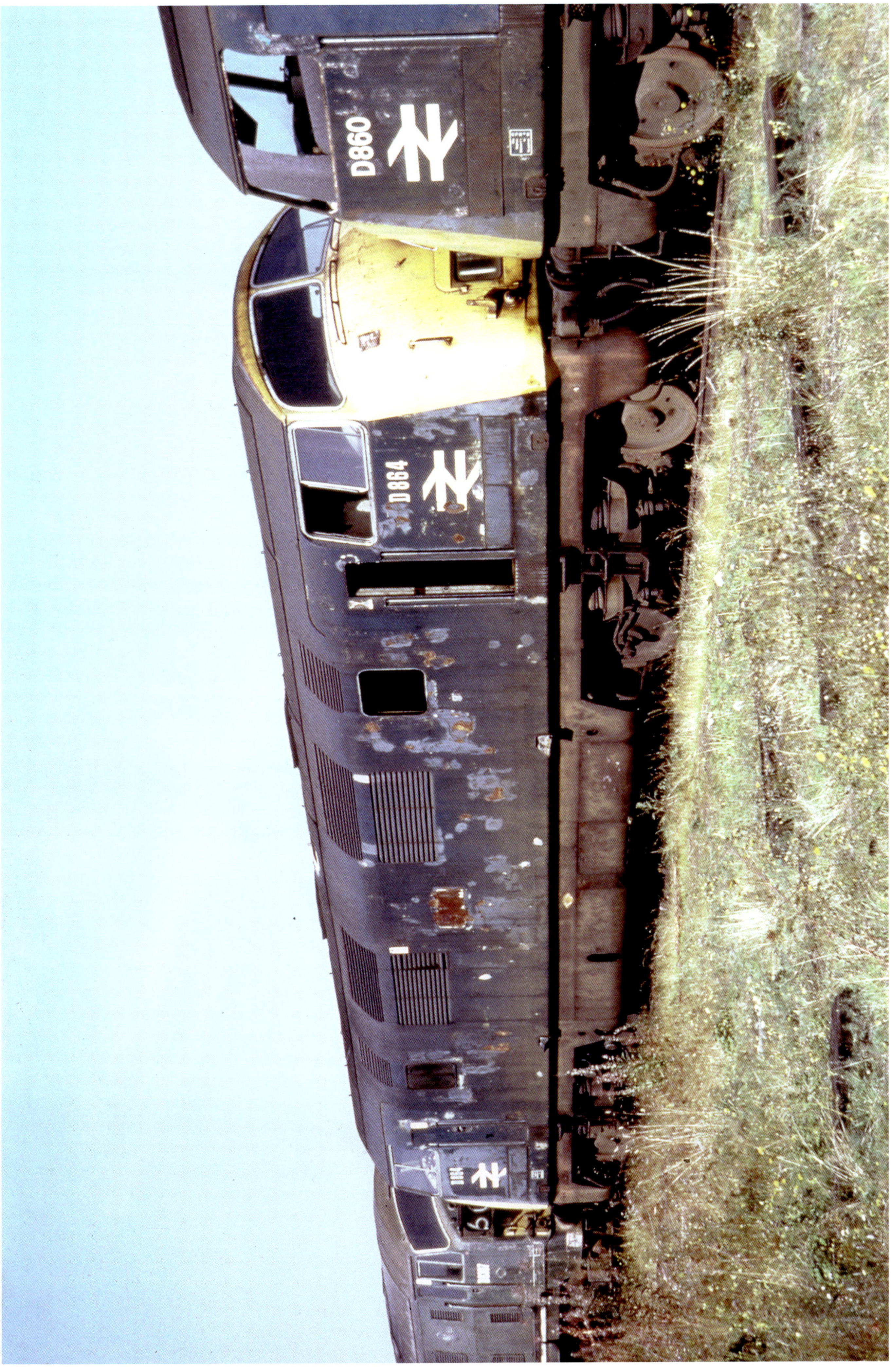
D860
D864

Help To Preserve Our Railway Heritage

Strathwood not only publish books on our railway heritage but have also set up the Railway Photographic Preservation Association as a Charitable Trust to house an archive of images comprising over 200,000 photographic negatives and slides.

The archive was established to not only preserve the collections of over one hundred photographers both living and deceased, but to also make their work available to a younger audience for the future. To achieve this aim, we have begun an energetic programme to publish a considerable number of books. Allied to this we are making as many as possible of the photographs and slides we hold, available as copies to interested enthusiasts, individuals, societies and other publishers.

Many photographers have chosen Strathwood to care for their collections and to publish the best examples of their work for posterity.

If you have negatives or colour slides of transport subjects then we would like to hear from you. We purchase, accept on loan, or welcome donations of material to the archive. Photographers always receive recognition for their work when it is used by publishers (A N Other/Strathwood Library). To answer why so many images are just credited as Strathwood Library Collection in this volume, the reason is we do not know who the original photographer was. This is usually because their collection gets split up via auctions or collectors upon their death with no record of the late photographer for us to credit. Please do not let this happen to your collection. Make contact with us today to discuss what can be done to ensure you work is fully credited and recognised for both today and the future.

Please call us today if you would like to see your work in print, perhaps in a similar fashion to this publication. We also undertake publications to benefit charities and societies on behalf of our contributors. In addition we can store, and catalogue collections on behalf of clubs and societies by way of loan, thereby releasing such groups to concentrate on other aspects of their activities.

Strathwood Ltd,
Glenavon House,
Kinchurdy Road,
Boat of Garten,
Inverness-shire,
PH24 3BP.

Telephone 01479 831139

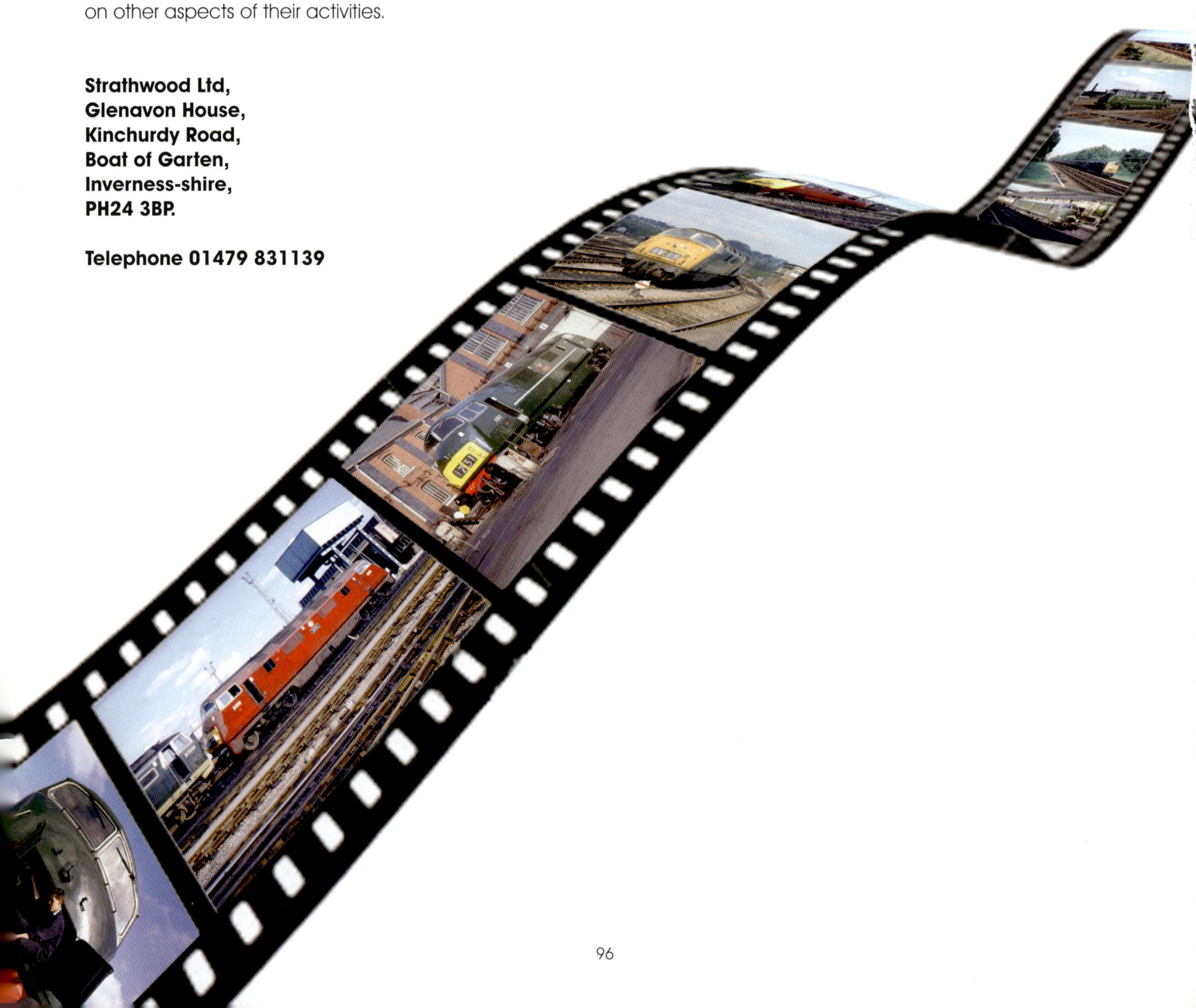